OUTDOOR LIFE
DEER
HUNTER'S
YEARBOOK
1984

Outdoor Life Books, New York

Stackpole Books, Harrisburg, Pennsylvania

Published by

Outdoor Life Books
Times Mirror Magazines, Inc.
380 Madison Avenue
New York, NY 10017

Distributed to the trade by

Stackpole Books
Cameron and Kelker Streets
P.O. Box 1831
Harrisburg, PA 17105

ISSN 0734-2918

ISBN 0-943822-20-3

Manufactured in the United States of America

Contents

Preface

Last year, I welcomed you to Volume 1 of the *Outdoor Life Deer Hunter's Yearbook* series. The first volume was exceedingly well received.

In your hands, Volume 2, like its predecessor, is designed to entertain you while helping you become a better deer hunter. Nearly all chapters originally appeared in *Outdoor Life* magazine. A few were selected from books. All have been updated. The writers, photographers, and artists represented here are tops in their specialties.

This volume's 42 chapters are grouped in nine sections that lead you quickly to the deer lore you're most interested in. As you'll find, the fare here is like a smorgasbord in a fine restaurant: Start where you choose, take what you want, return as often as you like.

Part 1, **Are You Prepared?**, deals with critical kinds of readiness. Dwight Schuh explains how to plan and execute hunts in new areas. Jim Carmichel, *Outdoor Life's* shooting editor, reveals his techniques for ensuring that he and his firearms are working well together. Bruce Brady shows how to become physically fit for hunting. And John Cartier tells the secrets for seeing more deer.

Part 2 is **Hunting for Whitetail Deer.** Carmichel takes you on three memorable hunts. Erwin Bauer coaches you on overcoming deer wiliness. And John Weiss provides a summary of astounding facts and figures from deer biologists. Larry Mueller probes "rattling." And Dwight Schuh tells you how to take advantage of the weather.

In Part 3, **Hunting for Mule Deer,** Ron Bishop gives you a ringside seat on a stalk with a surprise ending. Next comes an unforgettable chapter on the hunting horse by Jack O'Connor, the late and legendary shooting editor of *Outdoor Life.* Jim Zumbo tells how to hunt eight types of terrain. You'll also meet Old Crooked Horn, a big buck that gave fits to pursuers. Then, from Bruce Brady, you learn what it's like to be a western hunting guide.

In Part 4, **Guns, Scopes, and Ammo,** Carmichel presents a comprehensive guide on the hunting rifle. Cartier tells the advantages of combining an open mind with new equipment and techniques. And Tom Gresham explains how to select and use binoculars and spotting scopes.

Part 5 is **Outdoor Lore Improves Your Odds.** Here, Glenn Helgeland tells how to use tree stands, whether with gun or bow. Cartier tells you where to get the best maps and how to use them. Weiss unravels the mysteries of deer rubs and scapes, and explains fundamentals and fine points for enduring the wait in stands. Next, Schuh explains findings of a biologist who has been testing scents on deer 25 years. Wayne Fears gives advice on getting in and out of deer wood under tough conditions. And Norm Nelson tells how to exploit the rutting season.

Part 6 focuses on hunters **In Search of Big Trophies,** both the typical and the freak varieties.

Part 7, **Finding Those Hidden Bucks,** tells how to find those bucks after opening day, how to find spooked muleys and how to sneak up on bedded ones.

Part 8, **Secrets of Successful Bowhunters,** assembles the advice of three top hunters. One has taken a heap of record mule deer. Another reliably takes whitetail bucks when other hunters don't even get glimpses. Another tells you how to stalk bucks where cover seems nonexistent.

Part 9, **Meat for the Table,** is a marvelously illustrated guide to field-dressing, skinning, butchering, and cooking.

Now, begin by doing yourself a favor. Consider John Madson's thoughts on why we hunt deer, starting on the next page.

Chet Fish
Former Editor-in-Chief
Outdoor Life Magazine

Foreword: Why Hunt Deer?

It was at a conference for "nature educators" that the teacher asked me: "Why is it necessary to hunt deer in order to enjoy them?"

I can't remember my reply to her. It was probably lame enough. But her question jarred me into thinking instead of just feeling.

An often-used justification for hunting deer is that we do the deer a favor by killing them. This claim is unacceptable to most non-hunters, and it's not hard to understand why. We weaken our position as hunters when we rationalize our hunting as a clinical act of deer control. I doubt that any man honestly feels he is hunting deer for the deer's own good. He is hunting deer for *his* own good, and if the herd benefits, so much the better.

Well, I don't think I need to justify my act of hunting to any non-hunting educator, although I may owe her some proof that my hunting doesn't endanger her interests or those of the deer. No, I doubt we hunt deer to benefit them by trimming the herd. We hunt deer because we want to. So maybe the real question is not why we hunt deer, but rather why we enjoy it.

One of the most common reasons, I suppose, is the *meat reason*. The woods are full of guys who claim to be hunting for prime meat, although I've a hunch this is the standard alibi for busting the first deer that comes along. Still, there are some real meat hunters—men who can judge venison on the hoof, who have the patience and experience to pick and choose, and who take infinite pride in the quali-

ty of their venison. There are still some old hands who will pass up a real whangdoodle buck for a plump little yearling—although they are often experienced hunters who've already taken their share of whangdoodle bucks.

Then there's the *trophy reason*.

Those antlers on the wall are a man's effort not only to possess beauty but also to keep something important from slipping away and being lost and forgotten. And if the trophy testifies to the world that here is a strong and skillful hunter—well, why deny it? And so the great stag is stalked and taken. And although the hunter may drip with modesty and seem reluctant to speak, it's not hard to wring his story out of him. The hard part is turning him off.

Ten thousand years ago, that hunter would have stood by a fire and recounted the great deed to his clan brothers while the old men nodded approval and the stripling boys back in the shadows listened in wonder. It hasn't changed much. The trophy hunter, the ethical killer of the great stag or the great bear, still commands attention by the fire as he recites his deeds. His peers still salute him; the old men still nod and remember, and young boys dream of hunts to come.

The days of the great trophies are not past; there are still big stags lurking in cedar swamps and along the ridges, even though most of us will never shoot them. Yet, we've all taken deer that held special trophy value for us—and such value isn't always the measure of time and beam. It may be just a measure of hard, solid hunting in which both you and the deer conducted youselves well, so that neither was shamed. Trophy hunting has been bitterly condemned of late, but it can be worthy if the hunter is ethical and if he knows the best antlers are grown only in good habitat and then works to support such habitat, even if it sometimes means the hunting of antlerless deer.

Companionship is a strong element in deer hunting. For as long as man has hunted, he has done so in organized packs with special taboos, traditions, and rituals. There's that, and many other reasons as well.

One is that the deer is the ultimate game in most states, where it is the biggest, wariest, and most prized of all wildlife. But more than anything else, the greatest urge of the genuine deer hunter is his search for freedom, and for the genuine personal adventure that's the hallmark of such freedom.

Whatever it is that motivates men to hunt is distilled in deer hunting. Such hunting embodies the essence of hunting, for deer embody the essence of quality freedom within quality environments. The genuine deer hunter is probably as free as modern man can be in this technocracy of ours. Free not because he sheds civilized codes and restraints when he goes into the woods, but because he can project himself out of and beyond himself, out of and beyond the ordinary, and be wholly absorbed in a quieter, deeper, and older world.

You know how it is. You go into the woods and your presence makes a splash, and the ripples of your arrival spread like circles in water. Long after you have stopped moving, your presence widens in rings through the woods. But after a while this fades and the pool of forest silence is tranquil again. You are either forgotten or accepted—you are never sure which. Your presence has been absorbed into the pattern of the woods. You have begun to be part of things. This is when the hunting really begins.

You can always feel it when the circles stop widening. You can feel it on the back of your neck and in your gut, and in the awareness of other presences. This is when a man starts to hunt, and he always knows when it happens and when he is beginning to hunt well.

Such things are important to the man; they may be even more important to the boy.

There were those times when I was a kid, hunting and trapping and sometimes spending several days and nights alone in the woods, when I'd have a flash of insight that was usually gone as swiftly as it came—the vaguest sense of how aboriginal hunters must feel, and what real hunting, pure-quill, honest-to-God *real* hunting, is all about. One strong flash of this to a boy—one swift heady taste of this utter wild freedom and perception—is enough to keep him hunting all his days. Not just for meat or horns, but hunting for that flash of insight again,

trying to close the magic circle of man, wilderness, and deer.

Yet our critics sometimes say: "We could condone hunting if the hunter were hungry. But the modern hunter is not hungry; he simply kills for the joy of killing."

Nonsense. Of course deer hunters are hungry. We all hunt deer because we are hungry. The question is, hungry for what? Meat? Glory? Freedom? Personal proof? I contend that the genuine deer hunter (as opposed to the synthetic deer hunter, which is another case entirely) hunts to satisfy hungers just as sharp as the belly-hunger of Stone Age man. He is not hunting for the joy of killing; he is hunting for the joy of living.

And how about "personal proof" as a motive for hunting? Does a man prove himself by killing a deer? Of course not. The mere act of killing a deer proves nothing. It may not even prove that a man can really shoot. If there is any proof of a man in the hunt, it's not whether he has killed a deer but how he has hunted it.

Because the best deer hunts are not really contests between man and deer, but between man and nature. The man does not compete with just the deer, but with his own growling belly and freezing feet, with weariness, loneliness, impatience, discouragement, and the growing desire to quit. If a man can overcome these things, he has won an important contest with himself. And maybe the prize for winning that contest is a deer—and maybe not. So does a man prove he's *muy hombre* just by killing a deer? I doubt it. But at its best, the hunt can mean that a man has met some ancient tests that still wear true. He has used brain and spirit to rise above ignorance and weakness. And if that isn't proof of something worth having, then fifty thousand generations of hunters have been wrong.

To some people, of course, it proves only that the hunter is a rather dangerous barbarian whose actions clash with civilized values. And there is some truth in this, though not in the sense that our critics mean.

James Fenimore Cooper, who wrote a lot about people in the woods, was deeply concerned over the tragic clash between wilderness and civilization. He observed that the wilderness had one set of values which should be preserved, while civilization had certain values which might be brought into the wilderness but which usually destroy it. This may be the greatest single challenge to modern America: to preserve the intrinsic values of wildlands while enjoying the benefits of urban culture.

It was over a century ago that Cooper lamented the impact of civilization on wilderness. But at the same time, without knowing it, he was writing about the special breed of man who would someday cushion that impact—the figure which he made famous as Leatherstockings, "The Deerslayer."

John Madson

PART 1

ARE YOU PREPARED?

Hunting the Unknown— It Takes Planning

Dwight Schuh

Having a plan that takes into account where, when, and how to hunt is the key to deer-hunting success. To develop such a plan, you must know your country and the game you're after.

That's why you can hunt most effectively in areas you've hunted for years. You know the lay of the land, the trails, bedding and feeding areas, the habits of the deer, and appropriate hunting methods. Lack of such knowledge is what makes hunting in new, unknown country tough. You're hunting blind.

But I say you can score your first time in any new deer country. It's just a matter of familiarity. If you can become reasonably familiar with unknown country, you can hunt it effectively.

One way to do this, of course, is to hire a guide. The guide has the familiarity; he can plan for you. But what if you can't afford a guide? Or you just like doing things for yourself?

During a recent October, I hunted blacktail deer in Humboldt County of northwestern California. I live in Oregon, and I'd never seen this region before. I knew little about blacktails. In addition, hunter success there is only about 10 percent. Yet in five days of hunting, I killed two bucks, the legal limit in that unit.

This was no accident. I learned the country deliberately, and then planned how to get those bucks. You can do the same.

Some of my tactics may apply only to blacktail

Against backdrop of the Western sky, I pack out the hide and head of a deer from country I'd never hunted before.

My wife Laura and I, at our camp in California's Humboldt County, talk over plans for hunt in area new to us.

hunting, but others apply to deer hunting anywhere. The range of these Pacific Coast deer extends from southern California to southern Alaska, and it reaches from the coast eastward to the summit of the Sierra Nevada in California and the Cascade Range in Oregon and Washington. In the coast range, habitat is dense and blacktails are brush-huggers, much as whitetails are. But in the eastern, inland part of their range, blacktail habits are much like those of mule deer. So is the habitat they range in. This was true where I hunted.

All deer have basic requirements. The key to hunting them in any country is to learn these requirements and find places that provide them. My approach, a systematic familiarization process, makes this possible in a short time. Of course, some modifications may be in order, depending on the nature of the land you're hunting. But the principle remains the same. You must have a hunting plan. And to develop a plan, you must know the land and the animals. Five steps must be taken prior to your hunting.

1. Study maps. One thing that makes hunting new country difficult is a lack of familiarity with the land and the road system. Map study helps solve this problem. Two kinds of maps are essential. One type is put out by major landowners in the area. These show ownership boundaries and road numbers, and they're often the most up-to-date maps available. In most cases, these will be U.S. Forest Service, Bureau of Land Management, or other government agency maps. However, in some localities, primary landholders are private companies, many of which publish maps available to the public.

The other type of map you need is the topographic map. These have contour lines, showing the lay of the land, and they indicate woods, meadows, buildings, and other features you must become familiar with. Topographic maps are prepared by the U.S. Geological Survey, and distribution information and indexes to these maps are available from USGS Distribution offices at 1200 South Eads Street,

Arlington, VA 22202; Federal Building, Box 25286, Denver, CO 80225; and 310 First Avenue, Fairbanks, AK 99701. These maps are also sold by private map dealers.

2. Talk with people. Game wardens, biologists, surveyors, timber cruisers, and hunters are likely sources of information. Don't expect all of them to be helpful. Some might not know where to hunt; others aren't about to reveal their secrets. Most people want to be helpful, however, so talk to everyone. Eventually you'll come up with some useful information.

3. Drive all roads. The road system may have been altered since your maps were printed, and the only way to find this out is to drive every road within your chosen area. Update your maps according to your findings.

4. Go to all vantage points. The view from most forest roads is restricted, offering limited perspective. Short of flying, the best way to get an overview is to study the land from vantage points. Fire towers usually offer the best views, but cliffs and ridgetops will do. Study vegetation, terrain, logging patterns, and other features that might affect your hunting decisions.

5. Look for deer. Many hunters scout by looking for sign alone, but sign can be deceptive. In brushy country, it can be so localized that you might unknowingly pass by a concentration of deer. In open country, it may be so scattered that deer will seem scarce. And you can't be sure of the size and sex of deer leaving the sign. But the sighting of deer is unquestionable, and you can cover more ground quickly with binoculars from a vantage than you can by walking while looking for sign. Observe at daybreak and dusk when animals are moving.

These five steps deserve credit for my success in California. They were carried out *before* I started hunting. Here's how it worked.

Before leaving home, I had updated the maps. Topographic maps for my destination in Humboldt County were made in 1951, but my National forest map was printed in 1972. I transferred all new roads and other structures from the Forest Service map to the topographic maps.

Then I studied the land and vegetation patterns on the topographic maps. It was obvious the major landform was a long, north-south ridge bisecting the area, and that an east-west ridge met the main ridge from the west, forming a T. The maps showed primary access roads along the tops of these two ridges and campsites along the roads. So I would be camping high, hunting downhill.

I looked for steep spots and blocks of land far from roads and located the county lines, an important detail since the county adjacent to Humboldt was closed to hunting. In addition, map study revealed small towns where supplies were available, and fire-guard stations where I could get information and emergency help. Before ever seeing the country, then, I had some idea of what to expect.

My wife Laura and I drove to the hunting area on October 7. The season had opened September 24 and would close October 16. I planned to hunt through the end of the season if necessary. In California's Zone B, the limit that year was two bucks, forkhorn or better, so I had two tags. Laura wasn't hunting, but being a great observer and deer spotter, she helped with scouting.

I'd originally got the idea for hunting here earlier in the summer when I talked with a game warden in another region who'd formerly worked in Humboldt County. He told me of impressive deer counts there.

When Laura and I arrived Friday afternoon, we found plenty of campsites along the top of the main ridge. One thing the maps didn't tell us, however, was that all of these were dry. We had to find water, but an hour of searching proved fruitless. Finally we stopped at another camp. The two hunters there sent us directly to a spring we'd never have found on our own.

Throughout that afternoon and the next few days, we talked to many hunters. One dispelled our confusion over certain roads and pointed out shortcuts not shown on maps. Others offered hunting advice. In this strange country, I didn't know where to look for big bucks. Would they be high or low? In dense timber or open oaks? In rough canyons or on gentle hillsides? And what were the best hunting methods? Stillhunting? Driving? Taking a stand?

One man told us the bigger bucks were on west-facing slopes in heavy brush and old-growth conifers. On east- and south-facing slopes, bucks were generally smaller, he said. We talked with 10 different people who'd been hunting clearcuts. All had hunted several days; among them they'd seen only two legal bucks.

And one veteran offered this: "At this time of year, bucks are fat and have their thick coats. They bed in the coolest places they can find, so they climb to the tops of steep ridges and lie at the edges of flat spots or rock outcroppings. The breeze blowing up the ridge cools them and keeps the flies away. Hunt these places slowly. Take two steps; then stop to look for the flick of an ear or tail, or a patch of brown hair, and use your binoculars a lot. It should take you three or four hours to hunt a quarter acre. Keep at it and you'll find a good buck."

When Laura and I arrived, we'd noticed a brush

Discussions with people in new area can be rich source of information. Here, in fire tower, Laura gets tips on terrain.

patch that probably held deer. I was tempted to hunt there Saturday morning. If this had been opening day when deer were being pushed, that might have been feasible. But since bucks had been educated by three weeks of hunting pressure, my chances of lucking into one were remote. Besides, if I'd begun hunting the first likely looking spot, I'd have had no idea of other opportunities. So on Saturday and Sunday, I left my rifle cased. This, I believe, is important. If I'd set out to scout but had taken the rifle, I'd never have learned the country. I'd have ended up hunting.

For the first two days, Laura and I drove every road within our hunting territory, an area of about 10 square miles. We found that trying to relate roads to maps was confusing if not impossible. Many new logging roads had been built since even our most recent map was published. A number of "trails" on the maps turned out to be jeep roads, and some roads shown no longer existed. As we drove, we

Before doing any hunting, I went out to vantage points, marked likely spots on maps, and then made my choice.

updated our maps. By the end of those two days, we had an accurate picture of the road system.

Driving in itself wasn't sufficient to gain the familiarity needed for solid planning. So we spent time at different vantage points looking over the countryside.

From a fire lookout, we saw that stands of oak covered all south-facing slopes and that old-growth conifers coated most of the west side of the north-south ridge. The east side of this main ridge, however, and the north slope of the east-west ridge, had been opened up by large clearcuts. Finally, we could see that a jungle of manzanita and live oak choked two steep canyons at the juncture of the two main ridges. Thus, from this one viewpoint, we defined four types of vegetation.

From this and other vantage points, we pinpointed additional features such as steep ridges with flat spots and rock outcroppings where bucks might bed, and areas of good forage. We also noted rugged terrain that might discourage other hunters. We used binoculars to look for deer, concentrating our efforts at daybreak and dusk.

On the topographic maps, we marked potential bedding and feeding locations with red X's, and we drew in vegetation and clearcuts with blue ink for quick reference later.

Most hunters get out early and late, knowing their chances of seeing game are best at these times when the animals are active. But when scouting, many hunters drive the roads at midday, casually looking for animals. That doesn't make sense. To see animals when scouting, you have to be out early and late, the same as when hunting.

While glassing clearcuts, Laura and I saw a number of does and fawns, but no legal bucks. Our findings were similar in the oak forests. But in one of the steep canyons filled with live oak, we spotted one big buck. I've generally found that does, fawns, and young bucks inhabit certain localities while bigger bucks congregate in others. So the sighting of this buck seemed significant.

At the end of two full days of talking, driving, and looking, I felt ready to adopt a hunting plan. This plan was arrived at partly through the process of elimination. Clearcuts, even though they held many deer, seemed to offer few legal bucks. With midday temperatures reaching the 70's, the oak forests on parched south slopes seemed less than promising And the expanse of old-growth timber on the north-south ridge was featureless and had no obvious bedding ridges or pockets of forage.

So I decided to concentrate on the small section where the juncture of the two main ridges formed rugged canyons. This area had promising characteristics. As I first noticed by tight contour lines on the

The antlers are from the two bucks I took on this hunt, and the "tools" were vital ingredients in my strategy.

topographic map, and later confirmed by firsthand observation, it was precipitous. Then hunters in a camp near ours further whetted my interest when I questioned them about this place.

"Yeh, we know about the 'hole,'" one of them said. "But we're not about to hunt over there. We might see something and shoot it. Then we'd have to pack it out."

"Hmmm," I thought to myself. "Maybe everyone else is avoiding it for the same reason."

Two days of driving, glassing, updating maps, and talking to outdoor people gave me big edge in actual hunt.

In addition, Laura and I discovered that the "hole" wasn't visible from any nearby point. The main road along the top of the north-south ridge did border its upper side, but thick brush screened the canyons and ridges from above, making it impossible to see deer from the road. And no roads crossed the bottoms of the canyons.

Only from the fire lookout, over a mile distant on the east-west ridge, could we observe this area. From there, studying it with binoculars, we could see that two ridges sloping laterally from the top of the north-south ridge divided the canyons. These ridges had small flat spots shaded by stands of dense fir, ideal bedding sites. And thick brush in the canyons offered cover and forage for deer.

The best approach, considering the terrain, access, and prevailing wind direction, would be to hunt downhill from the north-south ridge, along the backbones of the lateral ridges. I would move slowly, trying to spot bedded bucks during midday, glassing down into the canyons for feeding deer in early morning and late evening.

With this plan in mind, I started hunting Monday. Although I saw no deer, fresh tracks crisscrossed the area, and I saw no sign of other hunters. Tuesday was a replay of Monday until just before dark. Then I spotted a fine buck crossing an opening. There was no time for a shot, but my confidence soared.

Wednesday morning the wind was blowing wrong, so I had to wait until noon to start hunting. Then I worked down the top of one of the lateral ridges. After I'd done three hours of slow moving, my plan proved itself as I watched a forkhorn step

from his bedding cover on the far side of a canyon. One shot at 200 yards brought him down.

I still had another tag, and daylight remained. And bigger bucks lived here somewhere. So after taking care of the buck, I left him in the shade to cool and continued down the same ridge.

Within 200 yards I spotted another buck just standing up to begin his evening feeding. He was too far away for an offhand shot, the only possible position from where I was, and a wall of live oak blocked the way to him. So I found a tunnel under the brush and started crawling. For 75 yards I could see nothing but tangled branches all around. Then daylight appeared ahead. Wrestling my way to a small, bare cliff, I stood up to see over the brush.

The buck was in the same position, now about 100 yards away. He was staring my way, but he wasn't spooked, just curious about the rustling he'd heard in the shrubbery. As I brought the .30/06 to my shoulder, I nearly had to stand on tiptoes to clear the bushes. The crosshairs centered on the buck's chest, and I squeezed. He dropped instantly. With my rifle ready to shoot again, I waited for five minutes. But the buck lay still.

Then I bulled my way through the jungle and found my trophy, a beautiful animal weighing about 140 pounds, with four symmetrical points on each side of his 16-inch rack, lying in the same bed he'd rested in only minutes before.

It was dark now. Laura and I would have to return the next day to pack the two bucks out of this hole. It would be work all the way.

But how could I complain? That's the way I'd planned it. 🦌

Ready or Not?

Jim Carmichel

For more years than I can remember, I've been trying to discover why some deer hunters are invariably successful and why others with seemingly equal opportunities almost never connect. What common trait links successful hunters? Is it their choice of guns or calibers? Are they a more determined breed? More patient? Better marksmen? What? The difference, so far as I can tell, is the month of August.

August is the month that tests the souls of deer hunters. To some, it is a month of a thousand days that ooze together with such numbing subtlety that it is scarcely noted in which hour on what day breathes the last soft sigh of summer.

To other deer hunters, August is the eve of the season, a time to get ready. A time to soften boots and harden muscles. A time to wipe summer's dust from bright steel and to burnish walnut with hand-rubbed oil. A time to quicken the eye and steady the aim.

August is the month when the racks in gun shops are filled with the latest in shooting ware, ready to be picked like ripe berries. Yet, for reasons that deserve no explanation, the guns languish there until short days or even hours before the season's opening. One of the saddest places I know is a sporting-goods shop two days before deer season. It's crowded with would-be hunters shoving feet into stiff boots, working the actions of unfamiliar rifles, and peering through unmounted scopes. It is sad because the frenzied excitement is often followed by crashing disappointment. But hunters who start getting ready in August are often rewarded by sweet memories that last for years.

Another sad sight is the local rifle range the weekend before deer season opens. I've seen hunters lined up 10 deep, desperately waiting to fire new rifles and zero new scopes. They try to crowd days of necessary practice into short minutes at the bench. But did you ever visit a shooting range in August? It can be a lonely place. There's never a line of waiting hunters. You can take your time and get to *know* your rifle. We've all heard the statistic that most whitetail deer are taken at ranges shorter than 75 yards. Another statistic, one you never hear, is that the average *miss* is fired at less than 75 yards.

"Come on," you say, "who could miss a great big deer at so short a distance?" But it's true. My mail is full of letters from perfectly serious readers complaining that a deer they shot "in the heart at 25 yards ran off without even leaving a blood trail." Invariably they blame poor bullets, bad rifles, or unreliable scopes. Never does the shooter's marksmanship seem to be at fault. In truth, though, most misses are just that—misses.

This is a tragedy because marksmanship is a skill than can be mastered with relative ease and maintained with little effort. August is the month to practice marksmanship. I have a notion that you are not so good with a rifle as you think you are. This is not an insult—it's a challenge. I challenge you to do this:

MARKSMANSHIP TESTS

Take your favorite deer rifle to the rifle range in August, and be sure to take plenty of ammo. Also take someone with you, a spouse, son, daughter, or

8

friend. When you get there, sit down at the test bench and fire a few shots at a 100-yard target. Make any necessary sight adjustments to ensure that your rifle is on target, because I don't want you to have an alibi.

My test is simple. Put up a target about the size of a paper plate at 100 yards. Shooting offhand (standing with no artificial support), fire five consecutive shots at the target. You don't have to hit the center of the target, just hit it *anywhere*. If all five shots are in the target, I withdraw my challenge and apologize; you are a crackerjack.

Here's the catch. Whoever you bring to the range must understand the rules and witness your shooting. You see, just having someone watch not only makes you be honest with yourself but also adds a certain element of pressure—not nearly as much pressure as you'll feel when you're aiming at a trophy buck—but enough to make your pulse quicken a bit.

Hunters, as a group, are probably the most truthloving, devout, chaste, and saintly people who ever roamed the earth, but for some reason we refuse to be honest *with ourselves* about our marksmanship. It's not that we deliberately mislead ourselves; we simply tend to forget our bad shots. If, for example, a hunter fires 20 shots at a target and only one plugs the bull's-eye dead center, he forgets the 19 other shots and goes home supremely confident in his deadly marksmanship.

The five-shot offhand test will tell you if you are a good shot. Here's another test that will tell if you are a *bad* shot. Do everything the same way, but this time, steady your rifle alongside a vertical support such as a tree, a pole, or firing-line roof support. Don't let the rifle touch the support—cushion it with your hand. When hunting in whitetail woods, we can often make use of such aids, and hunters who can't hit a pachyderm in the patoot when shooting offhand can usually get steady enough with a little support to get a bullet on target. If you can't hit a plate-size target with a side rest, you *know* you're going to miss a deer. And finding that out in August rather then during deer season is wonderful good luck. In one month, the month of August, you can become a good shot.

PRACTICE

The problem with practicing with your deer rifle is that it's so godawful expensive. Ammo makers operate on one of the thinnest profit margins in manufacturing, but even so the cost of, say, 100 rounds of .30/06 ammo is likely to be upwards of $60, even at discount prices. Handloaders have a tremendous price advantage in this respect because they can put together 100 '06 reloads for less then $20. This is a leading reason why reloaders tend to be better shots and more successful hunters. Quite simply, they can afford to practice more.

Even if you're not a handloader, you can beat the cost. One way is simply to do a lot of practicing with

When I raise my rifle for a shot in a deer woods, the results depend on the kind of practice I've been putting in.

a .22 Rimfire rifle. One very effective way to practice shots at deer with a .22 is to shoot at longer ranges than you would in casual plinking. A middling-to-good .22 rifle is about as accurate at 100 yards as a good centerfire deer rifle, you'll discover, so why not shoot at longer ranges so you'll get the "feel" of distance? If you normally hunt with a telescopic sight, let me give you a hint. Take the scope off your deer rifle and mount it on your .22. Any properly stocked gun shop will have mounts that will adapt your scope to most .22 rifles. At most, this will cost you the price of a new mount and rings, but some systems make it possible to swap the scope from rifle to rifle, with only the additional cost of an extra base or bases. The reason this is such a great idea is that it gives you the chance to fire hundreds of low-cost practice shots with the very scope you'll be using when the chips are down.

Finally, two or three weeks before your big hunt, put the scope back on your big-game rifle and zero it to dead-center perfection, but don't stop practicing. Spend a few more hours at the range getting used to your full-power deer loads.

TAKING RECOIL

Lots of hunters don't like to practice with their deer rifles because they fear recoil. I have two thoughts on this. First, rifles kick most painfully when fired from a benchrest. That's because they are held rather loosely on the sandbags and because your torso is in a position that does not permit your shoulder to move with the recoil. After firing a few shots over the sandbags to check your sights, forget the benchrest and do your shooting from the standing, sitting, and kneeling positions. You'll find the rifle kicks a lot less. Second, rifles kick us in the ears more than in the shoulder. Wear good earplugs (not just a wad of cotton), earmuffs, or better yet, do as I do and wear plugs *and* muffs. You'll immediately discover that your rifle doesn't seem to kick half as much. I absolutely guarantee it.

It's exceedingly difficult to learn to shoot a centerfire rifle well without ear protection. I cannot overemphasize this simple point.

Consider this simple parable. Deer hunter Jack and Bob are each given 100 cartridges. Jack shoots 95 of his cartridges on the practice range and takes the remaining five hunting. Bob shoots only five practice shots and takes the remaining 95 rounds into the woods. Who gets a deer?

GETTING YOUR RIFLE READY

Every once in a while, a proud hunter confides to me that his beloved deer rifle is so unfailingly trustworthy that a dozen seasons have passed without any need to touch the sight adjustments. I don't doubt this, for I've owned a few such exceptionally stable rifles myself, but it troubles me somewhat. It troubles me because if a hunter is seduced into believing his equipment is totally reliable, he is courting disappointment. I have a wonderfully reliable rifle, made by the David Miller Company, that has endured everything from the desert heat of Africa to the foggy cold of Alaska without any measurable changes in its zero. Even though it has proven itself to be utterly stable, I would never consider taking it on a hunt without first checking the scope at my test range. There are too many factors affecting how a rifle performs to accept the reliability of its zero on blind faith. Even if the rifle has not changed, your favorite ammunition may have. Changes in manufacturing procedures, loads, and bullet shape or construction can result in a different point of impact in respect to aim. Thus, a box of ammo may shoot inches wide of last year's box, even though both boxes are the same make and the bullet weight is the same.

Give your rifle a thorough going over in August, before you begin practicing, and then check again a few days before your hunt. When I take a rifle out of storage, I check the tightness of the guard screws and go over the scope-mount screws with a proper-fitting screwdriver. Heavy storage grease is cleaned away and replaced with light oil. I also run a patch through the barrel to clean out grease or oil, and the bore is left dry for shooting. Uncovered scope lenses

have a way of getting dusty, even when protected in a gun cabinet, so they can stand a light wiping with a soft cloth. If the lenses are really spotted, you may need to use alcohol or window cleaner, but in any event, don't wipe too hard and don't use coarse-grained tissue, because the chemical coating on the lenses might be scratched. Use a fluff of cotton, lens tissue, or clean soft-cotton cloth.

When I began my shooting career, there was considerable controversy about the need or even the advisability of cleaning rifle barrels. Some shooters claimed that with the new noncorrosive primers, cleaning wasn't necessary, and that the longer a rifle was shot without cleaning, the more accurate it became. During that period, some barrels were never cleaned, but that was before the game of benchrest shooting developed into what it is now. One thing benchrest shooting has taught us about accuracy is that rifle barrels *must* be cleaned if they are to be accurate. That's why target shooters now routinely clean their barrels several times during the course of a tournament. I do not like to fire a centerfire rifle much more than 20 rounds without cleaning. Get a good cleaning kit, and use it often.

If you have not fired your rifle since last hunting season, don't be distressed or even surprised if your sighting shots don't hit where they did a year ago. Many rifles, especially bolt-action models, tend to have a "wandering" point of impact with respect to point of aim that can vary as much as several inches. So if your rifle isn't shooting where it did last year, don't worry. Go ahead and make the necessary sight changes to get the zero right. However, make a note of how much the point of impact shifted and in which direction. If the trend continues in the same direction, it is a warning of chronic stock warpage or related bedding problems. If a rifle tends to shift zero on a daily basis, it could be a sign that the sights or even the stock are loose. Check everything again. Discovering such problems while there's time for corrections is one more reason why August is so important.

THE SHORT-RANGE "ZERO"

At least once a week I get a letter from a reader who is planning his once-in-a-lifetime mule-deer hunt and wants to know how to zero his rifle at 25 yards so that it will be sighted-in to hit right on target at 300 yards. Several years ago, many other magazines printed articles about short-range sighting-in tricks that would put bullets on target at long range. Since then, various charts have been published that are supposed to eliminate the fuss and bother of actu-

Practice with proper ear protection and you'll notice rifle recoil much less.

Can you put five shots in a target this size when shooting offhand at 100 yards?

You can't hit plate-size target at 100 yards with side rest? You need practice.

ally shooting a rifle at long range in order to get the sights set right. It's a great idea, saves lots of walking back and forth to distant targets, and is especially helpful to hunters who have access to only short-distance ranges. The problem, though, is that the system is cursed with so many variables that it is *very* unreliable. In other words, forget it.

A TIME TO BUY

The yearly gun trade follows a set pattern. Around the first of the year, the various gunmakers show their new models to the trade and take orders from dealers. The guns are then manufactured during the spring and early summer and delivered to dealers by late summer. That's why the best possible selection of new guns is available in August. As deer season comes closer, gun sales increase. By the eve of hunting season, the most desirable guns have disappeared from dealers' racks.

So, if you're thinking about a new deer rifle, August is the time to start looking. If you buy then, chances of getting the gun you want are much better. Not only will you get the model dearest to your heart but you'll get the individual firearm you need. All guns are a bit different. If you look at 10 guns, all the same model, you'll discover that each one has certain unique characteristics. Stocks, in particular, are different. Early shoppers can sort through several guns to pick a special stock that has more figure, color, or better grain than the others. Late shoppers get what's left.

August is also a relatively slow month for gunsmiths. If you need work done—scope mounting, a recoil pad fitted, reblueing, or refinishing—that's the best time, because the wait is short. But if you wait until deer season is at hand to visit your gunsmith, as so many of our brethren do, you'll find yourself at the end of a long waiting list.

CLOTHES AND GEAR

August is the time to buy and break in hunting clothes and gear.

Boots are the hunter's best friend or his mortal enemy. I have some mighty strong feelings about hunting boots, and if I had my way, the makers of some of today's outdoor footwear would be condemned to wear their own products. We've all heard the old pro's advice about buying boots early in the season and breaking them in bit by bit. Sounds like good advice, and to a certain extent, it is. But I really think that whoever originated this gem probably never owned a really good pair of boots. The best four or five pairs of boots I've ever owned required no breaking in whatever and were ready for long hikes the first time I wore them. Price, in case you're wondering, is only a rough guide to quality, comfort, and durability. There are several brands of boots I would like to steer you away from, but since I can't afford the ensuing lawsuits, the best advice I can give you is to give a lot of

thought to your selection. Sales gimmicks that look good can be absolutely crippling.

We want our hunting boots to be as water-repellent as possible, but some makes and styles absolutely resist all efforts to make them turn water. I'm not talking about the "guaranteed" waterproof models—which, in my experience, pretty well do what the makers claim—but the more ordinary plain leather types. One of the first clues to how waterproof a boot can be made is the leather's exterior surface. If the boot has a slick, lacquered or polished look, it will be difficult to waterproof. The problem is the leather-finishing process, which usually involves a sprayed-on, plastic-like coating that provides the slick, shiny texture. This kind of finish won't turn water, but it *will* resist many waterproofing greases and compounds. The slick leather coating won't let grease soak in and protect the leather.

A good way to cure the problem is to soak the boots in water and wear them wet while mowing the lawn or going about similar chores. This serves the double purpose of conforming the boot to your foot in the fastest, easiest possible way, and it also scrubs away the cheap plastic coating. When the leather has a dull, almost suede-like surface, it will absorb warm grease and become reasonably water-resistant.

Another tip-off to leaky boots is excessive stitching. Some boots have rugged-looking stitching, which, on close inspection, doesn't hold anything together. Such decorative stitching is nothing but a lot of holes that let the water come pouring in.

Will you be using a portable tree stand? An ever-increasing number of hunting deaths and serious injuries are caused by falling out of tree stands. One major reason for these accidents is simply not knowing how to use the various portable tree stands, especially the climbing types. Another is failure to maintain permanent stands. I promise you that the time to learn how to use a portable tree stand is not on the first dark morning of the season. Using a tree stand is one of the most effective ways to hunt whitetails, but some models are not as simple to use as the brochures say. Using a climbing platform, in particular, takes some skill and requires practice.

So if you see a portable tree stand in your future, go shopping early. Practice with it a little at a time until you develop confidence. Get to know the anchoring and support systems so well that you can use them in dim light or even darkness. You don't want to spend the first all-important hours of deer season trying to figure out how your platform works.

Even if your state's deer season opens a month or two later, August is the month it should all start. That's the time to make lists of things to do. There is gear to check and repair, ammo to buy, and skills to be honed to razor-edged readiness. The pleasure of deer hunting is not felt only in the fleeting instant when a trophy buck bounds into your scope's field of view; it also can be enjoyed during your preparations for that wonderful moment.

Are You Fit for Hunting?

Bruce Brady

Over the years, I've had the good fortune to savor some of the best hunting grounds in the nation. All my hunts presented a challenge, not only in terms of game sought but also in handling some rough terrain. To enjoy the challenge, you have to be in shape for the hunt. Does your physical condition enhance or detract from your hunting success? The test that follows will help you judge while there's still time to shape up.

I have guided big-game hunts in the West, and after watching many poorly conditioned hunters, I can say without fear of contradiction that their two best days are the first day, before wind and muscles are taxed, and the final day, when all the torture is ended. It's difficult to become enraptured with a hunt or concentrate on a stalk when your back aches and your lungs are burning.

Keeping yourself in good physical condition just might mean keeping yourself alive. We've all heard stories of hunters felled by fatal heart attacks. Cardiovascular health is a major concern. So we'll start the "hunter's fitness test" by running, because running is both the best test of heart, lung, and blood-vessel proficiency and the most effective conditioning for the cardiovascular system. It's a good idea, before attempting the test, to have a complete physical examination, including an electrocardiogram.

THE 12-MINUTE RUN

The 12-minute run test, developed by Dr. Kenneth Cooper, is one of the best tests for cardiovascular fitness. To perform the test, you simply run as far as possible in 12 minutes. Establish and maintain a steady pace. The greater the distance covered, the better the score. Use Chart I to assess your fitness.

Unless you already run regularly, you will probably be shocked at your score on the 12-minute run test. Your cardiovascular fitness may not be the only disappointment; your legs probably aren't prepared for running, much less the rigors of a hard hunt.

Fortunately, such health problems aren't permanent. Your heart, lungs, blood vessels. and legs can all be strengthened if you implement a running program. I heartily recommend that you first read *The New Aerobics* by Dr. Kenneth Cooper (published by

Chart 1
12-MINUTE RUN TEST FOR MEN

(Distance in miles in 12 minutes)*

Fitness	Under 30	30–40	40–50	50+
Excellent	1.75	1.62	1.50	1.38
Good	1.62	1.50	1.38	1.25
Average	1.50	1.38	1.25	1.12
Fair	1.38	1.25	1.12	1.0
Poor	1.25	1.12	1.0	.87

Women should deduct .125 miles from the above scores.

If you rank below average on your track test, your body will suffer on a hunt

Unless you're in good physical shape, dragging or packing out a deer will be torture on your heart and lungs.

M. Evans & Company, Inc., 216 E. 49th Street, New York, NY 10017). The author offers solid programs and step-by-step procedures.

Regardless of your age, you should begin running slowly; it's all too easy to pull muscles or otherwise injure yourself. Always warm up thoroughly with stretching exercises. Sit-ups, side-bends, jumping-jacks, and half-squats are all good muscle extenders. Walk a quarter of a mile before running. After running, walk until you cool off a bit, and then do some more stretching.

Set goals for yourself. A good initial goal is to run a mile in less then 10 minutes. Next, try for two miles in less then 20 minutes. Gradually, you will increase your distance and speed. I believe a minimum of two miles in less than 20 minutes—five days a week—is needed to maintain good cardiovascular health.

In just a few weeks, you'll note a great difference in your wind, stamina, and leg strength. You will also discover that running relieves the tensions of the day, makes you feel better, sleep better, and work harder. Excess inches will begin to melt away, and you will note muscles in places you haven't seen them for years.

But more than good wind and strong legs are needed on most hunting trips. There always seems to be something heavy to lift or load. There's a buck to drag out, heavy sacks of decoys to tote, boats to load and portage, and dozens of other tasks requiring strength and endurance. So next, let's test the strength, endurance, and flexibility of several muscle groups.

BENT-KNEE SIT-UP TEST

This will test strength and endurance of the abdominal muscles. Lie on your back, hands interlocked behind your head, feet back toward your buttocks. A pal can hold your feet to the floor. A full sit-up is counted when you raise up, extend your elbows past your knees, and return to the floor. Your score is the number of sit-ups completed in one minute. You can rest on your back if needed. To determine your fitness level, see Chart 2.

Bent-Knee Sit-Up: With buddy holding your feet, raise up and push your elbows past your knees.

SIT-UP EXTENSION TEST

Flexibility is the ability to use a muscle throughout its range of motion. If you're inactive, or sit or stand for long periods, you may lose the ability to bend, twist, and stretch. The result is shortened muscles and tendons, lower back pain, and an imbalance in strength between opposing muscles. Shortened

Sit-Up: With your feet against books, stretch forward and measure how far fingers extend past books.

hamstrings in the back of the thigh is a common problem. Loss of such flexibility limits your ability to perform efficiently in the field, especially where brush is dense or the land precipitous. This sit-up extension test will provide a reasonable assessment of your ability to flex and stretch the muscles of the arms, shoulders, back, and thighs.

Sit on the floor with your legs fully extended and the bottoms of your feet touching a stack of books placed against the wall. Extend and stretch your hands and arms forward as far as you can, and hold for a count of three. Have your partner measure with a ruler the number of inches your fingers ex-

tend past the front edge of the books. Do not bend your knees. See Chart 2 to score.

DIP TEST

This test measures the strength and endurance of the extensors of the arms, shoulder girdle, and upper-back muscles. Begin at the end of parallel bars, supporting yourself with arms fully extended. Lower your body until your arms assume a right-

Dip Test: On parallel bars, you extend your arms fully, lower your body, and then push upward.

angle bend. Then push upward to return to the starting position. The score is the number of dips completed. No swinging, and don't count partial dips. See Chart 2.

PULL-UP TEST

A pull-up test determines the strength and muscular endurance of the flexors of the arms, shoulder girdle, and upper-back muscles. Use a chinning bar. Grasp the overhead bar with your palms facing away and let your legs hang fully extended. Pull up until your chin clears the top of the bar, then lower yourself to the starting position. Your score is the number of pull-ups performed. Be sure that your arms extend fully and your chin clears the bar. Do not swing or kick. See Chart 2 for evaluating.

Disappointed with your scores on these four tests? You can improve muscular strength, endurance, and flexibility by simply incorporating these same exercises into a daily conditioning program. A

Chart 2			
TEST FOR STRENGTH AND ENDURANCE			
	One-Minute *Sit-Ups*	*Pull-Ups*	*Dips*	*Sit-Up Extensions (inches)*
Excellent	40+	15+	15+	3 to 8
Good	35	10	10	1 to 3
Average	25	7	7	1
Fair	15	4	4	0
Poor	less than 15	less than 4	less than 4	0 to −6

A low score on these tests means you may not be able to handle tough camp chores

Pull-Up: Hold bar with your palms facing away, and then pull up until your chin clears bar.

host of other exercises and calisthenics will condition all the muscle groups you will use when hunting this fall. No expensive paraphernalia is required. Your local library is a convenient source of exercise books and manuals.

WEIGHT CONTROL

Excessive weight not only restricts your body movements but also damages your cardiovascular system by hindering your body's capacity to process and deliver oxygen.

Fat adds to the effort a hunter expends during a day in the field. Even 10 pounds makes a great difference. If you doubt it, just put a 10-pound weight into your hunting coat when you start out in the morning, and see how heavy it seems by late afternoon.

Fat is a dangerous burden: the death rate for people 15 to 24 percent overweight is 20 percent greater then for those who aren't overweight. The death rate for those who are 35 percent overweight is 50 percent greater.

Are you overweight? What should you weigh? To find the answers, look at Chart 3. This chart makes allowances for various frame sizes, but it fails to consider muscle content, and muscle weighs more than fat. For example, according to this table, a 6-foot, 220-pound professional running back with a

32-inch waist is 35 pounds overweight. This is an obvious inaccuracy.

The fat-pinch test is a more reliable method of measuring fat on the body. Your doctor can do this for you and instruct you on how to do it for yourself. Chart 3 should be used only to make a rough estimate of your proper weight.

Chart 3
DESIRABLE WEIGHTS
(Ages 25 and Over)
Men

Height (with shoes on)	Small Frame	Medium Frame	Large Frame
5' 2"	112–120	118–129	126–141
3"	115–123	121–133	129–144
4"	118–126	124–136	132–148
5"	121–129	127–139	135–152
6"	124–133	130–143	138–156
7"	128–137	134–147	142–161
8"	132–141	138–152	147–166
9"	136–145	142–156	151–170
10"	140–150	146–160	155–174
11"	144–154	150–165	159–179
6' 0"	148–158	154–170	164–184
1"	152–162	158–175	168–189
2"	156–167	162–180	173–194
3"	160–171	167–185	178–199
4"	164–176	172–190	182–204

Women

Height (with shoes on) 2-inch heels	Small Frame	Medium Frame	Large Frame
5' 0"	96–104	101–113	109–125
1"	99–107	104–116	112–128
2"	102–110	107–119	115–131
3"	105–113	110–122	118–134
4"	108–116	113–126	121–138
5"	111–119	116–130	125–142
6"	114–123	120–135	129–146
7"	118–127	124–139	133–150
8"	122–131	128–143	137–154

Reprinted from The Physical Fitness Encyclopedia © 1970 by *Rodale Press, Inc. Permission granted by Rodale Press, Inc., Emmaus, PA 18049.*

Fat can also be dangerous. Here's what you should weigh—or how much you should lose

Seek your doctor's advice. If you are overweight, he can supply a diet which includes all the necessary nutrients and still allows you to lose weight.

Running and exercise will take off inches, but diet is the key to weight loss. Get a calorie chart, and keep track of what you consume. Remember, one ounce of milk chocolate contains 150 calories—but only 120 calories are expended in running a mile in eight minutes.

Techniques for Seeing Deer

John O. Cartier

Warren Holmes and I were pass-shooting ducks on a knoll in North Dakota. Scattered clumps of brush varying from house-size to several acres dotted the prairie around us. During a lull in the shooting, my companion pointed to a small patch of thickets 300 yards away.

"Big buck," he said.

I stared at those thickets till my eyes watered. I couldn't see anything that even resembled a deer. I shook my head and said, "Warren, I think you're seeing things."

"Well, darn it," he answered, "he's standing right there next to the north edge. There, he's moving out. Surely you can spot him now."

I finally did see the deer, but not until his body began taking shape as a silhouette against the golden prairie. Even then it was difficult to spot his antlers till he turned his head to look at us.

Warren has worn glasses since childhood. I've never worn them. We're both in our mid-fifties. My eyes are better than his, but he has made me feel like a fool on several occasions when he had to point out game to me.

One time in Wyoming we were hunting mule deer. Our host was a rancher who had hunted deer in the West for many years. His idea of hunting is to drive back-country trails in a pickup while looking for game. He is accustomed to the system and to the terrain, but Warren often spotted deer before he did. I recall one time we were driving slowly down through a gully.

"Hold it," Warren said. "Back up about 15 feet. I think I saw the top of a buck's head in those rocks 100 yards to our right."

Ken backed up and stopped. Warren had been correct. He pointed toward a precise spot and told us a small three-pointer was lying flat out while trying to hide. Neither Ken nor I saw the animal till it decided to jump up and bolt.

"I'll be darned," our host said. "How'd you ever spot that little buck?"

Later in the day, Warren decided he'd have a better vantage point if he rode in the truck's bed instead of its cab. Several times Ken and I were surprised by his sudden pounding on the roof. It was Warren's signal that he'd spotted more deer.

That evening Ken told Warren that he was astonished with his game-seeing abilities, particularly because Warren had little experience hunting in the West. Ken asked what the secret was.

"Well, I guess a deer is a deer," my partner began. "Even though I don't have much knowledge of mule deer, I've hunted whitetails all my life. Most hunters make the mistake of expecting to see a whole deer. Most often you'll see only parts of a motionless animal. I seem to have a natural knack for recognizing cover where deer may be. I search that cover with my eyes, and I look for colors or shapes that could be parts of a deer. I often see a pair of legs, a flickering ear, or parts of antlers before I can make out the animal itself."

Larry Price, a guide with whom I've hunted in Colorado, also has a great facility to see deer. He explained his ability in another way.

"Most hunters fail to see deer in heavy cover unless the animals are moving," he told me. "Movement is easy to see, so I don't worry about missing it. I concentrate on looking for unnatural objects that aren't moving. When you think about it, you'll realize that most objects in the woods are vertical. Sure there are blowdowns, logs, and rocks that are horizontal, but everything that's growing is vertical. Deer bodies are not. So I pay special attention to horizontal objects, and I really scrutinize anything that approaches a deer's size or color."

Wayne Fitzwater, a Montana game warden, once told me that experience is the most important factor in seeing game. We sat on the edge of a mountain ledge one evening and watched mule deer by the dozens come out of forests surrounding a logged-off area across a canyon. He claimed it isn't much of a problem to see game if you've had enough hunting experience to hunt where game is likely to be.

I'll have more to say about this theory shortly. But first I want to mention that Wayne's system had to be more complicated. He was pointing out bucks that were several hundred yards away. Not only that, but also he was seeing the animals as they were just beginning to walk out of the timber. Often I couldn't tell deer from stumps until the animals were well into the clearing.

That night in camp, we discussed the art of seeing game, and Wayne mentioned something that I'd never thought about before. He just passed it off as matter-of-fact, but I believe it's an important principle most hunters are unaware of.

"Many hunters miss seeing detail because they take a wide-angle view of everything," he began. "That's because a panoramic view is naturally most interesting. The trick is to spend only half your time with the wide-angle view. The other half should be spent looking for detail. You were having trouble telling deer from stumps because you were trying to see everything at once. After you concentrated on a particular deer, it suddenly didn't look like a stump at all. That's because you narrowed down your field of view. You saw a lot of stumps that looked like deer, but after you focused your attention you didn't see a deer that looked like a stump. It's just a matter of training your eyes to see detail."

How important is the art of seeing game? It's all-important for deer hunters because modern deer depend far less upon running to safety than did the bucks of yesteryear. Today's bucks know their odds of staying alive are much better if they hide instead of run. Deer still panic and run, but they are apt to run for shorter distances, then hide sooner and longer.

When I started hunting mule deer years ago in the Western states, I was astonished to see so many deer in pastures, in fields along roads, and in plain sight in woodland clearings. That fact was brought home to me during a hunt with Ray Lyons, an outfitter in Collbran, Colorado.

We drove down out of the mountains one evening when a blizzard was brewing. In fields along the valley road, we saw quite a few deer, often several of them feeding in groups. I mentioned to Ray that I'd spotted no deer along the same route during the several previous days we'd been driving it.

"They're feeding early because a storm's coming," he said. "There are plenty of deer down in these valleys, but they normally don't come out of hiding till dark. Years ago you used to see deer all over the place, even during hunting season. They're much more secretive now, and they're wizards at hiding. You have to look a lot harder to see deer today."

You might conclude from a casual look at the scene on the left that it has no deer in it. Wrong. Study carefully the scene on the right and you will find evidence that will enable you to identify a deer in both views. Successful hunters make a practice of studying suspicious areas and forms. (Don Wooldridge photos)

That statement came from a man who had been a full-time guide and outfitter for nearly 50 years. It's some of the best advice a modern deer hunter can get.

As for seeing whitetails, I believe Warren Holmes's convictions are about as solid as any. His score for the past 18 years is 18 bucks. He took all of them in a heavily hunted area of Michigan, a state where the deer-hunter success ratio is only about 15 percent. How can he score so consistently when nearly 90 percent of the hunters around him fail to go home with venison? Well, he hunts hard, and he hunts only from stands. But it's likely that much of his success comes from his knack for seeing deer. One time he said to me, "The best shot in the world isn't going to eat deer liver unless he can see a deer to shoot at."

One of Warren's favorite topics is deer size. He points out that almost all hunters delude themselves into expecting the average whitetail to be much larger and taller than it really is. Tell a hunter that a big buck seldom stands taller than 40 inches at his shoulder and you'll have a doubter, but you'll be telling the truth. Warren claims that if a hunter thinks "small" he'll see more deer.

Incidentally, I happen to believe that the odds are pretty well stacked against many deer hunters who go after their whitetail bucks by using the stillhunting technique. But I know one guy, now an old man, who used to be fairly successful with the system before his area became crowded with hunters. Years ago, when I began to get serious about deer hunting, I'd often visit with this fellow and ask him about the tricks of the trade. I've never forgotten one comment he made, and it's better advice now than it was then.

"I'd tell any hunter to use his eyes more than his feet," he began. "Most hunters are in too much of a hurry to see what's over the next hill. The plain fact is that once you're in good deer country, your buck is just as likely to be in the thicket next to you as he is to be in one three miles away. You won't get a shot at him unless you see him before he sees you. You have to focus all your attention on the most suspicious things you see. That's the way to spot a deer. Successful stillhunting is about 90 percent looking."

I'll admit that my ability to see deer is not too good, but it's far better than it was 30 years ago. Not long ago, I downed a mule-deer buck that was almost invisible. He was standing motionless in a stand of timber so thick you could barely see the snow background behind the trees. When I first spotted him, all I noticed was a patch of gray that was out of place against the white snow and pale-green aspen trunks. Seconds later, I picked out part of a rack of antlers. Then I noticed another patch of gray that was part of the buck's shoulder. That offered me a vital area to shoot at, and it was a big enough target since the range was short. My slug broke the deer's back, and he dropped on the spot. I'm just about positive I'd never have seen that deer unless I'd known what to look for.

Everything I've mentioned so far points out that much of the skill used in seeing deer is a skill that can be learned. I believe that most successful deer hunters develop much of this skill without being aware of it. In acquiring an extensive outdoor background, you automatically learn to interpret what you see. As warden Wayne Fitzwater told me, an experienced hunter learns to recognize good deer country. That skill presents the possibility of seeing

The scene below contains seven whitetails, but the casual hunter would probably spot only the doe at the left. The key to success is to look first for parts of deer not a whole animal. For proof of seven deer, see illustration to right. Then pick out deer below.
(Missouri Conservation Department photo by Don Wooldridge)

more deer. You learn to analyze where deer travel, feed, and bed; you literally think like a deer. In short, a hunter with lots of experience knows where to look. The most successful veteran hunters also know *how* to look.

The most obvious way to get a better view of what you're looking at is to inspect a questionable object with binoculars or your riflescope. Glassing for deer is especially important in Western states, where you're likely to see animals at greater distances than in the heavily forested East, Midwest, and South. Several guides have told me that average deer hunters have great difficulty putting their glasses or scopes on partially hidden deer even after they have located them with the unaided eye.

The reason is that most hunters seldom use their binoculars or scopes except during the few days each year that they are actually hunting. They aren't familiar enough with their equipment to use it efficiently. This is one fault I don't have. I'm a nut on using binoculars year-round.

My office windows face out on a large inland lake. I delight in studying migrating ducks in fall and spring, fishermen in summer and winter, and birds and squirrels and other interesting objects just about anytime. Scarcely a day goes by during which I don't use my binoculars several times. I'm as familiar with using those glasses as I am with touching a match to my pipe.

This familiarity often enables me to see game that would otherwise go unnoticed. I go along with the guides who claim that the average hunter would do himself a big favor by learning to use optics efficiently. A deer antler that seems to be a branch in the distance can be identified for just what it is with the use of glasses. I could list many such examples.

Deer hunters of years ago didn't bother much with scopes or binoculars because the early models were relatively bulky and inefficient. Modern optics are far superior, and they're among the most impor-

tant advances ever made in deer-hunting equipment. For today's deer hunter, a good binocular can be just about as important as his rifle.

A problem among Eastern hunters who go after mule deer in the West for the first time is that they don't look for deer in the right places. Most whitetails seen from stands or during drives are likely to be spotted 50 to 75 yards away. In the more open country where mule deer are hunted, it's common to see potential targets several hundred yards away. Also, whitetails are much more likely to hide than muleys. A whitetail may not bolt until you're practically on top of him, but a mule deer will seldom let you approach closer than 100 yards.

Hunters with whitetail backgrounds often go on their first mule-deer hunt and continue to use the short-range vision they used back home. They miss seeing deer that may be in plain view across a canyon, down in a draw, or up on a ridge. The cure is to get local advice on where to look when hunting a new area for the first time.

One of my Michigan friends joined five other fellows and drove to the Colorado Rockies for a mule-deer hunt. They had never hunted the area, they had no experience with mule deer, they had no guide, and they didn't bother to ask for local advice. They camped for six days, saw few deer, and scored on only one small buck.

In contrast, I booked a hunt in approximately the same area with a reputable outfitter. There were four hunters in my group, and we nailed four big bucks in only 2½ days of hunting. The difference was that our outfitter put us in the right spots and told us where to look for deer.

One of the main reasons hunters don't see deer is that the animals see or hear them first. Mule deer, more so than whitetails, are likely to spook and run when confronted by man. It's common sense to expect to see deer farther ahead if you're walking on crusted snow or very dry ground than if you're

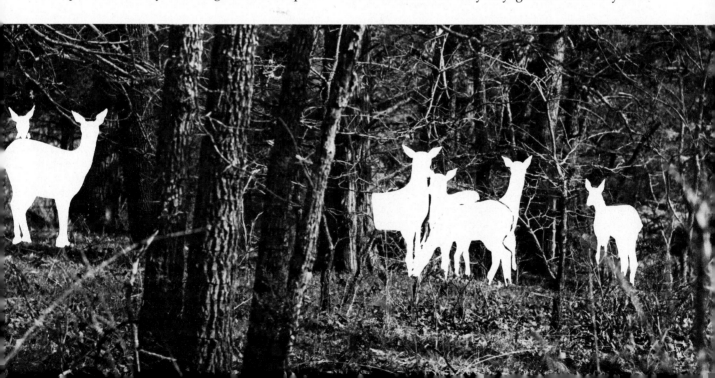

Many hunters fail to consider the weather's effects on game movement. In this photo, bucks have retreated into a hollow to escape heavy winds.

The most dramatic experiences that have shown me how weather affects deer happened within a few miles of where I'm writing these lines. Deer live all around my place in mixed woodlands of hardwoods, birch, brush, and conifers. These forests are fairly thick, except where they give way to huge areas of sand dunes along the Lake Michigan shoreline. The dunes are mostly rolling hills of sand with low areas that harbor scattered pockets of pine.

You could roam those dunes for days during spring, summer, and early fall and be lucky to see a deer track, let alone a deer. But as fall wears on, the herds begin moving into the dunes. When heavy snowfall hits, they converge on the area. Take a trip through there in winter on a snowmobile and you'll see deer all over the place.

It's likely that deer movements in your area are affected to some degree by weather, too. I can't tell you how your local deer react to changing weather conditions, because even the same species react differently in various parts of the country. But if you'll take the time to study your local situation and talk to local experts, you'll probably gain additional knowledge that will enable you to see more deer.

You need to develop the knack of "looking into" shadows to see bedded deer. If you're scanning the terrain too fast, you could miss a rack like this. (Don Wooldridge photo)

walking on wet or soft ground. You'll also make less noise if you eliminate noisemakers like keys or change in your pockets, canteens or binoculars banging against rifle stocks, or crinkly clothing and rain gear. The human voice is especially startling to deer. When you're hunting with companions, it's best to save talkfests until after the day's hunting is finished.

The time of day can be a very important factor in seeing deer. One time in the prairie portion of Wyoming, I wondered why my guide started the day stillhunting directly toward the brightening sky in the east. My unasked question was answered in a hurry when a three-point buck got up from his bed near the top of a rise 250 yards ahead of us. I'll never forget the coal-black silhouette the animal made against the dawn sky. Even his antlers were outlined in perfect detail One of my companions shot the buck. When we reached the kill site, I commented that the deer must have been stupid to let a hunter in plain sight shoot him.

"No, we weren't in plain sight," the guide answered. "Look back down to where we were when he stood up. It's still in shadows down there. He couldn't see us nearly so well as we could see him. If you can hunt upwind, you should go east in early morning and west in late evening. You'll see a lot more deer that way. On clear days, with the sun up, it's best to hunt with the sun behind you because it will shine on the deer. That's when the flick of an ear or flash of an antler really shows up."

The smart hunter knows where to look for the animals in various kinds of weather. On warm days, deer seek shade. On cold days, bucks often bed on slopes or ridges, facing southern exposures, where sunshine filters through the cover. Deer don't like windy places. When a strong wind is blowing, your best bet is to look for them on the lee side of hills and ridges or in lowland pockets of cover.

I believe it's possible for you to train yourself year-round to see game better. For example, I get a kick out of watching squirrels in the clearings and trees around my bird feeders. Sometimes they approach with caution, hiding against a tree trunk, flattening out on a limb, or jumping into a bush and freezing motionless for minutes. You learn something about the motions and movements of game by watching any wild animal or bird. I'm not saying you could train yourself to see deer by watching birds and squirrels in a big-city park, but I do believe that the more movement of wildlife you watch, the more you'll train your game eye to see those movements. Also, you'll be training yourself to understand what you see, and the benefits of that type of education can add up fast.

How to Shoot Big Game

Jim Carmichel

How many times have you heard a hunter say, "I'm not so hot at target practice, but when it comes to the real thing, I really pick them off."?

I've been hearing this old tune for more years then I care to remember. Frankly, I don't buy it and never have. Over the years, as I've watched more and more hunters and target shooters in action, I've become completely convinced that hunters who miss targets, be they paper bull's-eyes or beer cans, also miss shots at game. By the same token, some of the best target shooters I know are among the deadliest shots on game.

Before we start arguing, let's be sure we're talking about real target shooters. Informal plinking at a tin can or paper target tacked on a post is not target shooting. Real target shooting with a rifle is a highly organized, rigidly regulated, semi-athletic sport that calls for difficult shots at difficult targets from several different shooting positions at a variety of ranges.

Top target riflemen train like athletes. For example, the 200-yard rapid-fire phase of the standard National Match course fired with high-powered rifles (usually .308 or .30/06) calls for 10 shots from the sitting position in 60 *seconds.* During this time, the competitor must *reload.* Yet, even with the mandatory iron sights (nontelescopic), the better competitors keep most of their shots inside the seven-inch 10-ring, and quite a few hit inside the three-inch X-ring. This type of shooting develops good gun-handling, aiming, and trigger-squeezing techniques to the point where they are second nature. And the pressures a target shooter must deal with in competition provide good training for controlling himself during the inevitable excitement of shooting at game. In a nutshell, this is why many target shooters are excellent game shots in virtually every circumstance you can name.

Target shooting as we hunters generally tend to know it, however, is a Saturday afternoon trip to the local club range where we rest our big-game rifles on solid supports and snipe away at big fat targets. This is a thousand times better than no shooting practice at all, but its chief value is to tell the hunter how well his rifle, ammo, and sights are performing. After punching half a dozen neat little holes in the center of his 100-yard target, the typical hunter gets up from the benchrest and remarks: "Well, that's good enough for a deer," and goes off on his hunting trip with complete confidence.

A few days later, he's easing through the brush in his favorite deer territory and spies a nice eight-point whitetail across a clearing at about 80 yards. Now that buck has a chest depth of about 18 inches and a brisket-to-last-rib length of some 20 inches. That's a big patch of deer hair to aim at and shouldn't be any problem for someone who just a week before cut the center out of a three-inch X-ring at 100 yards. But there's one big difference. Suddenly, our hunter is without his benchrest, and the only way he can get a shot is by standing up on his hind legs and supporting the rifle by muscle power alone. What's more, his heart is thumping like a wrecking ball, and his arms feel like cold spaghetti. The crosshairs of his scope run amok. They race wildly across the deer's heart-lung area and skitter into empty space just as his finger convulsively stabs at the trigger.

Minutes later, when his heart has slowed and his

breathing has steadied, one thought occurs to him: "I can't understand it! Even after all that practice, I bungled the shot like a beginner."

The point is that our hero never really practiced. He only did a little shooting under much more favorable conditions than one ever encounters in real hunting.

I've long noted that otherwise experienced hunters, men able to find their way through the woods and follow a set of tracks into next week, are not necessarily experienced riflemen. Being an experienced hunter and an experienced rifleman are two completely different things. Each requires an application of acquired skills, but these skills, in today's hunting picture, must be acquired separately. Time was when an ace wingshot or big-game hunter could sharpen his shooting skills to razor keenness simply by continued shooting at living targets. Professional buffalo hunters of the last century no doubt kept their marksmanship sharp simply by shooting hundreds of the great shaggy beasts every season. But a modern big-game hunter who *averages* three shots at live game per year over, say, a 10-year period, is getting more shooting than most. Obviously, this is nowhere near enough shooting to make anyone an experienced rifleman, so we have to get our experience elsewhere. And that means practicing on the target range.

I've heard it argued that there's no substitute for actual shooting at game, but every firearms-training agency I know of disagrees, including our armed forces, the FBI, and the police academies. Their trainees don't become proficient by shooting at live enemy soldiers or criminals, of course. They do so in simulated fire-fight situations. Some of them become capable, experienced marksmen who are able to perform effectively under "field conditions."

Similar experience is available to the big-game hunter, and it is of enormous value. The problem is that most of the plinking games we play don't do any good where it counts. Shooting from a bench-rest to get experience for a deer hunt is like twiddling your thumbs as a means of training for a marathon run.

I train for a big-game hunt by firing 10 or 15 shots every day in the offhand position and again in the sitting position. A hundred practice shots stretched out over five days are far more effective than firing them all in a single session, because you quickly "saturate" or start to lose your concentration.

If you are a beginner, it's also a good idea to practice shooting from prone position with and without a padded rest. Prone is the steadiest possible position, and if you can use it when shooting game, it is the best bet.

I like to practice with another hunter or at least have someone look on and note my misses. This adds an element of pressure that is not unlike the

When I do my practice shooting, I like to have somebody else look on. To add a little more pressure, I have some of my actions timed. In practice from sitting position, I take first shot and one fast but deliberate follow-up.

The value of benchrest shooting is mainly to tell you how well your rifle, ammo, and sights are performing.

A qualification for big-game license in Sweden is to fire at "running moose" moving on cable. (Gun Digest Co. photo)

pressure of shooting at game. I don't think it makes too much difference what you use for a target. I use old-fashioned black bull's-eye-type paper targets simply because that's what I usually have on hand. To add a note of realism, though, you might try using a full or three-quarter-size deer-profile target. These are usually available at shops specializing in archery equipment. Whatever target you use, it is important that you have a dirt backstop or a large paper backer that will give you an idea of where your bullets go when you miss. A tendency to miss in a consistent direction usually is a sign of a fundamental shooting error such as flinching or trigger jerking.

When I practice shooting from the sitting position, I always begin by standing with the rifle slung over my shoulder and the safety on. As I drop to sitting position, I snap the sling under my arm for a better brace. And as the butt plate hits my shoulder, I flip the safety to off and I'm ready to fire. The first shot is followed by a fast but deliberate follow-up, but no more. Then I check where my bullets hit and start all over from standing.

When it comes to shooting offhand, I frankly admit that I can't hold the crosshairs very still. But I can *deliberately* move the crosshairs in a fairly straight line. Therefore, I've developed an offhand-shooting technique in which I start out with the

crosshairs below my intended target and then steadily raise the rifle. I touch off the shot when the crosshairs are crossing the target. The system is a matter of timing rather than steady holding, but it works fine for me.

A few years ago, I was presented with an offhand shot at a big snarling African lion at long range. Without even thinking about what I was doing, I automatically went through my paper-target practice routine, raised the crosshairs across his chest, and pulled the trigger at the right place. His hide is in my den, and I'm more convinced than ever that paper punching pays off in the field.

Shooting Metallic Silhouette is a truly wonderful target game for hunters. It's all offhand shooting, the time limit is 2½ minutes for five shots, and the targets are life-size steel profiles of animals. When hit solidly, they fall over with a satisfying clatter. Shooting clubs that don't have enough ground for a full-scale big-bore rifle silhouette setup should at least have the smallbore (.22 Rimfire) version.

Even if you don't like the idea of submitting yourself to organized rifle competition, the silhouette range is a great place to get tuned up for hunting. And I'll bet a pretty penny that after a few warmup sessions on a silhouette range, you'll get an itch to enter a tournament. Shooting silhouettes shoulder-to-shoulder with other competitors is the best practice of all, because it teaches you to shoot well when the pressure is on and your heart is pounding.

I have invented a perfect training game for the hunter. But alas, no one has seen fit to build the required setup. It would consist of a series of deer-size pasteboard cutouts of game spaced at uneven distances across a 200-yard range. Made to pop up and fall by means of a simple pull-string arrangement (like the pop-up targets used in infantry training), the closer targets should remain standing only three to five seconds. This would be just enough time to raise your rifle or unsling it and fire from offhand. The longer targets, say beyond 100 yards, would remain visible just long enough for the shooter to get into a solid sitting position and fire. Facing a series of pop-up paper deer, turkey, bear, elk, and other targets would give hunters an authentic feel for real game shooting and would help to develop an automatic reaction to a variety of shots. That's what *experience* is all about, and shooting this game would be a lot of fun, too.

Note that I've been talking about stationary targets and stationary game animals. What about moving game? My advice follows: Unless you are a very accomplished game shot and have practiced recently on moving targets, don't shoot at moving game. To do so is to risk wounding the animal or missing entirely. If you miss, you may spook the animal out of the country and never see it again. If you don't shoot, there's a good chance that another opportunity will come your way again. Oh, you might take a shot at very close range at an animal that is moving very slowly, but don't try anything that is really beyond your proven ability.

PART 2

HUNTING FOR WHITETAIL DEER

Whitetails I Have Known

Jim Carmichel

When I was a skinny, big-footed kid in grammar school, I had the unbelievably good luck of being yanked out of school for several days to go on a deer-hunting vacation with my family. Nowadays,thanks to the game commission's deer-stocking and management programs, deer are plentiful in the mountains of east Tennessee, but in the 1940s they were nonexistent. That meant that going on a real deer hunt involved traveling hundreds of miles and visiting places as far removed from our farm as was the back side of the moon. It was, to my mind, an elegant adventure, sort of like going to Europe or taking an ocean cruise. Nothing could be finer. My chums were green with envy.

Our hosts were old family friends who had struck it rich and bought a historic plantation in Virginia, complete with antebellum mansion and miles of sweet-scented hardwood forest.

On the day we arrived, dressed in our Sunday best, in a gleaming pickup truck, our host had shot a nice buck. It hung in the smokehouse. I remember inspecting the animal in elaborate detail; feeling the texture of its hair, looking at its teeth and bones, and—most of all—marveling at the wonder of its gracefully curved antlers.

Horns, as they grew on cows and bulls, were familiar to me. But antlers were something entirely different—harder, more graceful, and certainly more dangerous looking. I nearly lost my senses when told they were shed and regrown every year. For a while I simply didn't believe it and only gradually allowed myself to be convinced.

And deer could jump, too, higher than a cow or

even a horse. My imagination reeled with stories of these wonderful animals.

"Come on," I said, "nothing can jump a high-wire fence." So my host took me to a crossing place and showed where the deer-tracked path led up to a fence, then continued on the other side. "Wow, they really can do it. Wait till I tell Mom."

Next day, after breakfast of deer loin, rich gravy, and biscuits, I stood in front of the gun rack, itching to get my hands on a genuine deer rifle and go hunting for these wonderful animals. Already, visions of great stags were dancing through my head.

My dad took the first rifle, a Model 99 Savage in .250 caliber, and my brother selected a shortened .30/40 Krag. Why, I wondered, had he passed over a

did something that still has me wondering. After running dead away for about 100 yards, he spun around and headed right at me. Clearly, he would pass by within a few feet, and even at full tilt I'd have a fairly easy shot.

Closer he came, and the rifle was at my shoulder. My teeth were clinched against the fearful recoil, and my eye squinted over the sights.

"There he is, *pull the trigger!*"

Click.

"Hurry, he's getting away. Try another shot!"

Then the buck whirled again and *headed back* to me again! He was passing by close enough to hit with a hoe handle.

Click. And he was gone.

During a hunt in south Texas that had its ups and downs, I shot this whitetail buck. The right antler is large and well formed, but left one is oddly palmated.

truly beautiful Model 141 Remington pump-action rifle in .30 Remington in favor of the Krag? Anyway, I liked the pump and was glad I had a chance to use it. But when I was clear of the barn lot and stopped to load the rifle, his motives became clear. Nearly all of the cartridges had a sharp indentation on the primer, meaning they had previously misfired and were now useless. Of the lot, only three had virgin primers, and these I fed into the rifle with the optimism of youth.

Less than an hour later, I "jumped" a deer literally in his bed. He got up so close to me that for an instant I was so startled I almost turned and ran. He was not the stag of my dreams, but he did have antlers—perhaps six points—and he could be mine! At first the buck ran away so fast that it looked as though I wouldn't have time for a shot. But then he

Tears streamed down my cheeks. Tears of disappointment, tears of frustration, and tears of anger. I'd had a better than fair chance and lost it because of grown-ups who'd palmed off a bunch of useless cartridges on me. On the way back to the house, I tried the last cartridge. But like its brethren, it only clicked in dismal failure.

As it turned out, I was the only hunter who'd had a "shot" that day, meaning that on the following morning the gun rack was again emptied of all workable deer rifles. All that was left was a little Mossberg Model 151 Rimfire Autoloader complete with a 4× scope (don't ask how I remember these details, how could I possibly forget?) and several boxes of Super-X ammo.

The day before, I'd passed a newly disked and seeded field of winter wheat that was covered with crows. Surely they would be there again. "If I can't shoot a deer, at least I'll shoot some crows," I told myself as I lifted the .22 from the rack and pocketed a box of ammo.

The crows were there, within easy range, but my first shot kicked up dust far to the left and lower than where I'd aimed. When the crows settled back, I missed again the same way. Clearly the rifle didn't hit where the scope aimed. Why? The rest of the day, and the days following, were spent unraveling the mysteries of sight adjustment and bullet trajectory. A whole new world of excitement lay before me. So many things to learn about guns, and only a lifetime to study them.

It started with a deer rifle that wouldn't fire and a .22 that missed crows, and I'm still at it, studying, asking questions and—bit by bit—unraveling the puzzles.

A small boy can do worse than go deer hunting, even with a rifle that won't work.

Every time I look at the 12-point whitetail mounted on my trophy-room wall, I wonder if I'd do it over again if I had the chance.

It was a December hunt, and I was after big whitetails on the Guajolota (translates to female turkey) Ranch in deep south Texas. When I say big whitetails, I don't mean just big, but big-big, Texas-big, the kind of big that makes vaqueros (cowboys) whisper *"muy grande"* in wide-eyed wonder. The Guajolota is a working cow ranch, but—like most big spreads in south Texas—it swarms with quail and so many big-antlered whitetails that owner Jim McAllen got the idea that he could make more money "farming" deer than beef. So true to his stock-breeding tradition (McAllen, Texas, is named after Jim's pioneer family), he set out to make his herd of deer bigger and better by using the same selective breeding techniques proven in the development of superior beef herds. In Texas, just about everyone who hunts deer either owns land, leases hunting rights, or hunts on a "pay per day" ranch. (That "per day" arrangement is not the same sort of operation as the exotic game ranches, which also flourish in Texas.) Accordingly, McAllen figured that if he could breed a "super" race of elk-headed whitetails, hunters would just naturally pay more to hunt on the Guajolota.

The first step in his program was to kill off the "culls"—bucks with skimpy antlers and a tendency to pass on this trait—and save the giant bucks for a while for breeding. The program had been in effect only a few years when I hunted the Guajolota, but signs of its success were abundant on my first morning of hunting.

Accompanied by my pal Jim Nolen, maker of the well-known Nolen knives, and guided by Ed Dutch, who at that time was the ranch's game biologist but has since become a top wildlife photographer, we hid under a mesquite tree where we could look out over a 60-yard flat of open grassland.

With a bit of imagination, you might call the south-Texas terrain "brush country," but it's not the kind of brush hunting one gets in, say, Pennsylvania or Missouri. Just about everything that grows wild in that part of the Texas empire either sticks, scratches, bites, or poisons, so stalking deer through the cactus and catclaw isn't all that much fun. That's why hunting is usually done from a quick stand or from a high seat that lets you look over the thorny chapparal. Fortunately, there is a high buck-to-doe ratio that makes the bucks especially aggressive and eager to challenge other bucks for available does.

The sound of these bucks doing battle is a distinctive clicking and rubbing of antlers that can be heard a pretty fair ways and has the effect of calling other bucks to join the fray. If you ever happen to come upon a couple of bucks fighting it out over some does, you'll probably spot one or two more waiting their turn. And while the fighting is going on, a smarter-than-average Romeo may be trying to make off with the harem.

Many years ago, some deer hunters had the clever idea of banging a couple of deer antlers together to imitate the sounds of a fight and thereby call bucks to the gun. It worked like a charm, and "rattling" up bucks has become an accepted form of the hunting arts.

I've tried rattling bucks from Maine to California, but the only places I've had much success were in areas of dense deer population where there were plenty of aggressive bucks. South Texas is the home of rattling, with both the terrain and temperament of the bucks ideally suited for the technique. The trick, though, in addition to knowing how to rattle the antlers together, is finding a stand that gives you a fairly good view of at least an acre or so of relatively open space.

Some bucks apparently lose all reason at the sound of a fight and dash right in where at any other season they would fear to tread. Some rattlers report having snorting bucks right in their laps after only a moment or two of clicking the antlers. Wiser bucks will come in more cautiously, perhaps circling the stand, wanting to get sight or wind of the combatants. Thus, if you position yourself on the edge of a clearing, you get to see the deer before he gets too close. This also gives the deer a bit of breathing room so he won't have to get too close and overly spooky. You'll see deer heads poking out of the bush around the clearing, ears forward, and too curious—or determined—to bound away. More often than not, there's time for a well-aimed shot, but be sure to keep your rifle close to your shoulder and ready to fire. If they see you move, they're gone in a flash. Man, deer, or fowl, there's something about poaching on another's territory that makes any male more than a little spooky.

I settled back against the forked trunk of the mesquite tree with my rifle resting on my knees. It was a trim little .250/3000 bolt gun stocked by Don Allen and built on a Mauser action that had been short-

While I wait on a muddy Alabama road, hounds run across after imaginary buck. They also turned up two genuine deer.

ened a full inch by ace metalsmith Ron Lampert. Nolen, who was to take first turn playing the antlers, was just to my right, and Dutch, who wanted some pictures, was a few yards behind, manning a telephoto lens.

Results were almost immediate. Nolen had banged the antlers no more than twice, twisting and rubbing them together to make the characteristic *scrape-click-scrape* sound of fighting deer, when there, right in front of me, snorting and stomping his feet, was the biggest whitetail buck I'd ever seen on the hoof. He was huge, with perfectly symmetrical antlers. The main beams seemed to grow straight out in a horizontal line before hooking in at the tips. His points stood straight up like rods in an iron gate, and the whole picture was a deer-hunter's fantasy. The buck of a lifetime, too big to be true, perfect. It has to be a lie, a tale told in a deer camp, vividly remembered.

But he was there, stomping, snorting, beautiful. All I had to do was put the crosshairs on his chest and touch the trigger and my whitetail-hunting days would be over, for never would I see a bigger buck. For long moments, I held the crosshairs on his chest, poised to shoot, listening for the click of Dutch's camera, *Click-click-click* it went. Now I had a

record of the moment, a deer hunter at the gates of paradise. Every nerve in me howled "pull the trigger, pull the trigger," but I didn't.

Greed had slithered to the surface of my consciousness. Greed, unbelievable, unforgivable greed. "Look old boy," it said to me, "this is only the first deer. Think about the *really* big ones that are waiting back there in the thicket. We've got lots of time to wait for the absolute world beater."

Incredibly, I lowered my rifle, worked the bolt, and emptied the chamber. Then, settling the crosshairs back on the buck's chest, I tickled the trigger.

"Click," it went, and the buck was gone.

"Just wanted to know what it felt like to pull the trigger on a giant buck," I explained to an absolutely astonished Jim Nolen.

"Why didn't you shoot?" Dutch asked.

"Waiting for something bigger," I allowed.

"That's as big as they get," was his answer, and I knew greed had done me in.

That morning, we rattled in a couple more trophy-size bucks, but nothing nearly as grand as the first, so I couldn't bring myself to raise the rifle. That afternoon, after a lunch of chili and frijoles served on a tortilla, cowboy-style, followed by a siesta, we tried again—but the antlers were cold, and nothing answered the challenge.

That evening, a few of McAllen's vaqueros stopped by the bunkhouse for *cerveza* and conversation. "It is true," they asked, "you had *El Macho Grande* in your sights and did not shoot? Why?"

I really couldn't answer, but one thing for sure: if I ever saw him again, I *would* shoot.

Next day, the antlers were still cold, so by mid-afternoon we changed tactics and climbed into a tower where we could watch for deer crossing a narrow *sendero* (a rough, clean-cut roadway). The view from the tower allowed us to look down into the endless thicket, but no deer were moving. By early evening, I had counted dozens of javelina, the small wild pigs of the Southwest, and had seen more quail than I thought existed, but no deer other than an occasional doe.

The sun hung low over the deep Texas thicket and a soft haze had wrapped itself around the evening air when the buck stepped into the *sendero*. The distance was just a bit more than 200 yards, but even with my 7× binoculars, the antlers were hard to judge because the sun was behind the deer, reflecting through the haze so that the deer seemed to be the center of a psychedelic burst of rainbow color. It was not a vision of earth, but a dream in pastel colors with quail calls for background music.

The buck moved slowly, a step at a time, nibbling shoots of greenery. But his antlers remained a mystery. We could see that they were big and exceptionally high, but the way they reflected shafts of gilded light made rational judgment impossible.

"I can't see his antlers clearly," Nolen whispered, "but I can see points everywhere."

The buck was nearly across the *sendero* now, and in a moment he would be gone, perhaps forever. I'd already let the trophy of a lifetime slip through my fingers. Did I dare risk losing a second chance? My trigger finger tightened, and the little rifle spoke gently to the soft evening.

The buck was a freak, wearing incredible antlers that had grown to typical, though huge, shape on the right side but with an oddly palmated branch on the left. Is it the trophy of a lifetime, a one-of-a-kind specimen never to be duplicated? Or just a freak with outsize antler growth? I wonder. I wonder every time I look at it on the wall.

Alabama, for instance, in addition to having liberal season and bag limits, has some of the biggest-antlered and heaviest-bodied whitetails I've ever looked at. One Alabama trophy deer I saw a few years back got me so excited that I spent several consecutive seasons there trying to bring home the granddaddy.

And I saw lots of bucks, some eight and 10-pointers with such seductive racks that I was often tempted to touch the trigger. Patience prevailed, though, and as days turned to weeks, I became more or less accustomed to the sight of the Alabama sun setting over a hardwood thicket in which, from a tree stand, I might be glassing from two to six big-antlered bucks at one time. But as I said, I wanted only the he-coon of the hardwoods, and nothing else would do. How was it, then, that I eventually shot a little eight-pointer?

Hoping to relieve the tedium of my daily wait-and-watch routine, I got myself invited to a party hunt, and on the appointed morning found myself in the midst of an incredible spectacle. The setting was a beautiful Southern mansion complete with curving driveway and vast, oak-bordered lawns. What made the scene so bizarre was the unbelievable variety of humanity strolling or squatting about the neatly clipped grounds. Tweed shooting jackets and English riding boots mixed with faded overalls and run-down clodhoppers while the elegant accents of aristocratic Southern speech were punctuated with the staccato *"patoos"* of well-aimed tobacco juice. There had been a violent thunderstorm during the night, and judging by the smells of wet wool and soaked leather, many of the attendees had passed the night in the rain.

A metal tub about the size of a horse-watering trough was being set up on a stone foundation, eventually to be filled with gallons of cooking oil, and nearby a wild-eyed chap was tugging at a heavy chain leash in a futile attempt to separate two snarling dogs. "Get back," he yelled when I approached to help, "these dogs are killers."

"Then why don't you leave them alone?" I asked.

"I'm trying to keep them from killing each other until Big Bob wakes up."

"Who is Big Bob?" I had to ask.

"That's him over yonder," he responded, waving his free hand in the direction of an inert form stretched out in the tangled remains of what appeared to have once been a rose garden.

I meant to take a closer look, but at that moment a silence fell over the assembly as a spry black man of uncertain vintage, his hair as fluffy white as a ripe cotton boll, came down the brick-paved path leading from the big house.

"Mista William is a commin'," he chanted. "Mista William is commin', here he come now."

Sure enough, there was the great one himself, Mister William, owner of thousands of acres of prime farmland and hardwoods, home to the biggest whitetails to be found anywhere. Obviously, Mister William had reached that unique station in society where elegant or even proper attire was no longer required as an emblem of station or success. Accordingly, he was outfitted in soiled chino work pants and shirt, the tail of the latter flapping loosely about his backside, muddied work shoes with, as I remember, only one sock, and crowned off with an ancient straw hat that was liberally ventilated with odd-size holes. Yet there was no denying his regal presence. As he puffed unsteadily along the brick pavement, pausing occasionally to scratch, spit, or realign his direction, there was a chorus of salutations, and more than a few caps were doffed by whites and blacks.

"Mornin', Mista William." "Fine day Bill." "Good to see you, Mista Bill."

Each greeting was received with a wave, and every face was recognized by name.

"Glad to see you, Jack." "Nice of you to come over, Pete. How's Mary and the kids?" "Hi, Ralph."

When at last he faced me, his eyes narrowed, searching for a name.

"Nice to meet you, sir," I said. "I'm Jim Carmichel, and I appreciated the invitation to your deer hunt."

"Glad to have you, glad to have you," he said as he gestured grandly. "This hunt ain't much, just something me and the boys like to do every year about this time.

"Hey there you, Jake, tell Big Bob I said to put Mr. Carmichel here on the road where the deer cross."

With that, he ambled back up the walk, mounted the porch steps, and turned to face the breathless assembly. "Boys, the hunt's on."

The next few moments were lost in a bedlam of shouts, cheers, running feet, and spinning truck tires. Seated in the back of a pickup (I almost made the fatal mistake of climbing into a truck full of savage curs) that fishtailed out of the driveway in a shower of mud and gravel, I caught a glimpse of Mister William as he turned and reentered the great house, aided by his white-topped butler. Apparently he was not attending his own hunt.

Positioned as I eventually was, on a muddied logging road, I could hear the baying pack of Catahoula curs as they topped a ridge nearly a mile away. As the baying grew louder, it was apparent they were coming my way and would cross the road in front of me. Mister William had indeed given me the best stand on the hunt, and in just a few moments I would have a shot.

In long waits on many a hunt, I dream of whitetails with racks like this one.

I was using a borrowed shotgun loaded with No. 000 buckshot, and the deer would be crossing from right to left, a dead-easy setup. When the deer broke from cover and bounded across the road, I swung the bead some two feet ahead of his chest and was tightening on the trigger when I realized that it wasn't much of a buck. An eight-pointer, perhaps, but it was a bucket-head without much width, height, or thickness of beam. The buck certainly wasn't the world beater I wanted. With another bound, the young buck disappeared right into more timber.

By then, the road was covered by a blanket of howling and snarling beasts with their owner, Big Bob, not far behind.

This was the first time I had had a close-up look at Big Bob, and he was, to be sure, an awesome apparition. Clad only in bib overalls and a white T-shirt, despite the chill of the day, Big Bob stood a good six or eight inches over six feet and was as wide as a church door. His hair, probably waist length, was knotted behind his head in the style of a samurai warrior. And when he spoke, I could see that every tooth in his head was covered in gold. His bout with the rose garden had crisscrossed his arms and face with bloody lacerations, and at his side swung a

hunting knife as long as a Saracen scimitar.

As he strode toward me—eyes wide, face blood-caked, and mouth flashing of gold—the sword banged against his knee. It was the only weapon he carried. Considering his size, the obvious strength of his hands and arms, and the fierceness of his countenance, the knife was more of an affectation than a necessity.

"Where's the deer?" he asked. "I didn't hear you shoot."

"I didn't shoot."

"How come? His tracks is right there in front of you."

"He wasn't a good trophy," I answered.

At this, his eyes narrowed, "Mister, we ain't huntin' trophies, we're huntin' meat. We got a lot of people to feed tonight. If you don't shoot somethin', these dogs get meaner than they already are." Big Bob made his point very convincingly.

"The next time something comes by, I'll be sure to shoot," I promised.

And that's exactly what I did. A couple of hours later, the howling pack came by again in violent pursuit of a distinctly undistinguished little eight-pointer.

That evening, my buck and two others that had been killed during the hunt were sliced into bite-size chunks, rolled in batter, and deep-fried in the gas-fired horse trough I'd noted earlier.

In time, huge platters were stacked with the delicious-smelling venison tidbits. But, for some reason, no one took so much as a single bite. This struck me as curious because no one had eaten since breakfast, and I assumed that everyone was as famished as I was. Not wanting to violate local custom, I decided it best not to serve myself until someone else had done so.

The reason for the holdup was soon apparent, however, when Mister William's butler appeared and announced the immediate arrival of his benefactor. "Here come Mista William, ever'body git ready, here he come now."

Mister William's appearance was greatly improved; not only was he better turned out than several hours previous, but his gait was markedly steadier.

Without a word to the hushed onlookers, he marched straight to the deep-fry trough and extracted a crispy brown morsel of batter-dipped venison. For a moment he chewed thoughtfully, eyes cast heavenward. Then, with a sly smile, he made his pronouncement, "Boys, this meat is fit to eat."

Later, food and drink in hand, I was buttonholed by Big Bob, his countenance no less ominous than earlier and his face still blood-caked from his personal war of the roses.

"If you had shot that other deer," he allowed, "we would have had some extra meat for my dogs. Now I have to feed 'em dry dog food, which makes their bowels tight, and they get meaner than ever."

"Here," I answered, handing him my half-emptied plate. "They can have mine."

Games
Whitetails Play

Erwin A. Bauer

For the last three decades and more, I have spent many days each fall in hunting, filming, and just watching whitetail deer. During that time, I've learned some of the games whitetails play. Many of those games were played on me, but not long ago, I had a ringside seat at a game played on somebody else.

It was a bright day in November, slightly warmer than normal for that time of year in the Midwest. I had built a platform blind in an oak tree near a point where two heavily used deer trails crossed and bordered an abandoned apple orchard. It seemed to be a good spot both for filming and for getting a good shot with bow and arrow before the firearms season opened. I climbed into the blind and sat down to see what might happen along.

I hadn't been in the tree long when a good buck came mincing down the trail. He moved slowly and suspiciously, his antlered head held low, looking in every direction except up at me. About 75 yards away, he stopped in some tall grass beneath an apple tree and began pawing the ground. Then, like a weary hound dog, he circled the trampled area several times, settled down in it, and remained still. I could see only his antlers.

Perhaps an hour passed. Then a station wagon stopped on a farm road several hundred yards away, and two men stepped out of it. Through binoculars, I recognized them as surveyors. One man set up a transit on its tripod; the other grabbed a range pole. The rodman then walked out into the apple orchard, following the buck's exact trail. He walked within 15 feet of the animal without ever seeing it.

The buck did not spook; he held fast!

For at least 10 minutes, the two surveyors worked in the surrounding area—the rodman very near the buck, both men shouting instructions. But not until they were back in the station wagon and driving away did the deer stand up and leave the scene. His nerves apparently couldn't stand the pressure any longer.

But that wasn't all. A moment later, a bigger buck, which had been bedded near the first and which I had not seen, stood up and hurried away. I can only guess that this second deer was already bedded down when I climbed the tree and that he had decided to wait me out.

Nothing else happened that morning, but I had seen enough to serve for many mornings. I wondered how many other times I had been close to trophy bucks without knowing it.

"Whitetails play amazing games," I mumbled to myself.

In the early years of my whitetail hunting, the only glimpses I had of bucks were of white fantails evaporating into the underbrush, usually just too far away for even a snap-shot. And even those glimpses were rare. So my personal experience seemed to prove what I'd read in every book I could find on deer hunting: that whitetail bucks invariably try to escape by running—that they run the instant they detect any false sound or smell in the forest. But now, after much more exposure to whitetails, I'm convinced that they don't always follow that behavior pattern.

The truth is that a good many of the biggest bucks escape by doing nothing at all. A recent trip furnished me with another excellent example.

I'd been photographing deer on a government reservation in Kentucky that contains a substantial whitetail herd. But each fall these animals are hunted hard during a series of weekend hunts, so they are as wild and wily as any whitetails anywhere. On the morning before the hunting, I'd had fair luck filming with the aid of a telephoto lens at very long range. But by noon, most of the animals had bedded and were hard to find. When I spotted an Osage-orange sapling that had practically been shredded by a buck's antlers, I parked my vehicle and walked the 100 feet or so to take close-up pictures of the damage.

The tree practically exploded. A splendid buck had been bedded unseen in grass just on the far side of the tree. He had waited until I'd approached to within 10 feet of him before he flushed out and raced for safety. Again I wondered how many other times I had passed very close to a stationary buck without seeing him.

On that same afternoon, I drove out onto a high ridge from which I could look down into a brushy, meandering creek bottom. There I stopped again, and through field glasses I soon spotted the ears of a doe bedded under a large sycamore. Then, just off to the right in a tangle of honeysuckle, I saw a bedded medium-size buck, which was staring directly toward me. Recalling my earlier experience, I figured I just might be able to approach near enough for close-range pictures. I picked up a Hasselblad

500C with 500 mm. lens (about 6×) and headed down the ridge, being careful not to walk directly toward the buck.

The doe spooked and bounded away almost as soon as I left the vehicle. I couldn't see the buck as I descended the ridge, but I could keep an eye on the telltale green of the honeysuckle. I would certainly see the buck if he jumped up—or so I thought.

What followed would have been comical to watch. I stalked up to the honeysuckle as carefully as I could, inches at a time, tense, holding my camera at ready. I *knew* I'd get a good shot, at least of a buck bounding away. But when I got there, the buck's bed—though still warm—was empty.

The escape was fairly easy to reconstruct. The buck, by staying on its belly and actually crawling, had retreated into a small draw that led away into the main stream channel. Its footprints were etched at water's edge. If whitetails could laugh, that one was probably guffawing.

I now have a couple theories to offer, for whatever they are worth. Bucks *do* prefer to escape by running—by evacuating the vicinity of danger. But the longer and more comfortably they are bedded, the more reluctant they are to make the break. Thus, a hunter who can locate a bedding area (or, better still, a bedded deer) is in a good position to score.

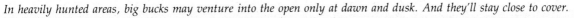

In heavily hunted areas, big bucks may venture into the open only at dawn and dusk. And they'll stay close to cover.

My other theory is that whitetails that live anywhere near human habitation or activity year-round become accustomed to human noise. Voices, for instance, alert them but do not unduly frighten them. So a noisy hunter has as good a chance as a stealthy stalker to approach close to such a whitetail in its bed—maybe even a better chance.

Perhaps I should mention another reason for that noise theory. In my years of filming many kinds of wild and semiwild big-game animals, I've found that my chances of getting close to them are better when I approach casually and openly, but not directly, than when I try to make a silent, hidden stalk. Animals with very good vision seem to be less apprehensive about what they can see than about what they cannot see. And whitetails have extraordinary vision.

The behavior of whitetails varies throughout the year. In spring and summer, they are most scattered. Bucks and the does with fawns are likely to be anywhere. In the winter, whitetails are most concentrated, with bucks and does grouping up where the foraging is best. In between comes the rut. Because the rut normally coincides with most state hunting seasons—and because it's the most active period in a whitetail's lifetime—it is the time that concerns hunters most.

First, let me explain something about the rut, or annual breeding season. It does not occur at exactly the same time every year, though very nearly so. In Ohio, for example, what might be termed the peak of the rut occurs in mid-November. North of Ohio it occurs somewhat earlier; south of Ohio, later.

Nor is the duration of the rut the same every fall. Occasionally most of the breeding activity may be concentrated in one week or so. More often it is spread out over a month or more. During the rut, short periods of great activity are interspersed with longer periods of relative inactivity. Cold weather seems to stimulate activity somewhat, and high temperatures may slow it down.

Technically the rut probably begins in late summer when bucks begin to shed the velvet from their fully grown antlers. Though the velvet falls away naturally, bucks hasten the process by rubbing their antlers against trees, shrubs, and one another. I have even seen them rubbing against telephone poles, as well as against an old outhouse at a long-deserted Michigan logging camp. This rubbing gradually becomes an aggressive display—a duel against a sapling or another deer—and continues for months after all the velvet is gone. Thus, the presence of many slashed trees from which the bark has been peeled should be a sure sign that many bucks are in the area.

But is it?

Not at all. It is only another game whitetails play.

One year in October, while I was on a weekend scouting and filming trip, I found an area of about 10 acres where trees had been slashed and barked wholesale. I have never seen so much slash damage concentrated in any other place.

"We'll build a couple of blinds," I said to Lew Baker, "and when the foliage is down, we'll do some serious filming."

The blinds were erected in ideal places. Two weeks later, most of the leaves had fallen from the trees. I went hopefully into the woods.

I have always wanted to film whitetail bucks fighting. Actually, fighting occurs far less frequently than most sportsmen believe. When it does, it usually happens at night. In all my time in deer woods, I have seen conflict only twice, and both incidents were merely brief pushing matches. Another time I saw two bucks with antlers locked; one was practically dead from the long struggle.

But now, as I entered my blind, I was hopeful from so much sign that I would see action.

I shouldn't have wasted my time. Not only did I fail to see bucks jousting; I didn't see any bucks at all. Only does. What happened?

On my desk is a beautiful scene on an outdoor calendar, very well done by the artist except for one thing. It shows a splendid whitetail buck with massive rack in a woodland opening. His swollen neck and his stance indicate that it is the rut. He is surrounded by three does. But the scene should be the other way around: during the peak of a whitetail rut, a single doe is far more likely to be surrounded by several bucks. Elk acquire harems; whitetails do not.

This doe and her fawn have noticed the photographer, but their low tails indicate that they aren't yet alarmed enough to make tracks toward heavy cover.

So where you find one good buck, you're likely to find others nearby. And all will be where the ready does (but not most of the does) are, rather than where they rubbed the tree trunks a few weeks—or even a few days—before.

This concentration of breeding bucks into groups accounts for the generally accepted belief among whitetail hunters that year after year certain places are "big-buck places." From my own experience, I'd say that theory is no more true than the elephant-graveyard theory.

On a snowy, gusty November evening, I spotted eight bucks in the vicinity of one doe at the edge of a hardwood forest. There may have been other bucks and does nearby, but my count in the failing light was nine deer. Four of the bucks were huge old busters; the others had pretty good heads. Each was trying to outmaneuver the others, but no actual head-on clashes occurred. It was too dark for photography, but I resolved to be on the spot first thing next morning. It was a very exciting prospect, and believe me: buck fever is possible even before the hunting season opens.

But as I've been saying, whitetails play games. In a whole year of Novembers, there wouldn't be more than a few days as perfect for photography as the next morning. It was crisp and clear. Shortly after daybreak, I drove out to the trysting spot, cameras ready. And found? NOTHING! Brush had been trampled, and leaves on the ground had been raked with sharp hoofs, but frost covered the evidence, and the deer were gone. Soon, so were my high and hopeful spirits.

Luckily I located those deer again late in the afternoon. I'm almost certain it was the same group because there were eight bucks and one doe. They were about 2½ miles as the crow flies from where I first saw them. My conclusion is that if there are big-buck areas, they are not necessarily in the same places day after day, let alone year after year. At least not during the turbulent time of the rut.

Perhaps I should make a further explanation here. After the rut subsides, the bucks in an area might very well retreat into deep winter cover and gather there. And these might be traditional wintering areas, most often very remote, where a serious deer hunter stands a good chance of getting a fine trophy if the season remains open long enough.

My whitetail filming during recent autumns has been in areas of both light and heavy hunting pressure. From these experiences, one fact has become very clear: the heavier the pressure, the more nocturnal are the bigger bucks in all their activity, and of course the harder they are to see. About the only chance you have of seeing them in the open in heavily hunted areas is very early and very late in the day, right at the edge of the forest.

At the tag end of my whitetail-watching one fall, on the eve of open hunting season, I sat in a tree blind a bowhunter had built several years before. It was flimsy, and I didn't really enjoy the precarious perch. But enough fascinating things happened on

Keep in mind a principle that this view illustrates: When you spot one deer, one or more others may be close by.

the ground to keep me up there awhile.

Around midafternoon, a handsome buck appeared from the heart of the forest and strolled toward the edge of the woods. He stayed in the shadows, moving quietly and scanning the forest all around. Eventually he vanished as silently as he had arrived.

Before dusk, four more deer, including two bucks, passed below me within point-blank gun range. Again, none of them stepped beyond the forest shadows. Then and there, I decided to spend opening day in that same tree, certain that I could collect my venison.

But I ended the first day without firing a shot. That time, however, I was tricked by other hunters rather than by whitetails. When I arrived on the scene opening day, five hunters were in the process of organizing a drive. Three of them were going on stand, one directly beneath my tree. The other two would make the drive from the opposite side of the woods. The strategy seemed to guarantee some shooting.

Later in the day, I again saw the leader of the hunt. I asked him if they had scored.

"Naw," he replied. "No deer in that woods. Scarce everywhere this year."

I wish I knew how the deer eluded those drivers. The next day I again saw deer from the tree stand, and I bagged one. It was so easy that I almost felt guilty. Because deer seldom look up, getting above them is one very effective game that hunters can play.

Science Unmasks the Whitetail

John Weiss

When the first white men came to North America some four centuries ago, they saw whitetail deer for the first time, since these animals are not present in Europe. But they learned little about whitetail deer, because scientific study techniques were not available. In fact, really penetrating study of the whitetail only began in the late 1960s or early 1970s, and much of what we have learned contradicts what earlier observers thought they knew. We advanced so rapidly in our study of whitetails that most of the highly respected biologists who carried out the work are still alive today. Here is a distillation of facts useful to hunters that arose from the new research.

1. Before the rutting season, each buck makes an average of 105 rubs on cedars and saplings. This activity takes place after the less-pronounced rubbing of velvet from antlers in late summer. The rut-rubbing has nothing to do with polishing the antlers, working off excess sexual energy, or preparing for battles with other bucks. It is a marking behavior, that tells other bucks in the area his ranking in the local pecking order. Young bucks tell their status by rubbing small trees averaging one inch in diameter. A middle-aged buck rubs slightly larger trees. The biggest trophy bucks use the largest trees (four inches or more in diameter). Once the marking of a tree is finished, a buck never returns to the rub, except by coincidence or when traveling a nearby trail.

2. Whitetails have little three-dimensional vision. As a result, it is common for them to look right at stationary hunters and not "see" them. Frequently they step over the edges of canyon rims and fall to their deaths, run into fences and become tangled.

1
ANTLER RUBS
(bark scraped from saplings) are not *sure signs that a buck is nearby. See No. 1 in the text.*

2 **THE EYES**
of a deer were formerly thought to be color blind, but deer see well in dim light or moonlight, and they detect movement instantaneously. You can wear bright safety colors, but don't even twitch your nose on stand. See No. 2 in text.

3
THE NOSE
is able to detect odors at half a mile, but at long range, the odor is so diffuse the animal does not react. To find out how close is too close, see No. 3 in text.

7
SCRAPES
are made with the deer's hoofs. These bore patches on the ground are scented invitations to does during the rutting season, and some hunters make it a point to sit near scrapes. How to choose the right one is described in No. 7 in text.

ILLUSTRATED BY RICHARD AMUNDSEN

4 *THE EARS*
of a whitetail tell you what he's thinking. For instance, they can swivel around independently of one another, and if a buck is doing that, he's trying to determine the source of sounds that may mean danger, and it would be better not to breathe for a while. For more "body language" of the ears, see No. 4 in the text.

VITAL STATISTICS:
There are 29 recognized subspecies of whitetail deer in North America. About 14-million whitetails inhabit the U.S. Hunters harvest 1.8-million whitetails annually. Average length of a whitetail is 60 to 75 inches. Whitetail height at shoulder averages 38 inches. The average mature whitetail weighs 150 pounds.

6. *A DEER'S TAIL*
often tells you what the animal is about to do. Almost everyone knows that when the flag goes up and the flared white hair shows the deer is about to bolt. But did you know that when a doe holds her tail far to one side, she is ready to be bred by a trailing buck and that you'll probably get a shot? For more, see No. 6 in text.

26

16

12

27

22

24

9 *FOUR STOMACH COMPARTMENTS*
make the whitetail a ruminant — an animal that chews the cud. This does affect your hunting, but few sportsmen ever give it a thought. See No. 9 in text.

5. *THE FRONT LEG*
isn't attached to the rest of the skeleton with a ball-and socket like the one in your shoulder. Instead, the scapula is wide and flat and is attached by means of a very elastic cartilage. This is one very important reason why it is often almost impossible to hit a running deer. See No. 5 in text.

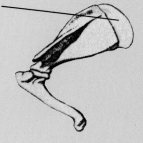

8 *TRACKS*
alone don't reveal a deer's sex, in spite of all the legends to the contrary. A deep set of prints, marks made by dragging hoofs, and dew-claw marks merely show that the deer is heavy or that the animal is sinking into soft ground. But there are some clues. See No. 8 in text.

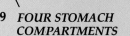

When running, they often collide with trees. Most of their feeding is done at dawn and dusk, but they feed after dark when the moon is bright.

3. Biologists say deer must be within 50 to 100 yards of a scent source before either a favorable or negative reaction takes place.

4. When a whitetail points one ear forward and the other back, the deer is checking the trail ahead while keeping tabs on his backtrail for something that may be following. When both ears are laid down flat behind the head, the deer is scared and about to run. The deer does this so that its ears won't be stung by the brush or other cover.

5. Because of the extreme flexibility of the whitetail's front shoulders, the legs can be turned at quite sharp angles to the body. The animal can therefore make very sharp turns while running, as every hunter knows who has ever contemplated shooting at a dodging buck.

6. When a whitetail feeds with its head down, and the tail begins to flick erratically from side to side, the animal is about to lift its head. Freeze! When the tail is sticking straight out, the deer is very nervous and will probably run.

7. Each buck makes an average 27 scrapes by using the front hoofs to paw away fallen leaves or other debris. The buck scents the scrape with secretions from glands on his legs. The size of the scrape indicates the age of the deer. Six to eight-inch diameter scrapes are made by young, immature bucks. Eight to 15-inch diameter scrapes are made by middle-aged bucks. The largest trophy bucks consistently make big scrapes, averaging 18 to 24 inches in diameter, and their scrapes are sometimes as large as three feet in diameter. Bucks come back as often as three times a day to check their scrapes for the presence of a ready doe.

8. Does tend to walk pigeon-toed, and they meander and wander much more than bucks. Bucks tend to turn their hoofs outward and walk in a straightaway fashion as though they had definite goals in mind. They often do. Bucks with the wide antlers tend to walk around closely grown cover because they cannot force their antlers through it.

9. Deer are most vulnerable to predation and hunting when they are feeding, because their heads are down and they see little. But because they are ruminants, they can feed very quickly and then retire to the safety of cover. The ingested food is held in the first, or upper, stomach. After the deer has bedded, he brings the food up into the mouth again and chews it more thoroughly, and then passes it into the second, third, and fourth stomach compartments.

10. The Pennsylvania Game Commission has learned that the best rack any buck is likely to have will grow sometime between the deer's fifth and seventh year. Yet because hunting pressure keeps most deer herds closely cropped, less than 4 percent of the bucks live to this ripe old age.

11. The rutting season is not triggered by cold air as previously believed. It is a post-Autumnal Equinox event. As the days begin growing shorter, decreasing levels of daily sunlight coming through the eyes of deer has a reverse-stimulation effect upon the pituitary gland near the brain, signaling a temporary slow-down in body growth and simultaneously an increase in the secretion of the sexual hormones.

12. The "metatarsal" glands (one on the outside of each hind leg) secrete an "alarm" scent when the deer is scared. Deer use this method of olfactory communication to warn each other of impending danger. The scent has a distinct garlic odor; if you smell it while deer are in the vicinity, they are probably aware of your presence or something else is beginning to spook them.

13. It is not necessary to cut a deer's throat during field-dressing to bleed the animal. In fact, this will ruin the cape for mounting and also will allow dirt to enter when you're dragging the deer out. If a neck, heart, lung, or liver shot has been made, the deer is bled, internally, and the blood will collect in the chest cavity and spill out when the body is opened.

14. Deer have such short memories they often cannot recall, only three minutes after the event, something that may have alerted them. If you cough or snap a twig, stop and remain perfectly quiet for several minutes. Nearby deer will go back to their previous activities, and you can resume your prowl, confident they are no longer suspicious.

15. Deer are not very intelligent. In fact, they are mental dimwits compared to birds of prey, members of the cat family, dogs, and pigs. But whitetails do

With tail up and rump patch flared, this buck's about to bolt. Such tipoffs help you act in time. (Erwin A. Bauer photo)

This buck makes tracks that might help you, but don't assume too much from such prints. (Erwin A. Bauer photo)

have keen survival instincts and are therefore clever at getting out of sticky predicaments.

16. A whitetail defecates an average of seven times a day. Therefore, finding large numbers of pellets will not necessarily indicate that many deer are in the area.

17. Radio-tracking studies have shown that a whitetail's home range averages 1½ square miles, but the crucial factor is the deer population in that area. When deer are few, the animals range over larger areas. A high population tends to restrict their movements.

18. When a deer sticks his tongue out of the side of his mouth, and at the same time holds his head lower than usual, he is exhibiting a fear response and is about to bolt. When a deer holds its head high, curls its upper lip back, and lays its ears down flat so they stand out horizontally from the side of the head, it smells something that it likes.

19. When bucks battle by clashing their antlers together, they are not fighting over nearby does. And whitetails are not territorial and so do not defend their ranges. Many bucks may even share the same home habitat with others. The fights are merely disputes over ranking in the local pecking order. The fights are usually brief since senior ranking is quickly decided. Bucks rarely inflict bodily harm on each other, but occasionally their antlers become locked and they die of starvation.

20. Deer are attracted to the scent of certain predators such as coyotes, weasels, bobcats, skunks, foxes. The reason is unknown. They often try to follow the scent to its source. But some studies indicate deer have a great fear of mountain lion and wolf scent. One of the best masking scents for hunters is skunk.

21. Deer instantly catalog sounds they hear, apparently without much conscious thought. A deer may not even raise its head from feeding, even though a hickory nut loudly thuds to the ground. But the metallic click of a cigarette lighter's lid or a gun's safety will bring their heads up in a flash.

22. Deer do not possess gall bladders. Since they are vegetarians, they have no need for bile (which is produced by the liver, stored in a gall bladder, and used in the digestion of animal fats). Because there is no gall or bladder, you don't have to worry about piercing it when you're gutting.

23. A deer's sense of taste is highly refined. The order of preference is for foods that are sweet, bland, sour, and then bitter. Deer also crave salt and like foods grown on fertilized ground because of the additional minerals it contains.

24. Although a deer will usually bed in the same general area every day, each animal selects a new site each time it beds.

25. Deer are not bothered by severe weather, except when finding food becomes difficult. When they retreat into dense cover, it's usually because wind impairs their ability to hear or smell approaching predators. When the wind blows, hunt heavy cover.

26. Does throw their tails high in the air far more often than bucks. It is believed the waving flag serves as a "flashing" signal to allow fawns to more easily follow their fleeing mother through dense and dark cover.

27. An average buck can make standing jumps of eight feet in length and running leaps of 30 feet. He can go as fast as 35 miles per hour. But a whitetail won't jump over anything it can't see through or over, because the animal always wants to know what's on the other side. A low, solid, board fence confines a deer, even though the deer could leap over it with ease.

28. Whitetails make a variety of sounds to communicate with each other. A fawn bleats to tell its mother its location. Bucks grunt when trailing a doe in heat. Bucks and does make raspy snorts to warn each other of danger. Bucks sneeze at each other as a threat gesture, especially if one comes too close to another's scrape or too close to a doe a buck is about to breed. Bucks and does also stamp their feet when they see or smell something that they are unable to identify.

29. Radio-tracking studies have shown that somewhere in a deer's home range there is always a "core" area averaging 40 acres in size, where the deer spends 80 percent of its time.

30. Radio-tracking studies have shown that when bucks return to check their scrapes, they do so five times more frequently during the early evening hours than at any other time of day.

And it should be remembered that all of the above is only a summary of the more-important research. Scientific research projects on deer are in progress throughout the United States, and what the investigators will discover during the *next* decade or so is impossible to predict.

How to Hunt North Woods Deer

Ken Gilsvik

I have never agreed with the popular idea that an old whitetail buck is smarter than an equally ancient mule deer. Long years of pursuing both have taught me otherwise. However, if a beginner who was seeking a trophy asked me which species he should hunt, I would recommend—without a moment's hesitation—the mule deer. When you're in mule-deer country, you can see an average of several hundred yards instead of an average of 30 yards, so your chances are bound to be better. The same situation applies to whitetails in farm country—it's much easier to push a good buck out of a 10- to 40-acre woodlot to a waiting gun than to move one past a stander in dense, endless forest.

In other words, it's the difference between being in approximately the right place to see your quarry and being in *exactly* the right place. This factor is what makes whitetail hunting in the North Woods so tough: learning to be in exactly the right place at the right time. This lesson is not learned easily. It takes time, patience, thought, and planning.

After a hitch in the service during World War II, I returned to civilian life. That same fall, 1946, I went on my first deer hunt in northern Minnesota. I was 20 years old.

I did not do well at first. In my first three years of hunting, I fired one shot at a forkhorn jumping out of a grass and alder swamp. I missed, shooting behind him. Even in failure I had learned my first lesson—shoot where the deer will be when the bullet arrives, not where the deer is when you shoot.

After hunting deer successfully for several years, I decided to keep notes to see if I could sort out a pattern in the best times of day, the best methods of hunting, and so on. Those notes show that I have now taken 56 whitetails in Minnesota in 34 years of hunting (Minnesota law allows all members of a party to hunt until all tags are filled).

I have more than made up for those early years when I was only learning about the greatest of all big-game animals. If a man's success does not increase with time, he's not profiting from past mistakes. I once told a young hunter, "Don't think about the deer you've shot. Think about the ones that got away and *why* they got away."

I learned this lesson myself many years ago when I was hunting a series of hardwood hills to the north of our hunting cabin. A ridge that jutted out into the center of a horseshoe-shaped valley commanded a good view in three directions. At the end of the ridge grew five huge white pines.

I stood with my back against one of the center pines. Minutes later, I thought I could see better by switching to a different tree, so I moved to the last pine at the point of the ridge. I soon realized that there was actually more brush obscuring my vision here than back at my last post. Again I moved, turning just in time to see a good buck, which had topped the far ridge, wheel around and go back the way he had come.

That deer had been heading straight for me, and I realized with disgust that I would have had a shot no matter which pine I had been standing under. Today I pick my stand just once, and I don't move until I'm ready to leave.

The second morning of another season found me standing against a white spruce. The surrounding country was alder and ash swamp, and I was stand-

To improve your deer hunting chances, it helps to analyze your past mistakes. (Erwin A. Bauer photo)

ing on a spruce ridge that branched right in front of me. A well-marked deer trail with numerous fresh scrapes branched off in three directions. There was no snow, but a heavy frost covered the ground, which made walking extremely noisy.

Like most spruce, mine had branches clear to the ground, so I had to break off a few limbs to get my back against the trunk. I was well hidden, but I didn't have much room to maneuver my rifle. In that situation, though, I felt camouflage was more important because any deer I'd see would be close.

I had arrived on the stand at first light. Approximately 45 minutes later, I heard a deer approaching from behind me, but not on any of the trails. I wasn't surprised. I knew that once the season opens, deer tend to stay away from trails.

Each step sounded as if the deer were stepping into a box of corn flakes, but I couldn't see him through the dense cover. All this time, however, I had been taking advantage of my concealment by slowly turning and maneuvering the .270 into position.

North Woods bucks can grow big. For instance, the 10-pointer I show here went 200 pounds field-dressed.

The deer moved up the low spruce ridge out of the dense alders and into my sight. He was only about 20 yards away, but I held my fire because there was too much intervening brush, mostly mountain maple. I picked out an opening about 10 feet ahead of the sneaking buck, and as he crossed it I aimed at his chest and fired. He dashed off. Seconds later, I heard his thrashes about 75 feet away. He was a dandy forkhorn, fat and round as a sausage.

This deer hunt sounds routine, but there are four different ways a beginning hunter might have botched the job—four things I automatically did right without consciously thinking about them. They are the profits of long and bitter experience.

The first important step was that I was downwind from the buck. If I had been upwind, he probably still would have come out of that swamp—somewhere on the far side, though.

Number two, I was well hidden. Concealment cannot be overemphasized, especially when hunting at close ranges. It is impossible to remain absolutely still for any length of time, so the better a hunter is hidden, the more free he is to make an occasional movement without being detected.

Third, even though the deer was very close, I didn't shoot until I was reasonably sure of sending a bullet undeflected through the brush. There is no doubt in my mind that more deer are missed because of bullet deflection than any other cause.

Number four, perhaps the most important of all, is that every action I took was in slow motion. A deer will always detect a quick movement but will not notice very slow movements unless he is extremely close. Yet moving is the most common mistake in deer hunting. So many times I've heard hunters of long experience say, "I spotted this deer and threw my gun up to take a shot." Throwing your gun up at a walking deer almost certainly

means taking a shot at a running deer.

If a deer runs toward me, I mount my rifle with caution, because deer in the woods will seldom run very far without stopping—and it's easier to hit a standing or walking deer than a running one, especially in thick brush. I've shot hundreds of jackrabbits and foxes on the run and don't find a deer in the open difficult to hit. A deer running through brush, though, is a different story.

I now have a tongue-in-cheek atttitude toward stillhunting. At the risk of hurting some hunters' feelings, I believe that most deer shot by hunters stillhunting in heavy forests are found by accident. Many of those deer have been spooked by other hunters, or are rutting bucks simply wandering around. Let me give a few illustrations.

Some years back, my brother Jim took up the trail of three deer one morning. He spent most of the day tracking the deer on new snow, jumping them twice but never getting a good look at them. Finally, late in the afternoon, he stopped briefly and got the surprise of his life. The three deer he had been straining his eyes to see all day long were suddenly running straight at him. He took the largest with several shots from his .300 Savage.

What happened? The three deer had wandered all over the area, finally walking in a beeline toward where I was on stand. Traveling into the wind, they caught my scent and immediately ran straight back at their pursuer.

A young chap who formerly hunted our area took up the trail of three deer one year. He also trailed those deer for most of the day without catching a glimpse of them in the dense timber. Suddenly, he came upon them standing in fairly open cover. At first he could hardly believe his good fortune. Then he heard human voices coming from a gang of hunters passing noisily along, 100 yards beyond.

The three deer were intently watching these hunters; as soon as they spotted this new threat, they forgot all about the danger behind them. The young man waited until the hunters moved out of his range of fire, then dropped the largest of the three whitetails.

Is stillhunting ever successful in the North Woods? Yes, but usually only under ideal circumstances. For instance, a few years back I was hunting off the Echo Trail in northern Minnesota, about a dozen miles south of the Canadian border. This is a rugged country of rolling hills, rock cliffs, and scattered huge boulders. I had entered the woods on a logging trail before dawn.

First light found me sitting on the edge of a pine-covered cliff overlooking a large expanse of varied terrain: half alder swamp with a little creek flowing through and half cut-over highland. After an hour or so, I spotted a small deer hopping through the cover. My scope told me it was a button buck—legal game but not what I was after.

Around midmorning, snow began falling. The flakes were huge and increased in intensity until I couldn't see anything. Then just as suddenly as the snow had started, it stopped. In a brief half-hour, what had been bare ground was now covered with three inches of snow.

Around noon, I decided to head out to the Echo Trail for lunch, taking the same logging trail. I was aware that my sorrel boots were making absolutely no noise in the soft wet snow as I cautiously walked along. A light breeze was blowing directly in my face as I rounded a ridge end. I took two more cautious steps, and a whistling snort rang out. I turned to see two big does bounding away and a huge buck following them. I shouldered the .270 and fired. The next thing I saw were four hoofs sticking up in the air.

As I fought my way through aspen whips and down timber, I temporarily took my eye off the place where the buck had gone down. Then I looked up to see him bounding up the ridge side. Cursing to myself, I brought up my rifle and fired just as he disappeared over the top. I fought my way uphill and stood on the crest, gasping for breath, straining my eyes to see the fleeing buck in the rolling terrain ahead. He was already out of sight. I knew my shot was a miss, but I searched for signs of a hit anyway.

Then calm and reason took over. That buck didn't look as big as the one I had originally shot at. Even his rack seemed smaller. And hadn't my buck gone down hard with all four feet sticking up? I walked back along the ridgetop and found him, lying in the new snow. The bullet had caught him dead center in the back of his neck as he went straight away. He had a beautiful 10-point rack, and weighed exactly 220 pounds field-dressed, the second largest buck I have ever taken.

During a recent season, I took a deer on our farm

under almost identical conditions. Melted frost made my walking absolutely quiet, and again I was on a logging trail. Two other times I have taken bucks by jumping them out of their beds in high grass. In all four of these situations, the walking conditions were ideal and there was no noisy brush to push through that could have alarmed the deer. Yet I believe that only about 10 percent of all the deer shot in the North Woods are taken by stillhunting or stalking. The rest are taken by standers and parties putting on drives.

Stand hunting has been the backbone of my consistent success on whitetails over the years. At least 75 percent of my deer have been taken with this method. You will notice I use the term "stand hunting" and not "trail watching."

We all hear plenty about watching well-traveled trails, or especially the junction where two runways cross. Trail watching is a good way to kill does and young bucks but not the old mossyhorns of eight points or better. Once the season opens, the big bucks seem to walk everywhere but on these heavily used trails. If you take up the trail of a big buck and follow it for half a day, you'll see that he may occasionally move onto a well-traveled runway. But almost without fail he will follow it only a short way before veering off into the brush again. The following hunt is a perfect example of this trait.

A long, narrow, grassy slough ran for several miles through a large wooded area about five miles northeast of our farm. I walked this slough for half a mile and finally found two trails that crossed the slough about 50 yards apart.

I took a stand behind the upturned roots of a big cedar blowdown midway between the two trails. But I could also see 50 yards in one direction to a bend in the slough and more than 200 yards in the other direction.

I took up my vigil behind the upturned cedar around 3 p.m. Red squirrels chattered and scurried in the brush while a woodpecker hammered off to my left.

By 4:30, I had just time to get out of the woods by dark. I checked the .270 and gave one last look west to the bend in the slough, then turned and looked the long way. There, about 150 yards away where there had been nothing only seconds before, a lone deer stood like a statue staring directly at me.

What a big doe, I thought, because in the tall timber and gloom of a cloudy late afternoon, I could see no trace of a rack. But there was something too familiar about the animal. I slowly brought up my rifle and peered through the scope. A wide, tall-tined rack showed clearly.

I had to aim high because of the tall grass, but at the roar of the .270, the big buck collapsed with a broken back. He had five points to a side and weighed 200 pounds field-dressed. Checking later, I saw that his lone tracks came out of the dense timber, well away from the trails, and ended in the snow where he lay—a typical North Woods buck.

Rain Dance
for Deer

Larry Mueller

Something was noisily coming down the hill. L.E. Goutierez tensed. He had just finished the ceremonial dance he expected would bring in a deer, and he was seated against a big, outline-breaking beech, his .50-caliber Hawken at ready.

Something moved in the trees. It was not a deer but L.E.'s host and hunting partner, Dr. Norman Ott. L.E. stood, assuming the hunt had ended, and checked his watch. At 8:07, it seemed early to quit, but perhaps the doctor had to make his hospital rounds.

L.E. pointed to the sacred ground that gave reason for his dance. The two men were silently pondering its implications when, suddenly, both heads turned toward a crashing sound coming from the swamp. "Here he comes!" the startled doctor cried out. The buck still came, swaying his heavy head like a bull elk, steam snorting from his nostrils in the crisp December air.

The buck was spellbound, and he charged the hunters without the slightest fear, caution, or good sense.

At 40 yards, Dr. Ott drew his bow. At 30, he let the bowstring slide smoothly from his fingertips. But just as the arrow launched, the deer turned. The shaft sliced air above the animal's shoulder, cutting nothing but the spell the buck was under. The big whitetail, now wildly alert, ducked slightly, reeled around, and put all of its energy into every jump.

"Shoot! Shoot!" yelled the doctor, knowing he'd never have time for a second arrow.

Dr. Ott is a man of science. Would he really hunt with a fellow who expects to attract deer by dancing around the woods like a wild man?

Yes, except L.E. performs his dance in specific places and with carefully thought-out choreography. The magic works anywhere whitetails live. L.E. had only been in this woods one other time before he enchanted the huge buck.

That December morning in southeast Louisiana had begun slowly. For a while it seemed that Dr. Ott wouldn't make the hunt. L.E. used the extra half-hour to work on three necessary items used to create the illusion that will undo the buck. One of those props, the antlers, will work without further adornment. As L.E. often jokes, the only requirement of a pair of antlers is that they come off a buck deer. But they do perform just a bit better with handles.

L.E. had shortened some bar-stool legs, providing him with several perfect five-inch maple handles. He bored two holes into the butt of each antler, bored two more (spaced the same) into the ends of two handles, cut the heads off four 8-penny nails to slide into the holes as pegs, and then glued a handle to each antler with fast-drying epoxy. With two pegs in each, the antlers couldn't turn on their handles. Long leather thongs were fastened to the handle bottoms so the antlers could be hung up or carried slung one on either side of a shoulder to prevent rattling. He finished just as Dr. Ott arrived.

At the hunting grounds, the morning drowsed on under a blanket of cold, misty fog. The virgin cypress swamp was silent. So was the eerie old vacant house that so long ago had been moved to the swamp's edge at the strange insistence of an Ott grandmother. Even the abundant squirrels were quiet in the surrounding hardwood hills. Owned by the family since the 1830s, and never completely logged, some of the virgin yellow pines stand so high that the old-timers used to claim they added salt to the shot rammed down their muzzleloaders "to make sure the squirrels didn't spoil on the way

I couldn't believe the amount of preparation L.E. went through or antics he used. Results were something else. (Steve Fritsch, art, Irene Vandermolen photo)

down." The tall, thick canopy delayed the woods' awakening.

At 6 a.m. L.E. hurriedly opened prop No. 2. The label on the little bottle said doe-in-heat scent, but half of its contents had been removed and replaced with pure vanilla extract.

Vanilla is a popular deer attractor in L.E.'s part of the country. Deer seem to follow it out of curiosity. But L.E. mixes it with the sex scent for both curiosity and enticement. When he smears the mixture on his boots and shoulders, he walks through the woods advertising an illusion, some say, of the sweetest-smelling doe in Louisiana.

"A fringe benefit to adding vanilla instead of using straight doe-in-heat scent," L.E. says, "comes after the hunt on the way home, when the heater is running full blast. Your buddies are willing to ride in the same truck with you."

Prop No. 3 comes out of a plastic bag: a pair of charms with solid biological reasons for working. They are scent glands cut from the hind legs of a buck deer. They can be fresh or frozen from last year. Holes are punched in the centers so the glands can be strung on L.E.'s boot laces.

At this point, as L.E. walks through the woods, he is still the sweetest-smelling doe in Louisiana, but now with a suitor in tow. When the swamp's chief stud smells this circumstantial evidence, he'll be infuriated by the notion that a rival buck has invaded his territory.

Dr. Ott strung the bow, his choice of weapons that day, and moved off to a stand 300 yards to the northwest. L.E. quietly laid a trail to another area they had previously scouted. Rubs were evident, but they only proved a buck had been in the vicinity. More importantly, there were scrapes, and that meant the buck would be back to see if his scent-and-hoofprint autograph in the middle of the bare dirt circle had attracted an admiring doe that might be waiting for him.

L.E. stood among the hardwoods in the scrape area, 100 yards from the swamp, his Hawken loaded with 90 grains of FFG behind 370 grains of pure lead. One chance. Everything had to be timed right. At 6:50 a.m. the sun was still taking its time lighting the swamp. L.E. decided to wait until 7:30 to begin his dance.

Every move was choreographed for maximum sound effects. The antlers would crash together, then rake apart. L.E. would jump up and down, kick a bush, and rub the antlers together, then scrape the leaves on the forest floor with one foot, then the other. Then he'd rub the rough, knobby bases of the antlers together, run into a sapling, and hook a small magnolia, shaking the leatherlike leaves. Bucks love to do that, and magnolia leaves make a terrible rattling racket.

After performing a three-minute unbroken dance that sounds exactly like two bucks fighting over a doe, the illusion is complete. The odors have told L.E.'s target buck that the sweetest-smelling doe in

Louisiana is being pursued by a bold buck out of its territory. And now the sounds are saying that a second buck, even bolder, has invaded the area and is challenging the other for a doe that the swamp stud, L.E.'s target buck, is certain should rightfully belong to him.

L.E. launched into his wild dance, confident that nothing more could be added to improve the illusion. But near the end of the planned course, he made an unnerving discovery: one of the nearby scrapes had been enlarged to five by eight feet and was torn up with hoof and skid marks. The buck had bred a doe right there! The illusion had grown from two bucks fighting over a doe in the target buck's territory, to mating right on the swamp stud's own bed!

L.E. grabbed his Hawken and ran for the beech tree to break his outline. The woods suddenly came alive. Squirrels chattered everywhere, 25 different ones by actual count, reacting either to the buck's presence or to L.E.'s realistic dance. He waited anxiously, but apparently the buck was out of earshot. Nothing happened. At 8 a.m., L.E. repeated the dance just one more time.

Minutes later, Dr. Ott walked up. L.E. was showing him the enlarged scrape when the buck came charging into the carefully built illusion.

"Shoot! Shoot!" Dr. Ott yelled after his arrow turned the deer.

One chance after all of this preparation, L.E. thought while cocking the hammer. He pulled the set trigger as he brought the muzzleloader to his shoulder, waited for the deer to be near the peak of a leap, and pulled. The muzzle flashed in the dim light, followed by a loud, flat boom in the heavy air. White smoke obliterated sight of the deer. But L.E. and Dr. Ott were quickly through it to find the folded deer, struck in the spine behind the shoulder.

"The buck weighed an estimated 200 pounds field-dressed and was three or four years old," L.E. said. "The neck measured 25¼ inches in circumference below the jaws and 36 at the brisket. The eight-point antlers had a spread of 21 inches with a four-inch circumference at the base and with 12-inch front tines. The taxidermist said it would take a magician to conjure up another buck like that in these parts."

However, the real magic about L.E.'s experience is that it can be repeated by anybody anywhere there are whitetail deer. Use fresh or frozen scent glands, and use pure vanilla, not imitation. Lay the trail. Do the deer dance near a scrape. Neglect no part of the illusion.

But what if you have no antlers? "One day I heard antlers rattling right in my own back yard," L.E said. "I ran to the window to see what was going on and found my son playing with two short lengths of bamboo. I had cut those big knobby ends off of the canes to make better fishing poles. Clashing them together, raking them apart, and rubbing the knobs together sounded just like rattling antlers. I'm going to experiment with those."

Weather Eye for Whitetails

Dwight Schuh

Most hunters know that whitetail deer move more on cool days than on hot, that they are active at night when the moon is full, and that in winter they feed heavily because that's when they need the most energy.

Actually, anyone who believes these "facts" is dead wrong. These and many other beliefs, regarded as natural laws over the years, are without foundation.

How do we know that? Because biologists have now studied whitetails and analyzed their behavior from Maine to Idaho. They have watched them for months from towers and blinds; they have used radio telemetry, track counts, spotlight counts, and other methods to keep track of deer. Countless hours of observation have enabled biologists to correlate deer movement and distribution with changing weather. In some instances, scientific findings reinforce age-old beliefs; in many other cases, they shoot holes in pet theories and provide fresh insights that could change our hunting practices.

Some elements discussed here, particularly time of year and time of day, aren't strictly "weather." But because they underlie all whitetail behavior, they can't be separated from a discussion of weather. Changing weather exerts its influence on whitetails within the frameworks of seasonal change and daily movement patterns.

TIME OF YEAR

Season exerts a major influence on deer behavior. The significant variable is length of daylight. According to scientists, daylight length affects production of the hormone thyroxin, which plays a large part in establishing the basic metabolic rate of deer. This means that in the winter, deer undergo a metabolic depression that lessens energy needs. In other words, whitetail deer are least active during the cold season because that's when their food requirements are the least.

In summer, when does are nursing fawns and bucks are growing new antlers, the metabolic rate rises to its maximum. As a result of increased food needs, deer are most active then.

Field observations bear this out. In New York's Adirondack Mountains, for example, Dr. Don F. Behrend found during a study of whitetails that deer are definitely most active in summer. Activity declined sharply, he says, from mid-August through September, and October marked the low point. The decline, of course, was interrupted in late October by the breeding season. At that time, activity increased and remained at a moderately high level through November.

Al Hofacker, record keeper for a nationwide organization of deer hunters called the Stump Sitters, reports a similar finding based on over 7,500 hours of field observation during two recent years. Looking only at figures taken from hunting seasons (summer activity is therefore excluded), primarily in the Midwest, the Stump Sitters' data show the greatest deer movement during September and the least in October, with an increase during the November rut.

An understanding of this seasonal pattern can help hunters with limited vacation time to make best use of it. Some states, because of their short open seasons, offer no choice, but others have long seasons. A few states have early deer seasons, many for bowhunters, that fall as early as August. Because deer are most active then, early seasons have a lot of potential, especially for stand hunting.

TIME OF DAY

Deer are inherently most active at dusk and dawn. That's no news to anyone who's spent some time in the woods. The point is that this inborn dawn-dusk pattern overrides most weather factors.

Of course, in specific localities, the daily activity may not be "normal." As Behrend points out, human disturbance, deer-population densities, availability of feed, and other things just may alter this pattern. Deer at a lake in the Adirondacks, Behrend discovered, were feeding on aquatic vegetation. These animals were most active at midday and did little moving in the mornings and evenings.

Even within the normal pattern, activity isn't necessarily equal during the morning and evening hours. Studying the nighttime behavior of whitetails in Idaho, biologist Lee Gladfelter observed that the peak activity each day occurred the second hour after sunset, with a lesser peak just before sunrise.

Another researcher, Arthur Tibbs, studying deer in Pennsylvania, saw more whitetails in open feeding sites during evening than during morning feeding hours. According to Al Hofacker, "Our records indicate that evening is far and away the best time to be on stand."

Of course, these reports don't necessarily mean deer are less active in the mornings, only that they're less observed at that time.

"Deer could be just as active in the morning, but at that time hunters are moving to their stand at the same time the deer are active. Deer may detect them and move out of the area," Hofacker says.

Nevertheless, most observations of deer indicate that hunters probably will do best on stand in the evening. As most hunters know, stands should be placed along forest deer trails between bedding sites and feeding grounds. And, of course, in the morning, hunters should move to stands well ahead of daylight to avoid spooking deer in the vicinity.

RELATIVE HUMIDITY

Under average conditions, humidity is lowest in late afternoon, when temperature is the highest. In the evening, the temperature drops and humidity rises. It reaches a peak in early morning just before sunrise, when the temperature is lowest. Of course, cloud cover or storms, which bring moisture and lower daytime temperatures, can raise humidity at any time of day.

Although temperature and humidity are inseparable, some studies indicate a stronger correlation between deer activity and humidity than between deer activity and temperature. Some biologists speculate that this has to do with body cooling. Others believe it's associated with a deer's scenting ability,

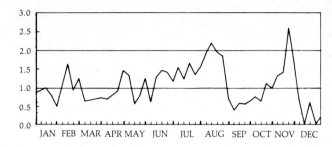

One unexpected finding is that deer activity (movement) is greatest in late summer and declines thereafter with the exception of a sharp peak during the rut when bucks seek out does. Graph is based on the observations in New York State by Dr. Don F. Behrend.

which is better when the humidity is fairly high.

Whatever the reasons, the following relationship evidently exists: the higher the humidity, the less active deer are; the lower the humidity, the more active deer are.

If humidity were the only factor involved in deer movement, mid-afternoon would obviously be the time of greatest activity. This is a case, however, in which the inborn early-and-late pattern prevails over the humidity factor. Still, humidity level is significant at any one period of the day. For example, a hunter is likely to see more deer moving on an evening of low relative humidity than on an evening of high humidity. Generally, you should also see more deer moving on a warm, clear day than on a cloudy, cool, or stormy day.

Probably no one will cancel a hunting trip because of high humidity, but humidity level could influence hunting method. On dry days, deer move more, so stand hunting is best. On humid days, stillhunting or driving may prove more effective.

TEMPERATURE

Relating deer movement to temperature is somewhat redundant because the general relationship is already clear—the higher the temperature, the more active the deer (within the normal daily movement patterns).

This applies seasonally as well as daily. In Pennsylvania, Arthur Tibbs found that as average monthly temperature rose from June through August, his average number of monthly deer sightings increased. In September, deer sightings declined along with the average temperature. This may be due to changing metabolism or to temperature alone, but one way or the other, the relationship is one that exists.

On a day-to-day basis, whitetails often are most active on warmer days. During early seasons, this probably relates to humidity levels; during the cold season when deer may stay bedded for several consecutive days, inactivity is necessary to preserve body heat and energy.

Whitetails are never totally predictable, and in snowstorms they may be in odd places. (Erwin A. Bauer photo)

Hunters traditionally think of cool, damp periods as ideal for hunting. As whitetail-behavior studies indicate, if the quality of hunting is measured by the level of deer activity, the warmer and drier the season and the day (within the tolerance range of deer), the better the hunting.

Here, however, a practical factor is important. During a warm, dry period, crackling leaves and twigs betray the stillhunter or tracker and getting a shot or even seeing deer is difficult. This is obviously why most deer hunters have always preferred cool, damp days for stillhunting. Hunting from a tree stand or a blind is the obvious answer.

WIND AND AIR CHILL

John Weiss, an Ohio writer, says that whitetails retreat to cover during heavy storms only because wind and precipitation dull their ability to detect predators and make them nervous and restless. "Whitetails don't need any protection from severe or inclement weather," Weiss says. "Physically, it doesn't bother them."

During early seasons, this statement seems to ap-

ply. At that time, air chill is not a problem, but strong wind does send deer into cover. Hofacker says the Stump Sitter figures show that as wind velocity increases, deer activity decreases. Under the category "light wind," members record an average of 70 deer sightings per 100 hours of observation; under the "moderate" and "gusty" categories, sightings decrease; for "continual strong wind," deer sightings average only 22 per 100 hours.

Once the cold sets in, however, air chill evidently does bother deer, and they do require protection from severe weather. Behrend reports that the "trend toward concentration (in evergreen shelter) is most closely associated with increasing frequency . . . of severe windchill in November and December. . . . "

Thomas J. Allen, studying whitetails in Maine, found that deer sought shelter when the air chill, a combination of air temperature and wind speed, was 9° F. or less.

"You may not be able to put it in exact degrees, especially from region to region," Allen says, "but any time the air-chill equivalent is lower than 20°, I believe it has an effect on the animals."

Concerning cold-weather cover, research only

During extreme cold and wind, whitetails often seek out small clearings and bed on the upwind side in the lee of trees where they can sun themselves.

verifies what most hunters realize—deer move into softwood stands. Dense evergreens moderate the effect of bitter weather. In Michigan, the temperature in softwood swamps can be 20° to 30° warmer than in surrounding uplands. In any conifer cover, temperature fluctuates less than in open habitat. And conifers can reduce wind velocity by 50 to 75 percent.

Deer also select protective terrain. In Maine, when strong winds blew from the northeast, Thomas J. Allen found that radio-equipped deer consistently bedded on west-facing hillsides, or at the upwind edges of sheltered clearings, where they could lie in direct sunlight. Generally, the animals stayed on south- and west-facing slopes where sunlight lasted longest. Allen says these findings held true during the rut as well as at other times.

The implications should be clear. During moderate to strong winds, especially during the late seasons when air chill is severe, hunters can expect to see little deer activity, particularly out in the open. At those times, it's probably best to stillhunt or drive cover that affords deer maximum protection.

SNOW DEPTH

Deep snow often forces deer to change feeding locations. In snow up to six inches deep, according to Hofacker, deer can still feed on ground foods such as fallen acorns by pawing the snow away. In deeper snow, the animals switch to woody browse and may change their location to seek it out.

"A hunter not aware of this may hunt in the wrong places," Hofacker says.

Deep snow also severely restricts mobility. In snow over 18 inches deep, about belly-high on a deer, the animals congregate in softwood wintering areas. Here, where snow is shallowest and crust

conditions are most stable, the concentrated animals beat down trails in a limited area.

Eighteen inches of snow is unusual during most fall hunting seasons, but snow depth could still be a factor in hunting. Allen observed deer moving into softwood cover, apparently anticipating deeper snow, when as little as three to five inches had fallen. Even when snow of 18 inches and more did force animals into wintering areas, Allen observed that deer would return to upland locations to feed just as soon as conditions allowed. For example, after strong winds had swept hillsides bare or had compacted snow into a strong crust that would bear their weight, the animals traveled up the slopes to feed. They returned to softwood shelter only during storms and periods of cold.

In West Virginia, where he now works for the Department of Natural Resources, Allen says that in the unusual event of heavy snow, deer concentrate briefly in conifer wintering areas, but as the snow melts, they disperse to good feeding ranges.

According to Lee Gladfelter, snow depths up to 12 inches don't restrict deer movement, but even at that shallow depth, the animals do choose paths of least resistance. In his study area, he discovered deer were walking in footprints he'd made in the snow, and deer traveled up and down creek bottoms and draws rather than across high ridges where snow was deeper.

In planning a late-fall hunt, therefore, take the restrictive potential of snow into account, but remember that the whitetails will take advantage of rich feeding areas whenever they can do so.

PRECIPITATION

Light rain or light snow apparently doesn't repress deer activity; heavy precipitation does. Most researchers agree that fairly heavy falling rain or snow forces deer into shelter. This could be the result of chilling, but most experienced observers believe it's because the heavy precipitation limits a deer's ability to hear and smell. Part of the reaction seems to be a desire to hide from predators.

The fact that fewer deer are observed during rain or snow storms doesn't necessarily mean they're less active. Stormy conditions make game spotting

Deer feed actively just before a rainstorm, but if very heavy rain falls, they seek "umbrella" cover and security from predators in conifers.

(and hunting) difficult. Arthur Tibbs says his observation points in Pennsylvania overlooked open feeding areas. Without question he saw fewer deer during heavy precipitation, but deer could have been moving within adjacent cover, where he couldn't see them.

At any rate, deer do seek cover types that offer umbrella protection from falling rain and snow, so that's where hunters should look for deer during storms.

BAROMETRIC PRESSURE

Most biologists have been unable to correlate barometric pressure with deer activity. However, a falling barometer (lowering air pressure) precedes most major fall storms, and as most hunters know, deer movement often increases greatly just prior to storms. So the evidence suggests that a dropping barometer does indicate greater deer activity.

Allen observed that deer in Maine became unusually active prior to and during the early stages of snowstorms. But when as little as three inches of snow had fallen, they congregated in softwoods.

"Generally, if deer moved to cover, the snowfall would be heavy and dropping barometric pressure normally foretold such storms," Allen says. "So deer did seem to move with a falling barometer."

Hofacker personally has observed a quite noticeable increase in activity just before storms, particularly prior to big snowstorms during the December bow season in Wisconsin.

Thus, the evidence is strong that when the barometer is dropping, hunters should hunt hard, probably from stands, waiting for deer to move to them. But once a storm has set in, they should change tactics and drive or stillhunt dense cover.

CLOUD COVER

The consensus is that deer are most active on clear days.

The Stump Sitter findings are representative of observations about cloud cover. During 5,000 hours of observation from stands, according to Hofacker, hunters averaged seeing 41 deer per 100 hours of observation on partly cloudy days; 45 per 100 hours on overcast days; and 59 per 100 hours on clear days.

"I had always assumed cloudy days were the best for hunting," Hofacker admits, "until I looked at our data. I find that we're seeing 40 percent more deer on clear days. This is a good example of how gut reactions don't always hold up. A wise hunter keeps accurate records of his observations."

Most research data substantiate the findings of the Stump Sitters. And the research is consistent with conclusions concerning humidity. Cloud cover implies the presence of high atmospheric moisture, and cloud cover during the day generally lowers air temperature. If high humidity is significant in retarding deer activity, deer should be most active on clear days.

MOON PHASE

We've all heard that deer move and feed more on moonlit nights than on dark nights. The implication is that hunting will be poor on days during the full-moon period.

According to research, that simply isn't true. Deer have excellent night vision, so lack of light isn't a limitation on nighttime activity. In fact, according to Lee Gladfelter, deer are likely to be most active on cloudy and moonless nights. He believes they feel more secure in the open during dark nights because they are less visible to predators. So forget the moon when planning a hunt.

It's widely believed that deer feed heavily on bright, moonlit nights, but statistics show they prefer complete dark or very little moonlight.

The foregoing reports of findings should be of help to hunters in many ways, but Al Hofacker made a very practical point when he said: "We don't use this information to determine when we'll hunt. Obviously, the best time to hunt is when you've got the time. Rather, the Stump Sitters use such information to determine *how* to hunt. If deer aren't active, there's no sense in stand hunting. Then hunters would do better to stillhunt or drive. We stress selecting hunting method according to the variables."

PART 3

HUNTING FOR MULE DEER

The Finest Stalk I Ever Witnessed

Ron Bishop

In the Santa Susana Mountains of Southern California, on the perimeter of a mania called Los Angeles, there is a section that is hunted only by truly absorbed hunters. There is a sizable deer population. It is on a vast ranch, but that has almost nothing to do with the facts that the deer are there and the hunting is dedicated. We call it the Devil's Crotch. The land rolls away and down to an immense basin. A thousand feet down, I suppose. A mile or two in diameter. Maybe more. It doesn't sound like much when you think in terms of Western "space"—but it's a lot. It's also a lot of trouble to hunt. The coastal deer season in California begins around the first week of August. The Crotch isn't splendid with breezes, and when the temperature settles in at over 100° F., you aren't so splendid either. That and the snakes, fleas, and ticks, and bringing the meat out on pack frames make you wonder what you're doing down there.

You're there because the deer are there. That's the surface reason. The real reason is that it is wild. Primitive. To have something so raw and basic close to a city of superficial pursuit is riveting, absorbing. In 30 to 40 years of hunting this region, I've seen one hunter in the Crotch. There could have been others. But maybe they saw me or my buddy and

didn't want to be seen, as a good hunter hunting strives to do, but I should have to imagine there were very few. The one was last year.

Looking at the Crotch from the top is a lot like marriage. You don't know what you're getting into. It looks to be a land of folding and enfolding ridges broken by great benches of grass and oaks.

But the ridges are high, thick chaparral. The trails go through the chaparral. Usually what's easy for an animal is hard for you. The trails become tunnels.

Once down into the hunting area, you must stop a moment. Not simply to reassemble yourself, but

to remind yourself that you are sane and that you do not—contrary to the misery of your joints—have a death wish.

After that most necessary moment—it might last a number of minutes—you begin to gain a balance of things again.

Now you see and care about movements distant and near, the smell of things, the drift and direction of breezes. It is barely light, and a day that will become a small life—as all true hunting days are—is about to begin. There is a sense of life-purpose. Down there is where the big deer are. If you simply wanted an animal, you could hunt the top country and the odds might provide a buck. With the rut, it would be a near certainty of seeing a fair selection, at least. But down there it is a man's world. There are battered, wise beings down there.

I crawled to the edge of a low, large sumac from which I could look down upon the lower benches and sage flanks. I got the spotting scope out of the pack and laid it on my packboard with my rifle, a Ruger No. 1/.270 with a 6× Leupold scope. A single-shot rifle appeals to me under such circumstances. It is specific—it asks only for precision, which is on-ly care. This is country with animals one cares very much about. I lay on the ground watching the brightening land through light 10× binoculars.

I watched a twist of even movement that was nothing and then became a bobcat immobile at the edge of some blue sage. It disappeared like light melting down a draw in shade toward some valley quail roosting in the scrub oak below. I could hear the quail. The cat was about 300 yards away, to my left, and slightly lower. Then a Cooper's hawk land-ed on a sycamore branch. He was below the quail in the stream bottom. At least some of the quail would die this day.

Then I saw three different bucks. They were about 500 yards away, maybe more. They were steeply below me, and that made them seem nearer than they probably were. They were big forkhorns, all well-bodied. About 200 yards apart, browsing on what looked to be plain sage. Old men. Old and un-concerned. They knew where they were. They had remained in cover, watched, and worked upwind and more downwind now. You didn't see them do this, but you knew they had. They were old men, weren't they? They had seen things. If they were capable, they could tell tales. Their ears flapped at the flies.

There is a central water hole in the Crotch—not a hole, actually, but a collection of small depressions holding water from the cliff-base seepage of the deep-rock inner wells. The water is stagnant and re-pugnant, but sustaining even in the driest of times. I glassed the water briefly. I had often seen moun-tain-lion pugs in the soft earth there.

Then I saw another buck emerge halfway out of shadow and stand for a moment. It was instinctive, without fear, a natural assuring caution. Then, be-fore I realized it, he was moving slowly between shade patterns and onto a small table of oats, sage, and small walnuts. He stopped again and watched carefully but placidly. Then he began to browse on the sage and some short buckbrush. He was a large deer with large antlers. He had three points on the left, four on the right, maybe more. High and wide and heavy. He could have been a Sierra deer. This was the deer I would shoot. I watched him carefully to be sure he was going to stay reasonably planted. Then I reached over for the rifle, worked into the sling, and tightened the keepers. I took two car-tridges out of my belt pocket and stuck them be-

tween the fingers of my left hand and rolled prone. He was down to my right and at an angle that al-lowed me to see enough intervening ground to judge distance. I usually underestimate range, but I thought he was a little less than 400 yards, maybe 375, which might seem like a long shot, but I knew the rifle perfectly. It was sighted-in carefully. Scru-tiny of loose brush and free limbs on all ridges and flats between us gave no indication of wind. It was a flat day. And it would be hot later. But after I shot him, I could quarter him or bone him out under the walnuts and hang the sacked meat from the limbs. It would cool in the shade. There I would nap until mid-afternoon, when the air would begin to cool and the pullout with the full packboard would not be complete torture and the evening breezes would begin near the top when you would have almost reached numbness. Just a faint passage of air across or into the streaming sweat of your body provides a bath that is impossible to describe accurately. It is life to something drowning.

All of these things were in place in my mind when I wedged prone and slid a shell in. Then, as I started to settle my cheek on the stock comb, I saw a flash of light from the corner of my left eye. I looked over at the far ridges. There was nothing. But it had been *something*. A flash that had been as quick and visible as a quick speck of light out of total darkness. Such things are man-made.

I slid the safety on and rolled out of the sling into a sitting position and inspected the area that had caught me. Slowly, slowly, bush, rock, tree, slowly, then the next ridge, slowly. Again the same, slow-ly. Then, there he was. A hunter was up under some low oaks in deep shade. I could barely make him out. He was not far from the three bucks deep below me. He was out on a ridge between them and the big buck. I couldn't shoot.

I extracted the shell and set the rifle back on the pack frame. I got out the spotting scope and a low, lightweight tripod. With the binoculars and the spotting scope, I could see the wide and the short of things. There came a warm pleasure, and for a while I didn't know why. Then I knew it was that whether I wanted the big buck or not, I wasn't going to get him and wouldn't have to labor with it. I had a valid reason for calling the game.

I found the hunter again through the glasses, marked him by the surrounding brush, and moved to the spotting scope. With the 20× scope, I could see him clearly. He had moved to the edge of the oak shade. He was a man in his 40's, perhaps; lean, tall, high shoes or low boots with thick soles and scuffed, journeyed leather. A dark blue work shirt and jeans washed to medium-light blue from use. An old felt hat rested on one knee. Dark brown or grey-black hair looked wet with sweat. It stuck to his head. On his back was an old and patched Maine packbasket that looked odd in this country. There was nothing odd about the rifle. It was a well-

THE FINEST STALK I EVER WITNESSED

used lever-action Savage 99 with open iron sights. The blueing along the sides of the barrel and action was worn almost white. He had a pair of very small 6× glasses and it was probably sunlight off a lens that had flashed. He was watching the three bucks, and they were watching him. Then, moving so slowly that I was barely aware of his change in position, he watched the big buck. Whether he realized it or not, he was being watched by the three bucks. If these bucks moved slowly from sight, he was safe. If they bolted, the big buck would be alerted and probably move into cover. The big buck was still too far away for his iron sights. Possibly 300 yards. Some shooters would have shot. This was a hunter.

The big buck browsed unaware and would stop from time to time and appear to stare at nothing. But you knew he was sensing. Instinctively taut-tuned to all frequencies. So was the hunter.

The three bucks moved from sight, unworried and unhurried. Now the hunter turned all his attention to the big buck. The hunter was "becoming" the buck, as you must if you hunt with passion.

He moved back slowly and down from sight. He was in a draw. I suspected he would move down the draw to close the range in half. Then he would go up a side draw and to the lip of a knoll that looked down on the big buck's flat. It was the only thing to do. And doing so he would never be sure he would not be betrayed by the breeze, shifts in the rising warmth. He could not be sure that the big buck would not move into brief cover, a matter of a few feet, a few yards. The animal would not stay in one spot, and shortly it would be looking for a bed. The bed would be on a rise under cover not thick enough to screen a breeze and facing the breeze, with an escape draw or thick brush. That is why it is far easier to team hunt: your partner stays back with overall vision and glasses, and you can learn by signals from him where the animal is or what has happened. But easier doesn't necessarily make it more satisfying. This hunter was playing it one on one. All the things I have mentioned, he knew and was thinking as he worked the draw. I was sure of it.

He was at the lip quicker than I thought he could be. A movement showed him on top and crawling, rifle cradled. He moved evenly—no dust whisped around him—and he was crawling over loose shale. He stopped and slowly gathered into a sitting position. He was now about 125 yards from the big buck. The animal had moved into an apron of brush, and the hunter couldn't see him. He glassed the ground the buck could have taken. He made up his mind that the animal was still there, only obscured from him. Slowly he smoothed back to crawling again and worked 20 or 25 yards up to his left behind brush. There was a clump of yucca at the end of the brush. Behind the clump he gathered back into sitting. The buck also had moved on. But the hunter could see his buck now. It also was now a little farther away, but it was no problem. I wondered why he didn't get into po-

sition. Then I realized that he could not move. The buck was angling toward him. And although the buck was browsing, the slightest movement—even the shine of the sun moving onto his face (he wore his hat low now)—would be seen by the buck. Both would be transfixed. This buck would be away instantly, and the merest movement, then, ruled out bringing the rifle slowly to shoulder. If he were going to shoot now, it would be a snap-shot.

Then the buck moved back and was away from the hunter. He could shoot. Slowly he raised the rifle. Again I expected the shot. Then I realized that the animal had moved around enough to offer only a raking shot. He probably could have driven the .300 or .250 Savage, or whatever caliber he had, into the lungs from that angle, but it was a shot that could never be neat. Then the buck moved into the brush behind the walnuts, out of sight. The hunter waited as though in decision; then he got down again and crawled back and up slightly—10 yards or so. When the hunter had gotten to his spot and back to sitting, the buck came out completely into the open. He had made up his mind to bed. This time the hunter had his rifle ready.

Far away, two ravens came over a ridge, squawking. They flew on squawking. The buck had heard such ravens squawk exactly this way countless times. But this time it bothered the buck, and he took two steps that were almost hops and stopped. Now for some reason he was unsure of everything. Everything looked right except everything felt wrong. He turned around. He looked up valley. Perhaps half a minute. An eternity. Then he turned back to the hunter. The buck was satisfied. Then he started walking without hesitation or fear exactly toward the hunter. Pictures are painted that way. Nobility is what is being painted.

When the buck was no more than 30 yards from the hunter, he saw the motionless man for what he was. The two looked at each other. Probably 10 or 15 seconds. Then the hunter started slowly to rise. At the first movement, the buck was off. Three immense bounds took him back into the draw the hunter had crawled up. With his first motion toward rising, the hunter continued without stopping to stand slowly erect. He was a tall man who looked taller standing there. He watched the buck as he removed the cartridge from the chamber of the rifle. Then the buck stepped out onto a shelf of ground. The deer had covered at least 100 yards very quickly. Explosively. But when he stepped out, it was with seeming deliberation. He stood looking back at the hunter. At that moment the buck looked larger, too. Then the buck vanished into deep oaks.

The hunter watched for a moment. Then he placed the rifle over his shoulder holding it by the barrel and started quietly out and up.

There was no need for caution. He was not going hunting. He could have banged along. But he was a woodsman. And he walked with the even-footed, calculated, effortless, slow-rolling rhythm of a woodsman.

The Hunting Horse

Jack O'Connor

One morning I started off alone for a hunt, and to make sure I'd go straight back to the camp, I took my bearings and found it was on a direct line between one of the peaks in the Picus and one in the Sierra Los Mochos. Outside of the hills and mountains, the whole country looked pretty much alike—sandy flats peppered with the tracks of deer and javelinas, scrubby desert trees, saguaro, cholla, dry sandy arroyos. Much of the time down in the brush it was impossible to see the landmarks, but they could always be located by climbing a little hill. The road from the ranch where we had borrowed the horses ended at the well. If a man went too far south and west he'd miss it—and there was not another road between the well and the Gulf of California.

When I started back that afternoon, I rode up on a little hill west of Los Mochos, took my line between the two peaks, and started out. About halfway to camp, my horse started veering to the left. I pulled him to the right, but again he began to drift over to the left. I rode up on another little rise, checked my line again. I was right. My knot-headed horse was wrong, something I regarded as odd because horses are supposed to have an infallible sense of direction. I had to fight the horse to keep him in line. Then suddenly I encountered horse tracks and the marks of a heavy limb being dragged. The trail was in the direction my horse had wanted to travel, and I felt very foolish indeed. That day I had told my Papago horse wrangler to go out and bring some wood to camp—and here was the sign that he had done so.

My horse started to trot now, and I gave him his head. In a few minutes we were in camp. I found later that I had taken a line on the wrong peak in the Picus and if I had kept going I would have missed camp by about a quarter of a mile.

I had always known that horses were pretty well equipped with built-in gyro compasses, and I had always been told that if I were ever out on a horse and lost, to give the horse his head and the horse would take me home. If I hadn't been so certain of my direction, so sure of my line, I would not have argued with the horse. Since that day, a great many years ago, horses have occasionally thought camp was in one direction when I thought it was in another. I have been smart enough not to argue with them—and the horses have always been right.

Once in northern British Columbia, my guide Frank Golata and I had been out on horseback to scout for sheep and caribou, and when we started back I suggested we give the horses their heads and see how they operated. Instead of traveling direct to camp, they followed their tracks back, taking every twist, every turn. They went over every little knoll where we had stopped to glass, around every point where we had looked into another basin, crossed every little brook exactly where we had crossed that morning.

A horse has a magnificent nose, and it would have been easy to follow a trail that fresh by smelling it out. In Alberta one time, my guide and I steered our horses a half mile into a tangle of down timber, and couldn't find a way out. We gave the horses their heads, and they worked their way into the clear, always exactly on their backtrack. Sometimes before going on, the lead horse stopped and sniffed the ground.

Horses also have a remarkable memory for country. Roy Hargreaves, who for many years outfitted in Alberta, told me that once an outfit of his was lost in a snowstorm at timberline. The head guide had no idea where the trail was, but Roy had told him that if he ever got into trouble to put a steady old packhorse named Red in the lead and to follow him. So Red was put at the head of the string. He turned around, started back, worked through some timber, and started down a long ridge. Presently the guide was conscious that they were on a trail. Presently he heard running water. Before long, Red stopped under a tree at the campsite they were looking for. The sense of smell cannot account for this, as Red hadn't been over that particular trail or at that camp for years.

The fact that a horse will return to camp if given his head is something which anyone taking a big-game hunt on which horses are used should store away in his memory. This uncanny ability possessed by almost any Western range horse has saved many a dude hunter, and for that matter

many a cowboy, from going without supper and sitting out all night in the cold.

The horse is about the most useful piece of equipment the Western hunter can have, and if it were not for the horse, many middle-aged, elderly, or out-of-condition hunters would have to stay at home. A horse furnishes the muscle, the wind, the endurance for hunters who don't have them. A horse also extends a hunter's range enormously. To hunt 10 miles from camp on foot and return in fairly rough and hilly country takes a young, tough man. But a 20-mile circle is a breeze for a good horse.

Carrying in the carcass of even a smallish deer is a backbreaker for a strong man but a cinch for a horse. I have carried in dozens of whitetails tied on behind the saddle with the saddle strings. I usually carry the larger mule deer across the saddle and lead the horse.

The easiest way to carry a big buck to camp on a saddle horse is to lay it across the saddle and button it to the saddlehorn by a hole cut in the flat of the belly skin. Then the head should be pulled back to

Here, early in his career, the late Jack O'Connor rides an animal whose savvy O'Connor often chose to rely on. During the several decades following this photo, O'Connor became a legendary shooting editor of Outdoor Life.

the cantle and the antlers tied securely with the rear saddle strings. Then the hunter should cut through the joints of the legs, break them so they will not catch on brush, and tie them down with the forward saddle strings. If the hunter has taken the trouble to balance the buck well, it'll ride nicely to camp.

A great many horses are allergic to having a deer put on them. They jump around, making packing the deer difficult, and sometimes they lash out with their hind feet. I cure this by blindfolding a horse with a large bandanna handkerchief, then covering my hand with deer blood and rubbing it over the horse's nose and into its nostrils. If the horse still feels like kicking (and he almost never does) I tie one hind foot up with a rope to the saddlehorn. When the hunter takes off the blindfold and starts leading the horse to camp, he is generally philosophical. I have even seen horses uncomplainingly carry mountain lions and black bears into camp after being blindfolded and given the blood-in-the-nose treatment.

But this magnificently powerful and gifted creature with his wonderful nose and eyes, his marvelous sense of direction is a relatively stupid animal. I am sure that the horse lovers of America will organize a posse to lynch me on reading this, but I'll stick to the sentiment. An article on my fellow native Arizonian Rex Ellsworth, the rancher and owner of one of the nation's most successful stables of race horses, quotes him as saying exactly the same thing. Caught in a barbed-wire fence, a horse will cut himself to pieces in his struggle, but the more intelligent but less appealing mule will remain quiet and wait for someone to get him out.

A horse is subject to sudden and unreasoning panics, as anyone who grew up in a small town during the horse-and-buggy era as I did can testify. When I was a lad, two or three runaways a week were routine, and they usually ended with broken buggies, torn harness, and often injured drivers and horses.

If a pack slips on a mule, that wise and cynical animal will almost always stop and wait for someone to come and fix it. If it slips on a horse, he'll go into a panic and strew everything packed on him all over the countryside. A number of years ago, Bill Rae, then chief editor of *Outdoor Life*, and I were on a sheep hunt in the Yukon. One of the packhorses was loaded with two pack panniers containing, among other things, the party's supply of whiskey. A bedroll was the top pack, and above that—held on by a diamond hitch thrown over it and the bedroll—was Bill's Dall-sheep head.

The head slipped, and the end of one of the horns tickled the horse in an unexpected place. Off he went, frantic with terror, wild eyed, bucking, knocking other packhorses down. Bill's sheep head sailed about 25 feet in the air, and every now and then a bottle of booze would go shooting out of a pannier like a shell from a mortar. Hoofs were drumming, the guides and wranglers were yelling, and the air was filled with the popping of brush and

the crash of broken pack boxes. Presently the horse had got rid of everything packed on him. The wranglers calmed him down, jury-rigged the broken panniers, and repacked him while Bill hunted down the sheep head and I backtracked the horse to the brush for the bottles. As miraculous as it may seem, not one of them was broken.

Another time in the Yukon, my party had come into a campsite after a long day on the trail and was making camp on Count Creek. Two packhorses were tied to an old stump, the roots of which had rotted. A fly bit one of the horses, he jerked his head, and the stump moved. This astonished the other horse. He snorted and backed away. This tilted the stump and bugged the first horse. He also yanked back. Now the stump was pulled from the ground and was suspended in the air between the two horses. Neither had ever seen a floating stump before. Wild eyed, screaming with terror, each put on all power and backed away from the stump. One of the ropes broke, and the horses fled in opposite directions, throwing their packs all over the countryside. As long as we were in that camp, those horses would snort and roll their eyes whenever they came near the spot where the stump had been.

A pal of mine has been a stunt pilot, parachute jumper, and wing walker. On his days off, he used to drive race cars for relaxation. He became a dude rancher, outfitter, and big-game guide. In his long and dangerous life, he has been seriously hurt three times—and every time by a horse. His wife wears store teeth because a tame and friendly horse was in a bad mood and kicked her face in one time. Another friend of mine, one of Arizona's famous lion-hunting Lee Brothers, was killed by a horse a couple of weeks after I had hunted whitetails on his ranch. He had been out looking at his cattle all day. He got almost back to his ranch house when he decided to ride back a quarter of a mile to look at a cow. The horse had been planning on getting the heavy rider and saddle off and kept trying to turn back to the ranch. He was on a steep sidehill when he decided to buck. He lost his footing, fell on his rider, and killed him.

Outfitters generally put their dudes on calm, patient, well-broken horses, and seldom do these novice riders have any trouble with them, but even the slowest old horse can panic. Once down in Mexico, my wife and I were riding out on a little afternoon hunt on a couple of pokey, half-starved old cow ponies. A half-mile or so from the camp, I discovered that some dogs were trying to follow us. That morning they had spooked a couple of deer, and I didn't want them along. I took after them to chase them back to the ranch. As I leaned over to whack one of them with a riata, the front cinch broke. The saddle turned, and I crashed to the ground like a load of bricks. With the saddle held under his belly by the second cinch, that horse really went into orbit! Kicking and squealing, he rushed around tearing down bushes and bumping into trees. In the saddle scabbard was my pet .30/06 with a superb French-walnut stock by Adolph Minar of Fountain, Colorado. It stayed in the scabbard for about five quick jumps. Then I saw it sail 50 feet into the air and land in a pile of rocks. From that time on, Old Betsy really wore the scars of battle!

A mountain-raised horse is a marvelously sure-footed animal, but there is nothing to the old saying that a horse can go anywhere a man can go. Even a fair climber can go places where the most sure-footed of horses would break his neck. The dude hunter who goes out on horseback should always bear that in mind, and if you come to a spot where a horse might lose his footing, you should get off and lead. After all, the horse is an animal which evolved not in the mountains but out on the plains. He is by nature not a climber but a runner.

The frozen ground of icy slopes is poison for a horse. Slanting solid rock is dangerous. Perhaps the worst of all is a slanting rock slope with loose stones on it. Once I was hunting with an amigo in British Columbia with an Indian guide who was allergic to walking. We were rimming around a steep hillside. It was mid-morning and the warm sun was shining, but it had been bitterly cold the night before and shady areas were still covered with heavy frost. Ahead of us was a steep frosty stretch, and I suspected that the ground under the frost was frozen. I suggested that the Indian guide get off, and I prepared to dismount myself. But the guide went on. The instant the horse stepped on the frozen ground, his feet shot out from under him. Horse and rider tobogganed about 300 yards down that frozen glassy hill and came to rest unhurt in a nice, soft, grassy meadow.

On another occasion in Arizona, a companion and I were coming in from a deer hunt. Ahead of us I saw a smooth steep slope of solid rock covered with scattered small stones and pebbles. I got off and was leading my horse when I heard a fearful clatter. Here came my pal and his horse, first one on top, then the other. Luckily neither was hurt.

A horse learns by experience to handle himself in soft ground and in rough country, and a plains horse is as inept in muskeg or mountains as a city-bred man is on snowshoes. I once rode on a long pack trip in northern British Columbia a very gentle and pretty little mare called Susy Q. She was farm bred and knew nothing about the bush. I had to lead her across every muskeg we encountered. If I did not, she was quickly bogged down and helpless. She learned to step exactly where I stepped. She was terrified of rough country. When we came to what she considered bad going, she'd stop and tremble until I got off and led her.

A horse may be shy on brains and subject to panics, but he has a wonderful nose and magnificent eyes. On dozens of occasions I have taken game that my horse saw or smelled first. One horse I rode in

This photo shows O'Connor on one of his last hunts on horseback—approaching what he called the biblical "three-score and ten years" of age.

Mexico associated the odor of deer with rifle fire, and every time he'd smell a deer he'd snort, roll his eyes, and jitter around. Such conduct always meant, I discovered, that deer were nearby. This horse also always ran away the instant I yanked my rifle out of the scabbard, and it was something of a handicap to wonder where my horse would wind up while I was trying to concentrate on knocking off a buck. I finally solved the problem by tying a knot in the reins so short that when I hauled back and put the reins over the saddle horn, the horse would stay put. His chin was pulled right up to his neck, and if he tried to move it hurt him.

A gifted packhorse that a guide and I used to take along to bring back heads and meat on could spot moose and caribou almost as far away as I could see them with glasses. I could always tell when he saw or smelled a bear because he would crowd right up to the guide and me, his eyes rolling and his nostrils distended.

A horse likewise has the night vision of a bat, and many times horses have brought me safely to camp when it was so dark I could hardly see my hand before my face. Once in the Yukon, a companion and I were seated by a little stream eating our sandwiches. Suddenly my horse's ears went forward. He snorted and gazed fixedly back into the dark shadows of some timber a couple of hundred yards away. With the naked eye I could see nothing. I picked up my binocular, and with the aid of its light-gathering power I could see the head of a black bear. He was watching us from the far side of a log back in the heavy shadows of the timber. My scope-sighted .270 was leaning on a tree beside me. I could also see the bear's head through the bright scope. I squeezed the trigger and hit the bear right through the brain just above the eyes.

In parts of the West, it is possible to hunt almost entirely from horseback. The hunter simply rides around likely looking deer country until he sees a deer. Then he gets off and starts shooting. This is a relatively easy, interesting, and exciting way to hunt.

In rougher and more wooded country, the horse-back hunter rides to likely looking areas, then gets off and hunts on foot. In many sheep mountains such hunting is possible. The best North American sheep I ever shot was a fine Dall. My guide and I located the ram about a mile away and then rode around and above the bunch of rams the big one was running with. Riding around in the open country above timberline in the Yukon and northern British Columbia, I have many times spotted caribou, moose, and even grizzlies while still in the saddle, and in Arizona and Wyoming I have piled off horses and shot elk. Once I stepped off a horse at the head of a packtrain, sat down, and knocked a fine ram off a ledge about 200 feet above me and 250 yards away.

Most dude hunters unused to riding get so saddle-sore they are miserable. The major reason for this is that the stirrups are not properly adjusted. If the stirrups are too long, the rider's weight rests entirely on his buttocks, and at the end of 20 miles on the trail, he is convinced that his bones are sticking through the flesh. If his stirrups are too short, his knees cramp most horribly. For trail riding, the best adjustment, for me anyway, is to have the stirrups long enough so that when I stand up in them my fanny clears the saddle by from four to six inches. They are then long enough so that knees do not cramp and short enough so that my leg muscles can take some of the shock and bumps off my rear end.

With my stirrups so adjusted, I can get on a horse and ride 20 miles the first day and be only a little sore at the end. Another thing the occasional rider should remember is to keep your back straight. If you don't, the continual jiggling of the horse will pull and twist the muscles of the small of your back and at day's end you'll feel as if you had been sawed in half.

One of the most depressing sights in nature is to see a line of dudes starting out with a pack outfit on horseback. They are perched on their horses as inert as so many bags of potatoes. Almost always their stirrups are too short. They sit there miserably with their backs bowed, their knees under their chins, their rifles either carried over their shoulders by slings or tucked away in scabbards at odd and impossible angles.

The chap planning a horseback hunt or a packtrip doesn't need to be a bronco buster or a hell-bent vaquero, but he should know how to adjust his stirrups and how to sit in a saddle.

A great boon to the hunter, this Western and Northern horse, but the hunter should never forget that he is a creature of flesh and blood and not a machine. He is magnificently strong and enduring and is equipped with marvelous eyes, a wonderful nose, and a built-in compass as good as that of the homing pigeon.

A little more advice for the horseback hunter. The rifle should never be left in the saddle scabbard when the hunter dismounts for lunch, to glass, or for any other reason. If his back is sore or the saddle happens to be uncomfortable, a horse often gets a notion to roll. A rifle or a camera that has been rolled on by a horse weighing 800 to 1000 pounds has generally had it.

Some more advice on horses: Don't overload your saddlebags, as they ride right over a horse's kidneys and are apt to hurt him. A horse with saddle sores or painful kidneys is a very unhappy horse. Take along a lunch, an extra box of cartridges, some film, perhaps a camera. Don't load the poor horse down with canned goods, bottles of beer, heavy movie cameras. Tie your stag shirt or rain jacket on behind the cantle with the saddle strings. If you have your camera and binoculars with you, it is best to carry them with straps across your shoulder. Don't hang them on the saddlehorn or tie them to the saddle with the saddle strings. If the horse plows through some brush, the straps may be broken and camera and binoculars lost.

Few occasional fall hunters are expert horsemen, and they are apt to be a bit in awe of the strange monsters they are given to ride. The horse quickly senses this and will take advantage of the timid rider. A hunter should have a quirt with him, but if he does not he can cut himself a good switch. The first time his horse starts lagging or decides to pause and refresh himself with a luscious bit of grass, the rider should belt the hell out of him. Then the horse knows who is master. It is remarkable how full of ambition and energy a good quirt or a pair of spurs will fill the laziest horse.

The hunter should take care not to get kicked or stepped on. Never startle a horse. Approach him so he can see you. If he is dozing, speak to him. A pal of mine had just killed and dressed a deer. He decided to go to his horse and get a pack of cigarettes out of his saddlebags. He approached from the rear, and suddenly the horse was aware of the smell of deer blood. It lashed out with a hind hoof and struck my pal on the thigh. For a week, he couldn't even hobble.

As a cowpoke friend of mine says: "Always keep an eye on a horse. You don't always know what he's going to do, and he don't neither. It's always them old gentle bastards that kill you!"

Mule Deer:
Read the Country

Jim Zumbo

Many mule-deer hunters haunt the high country, and that's where most Eastern hunters believe they'll get a buck if they go West. The best-known method is to glass with binoculars and a spotting scope, make long approaches and stalks, and shoot a scoped flat-trajectory rifle at long range. But mule deer are adaptable, and they inhabit eight quite different habitats.

Ever hear, for example, of float-trip hunting with a boat for mule deer? That's only one of the many methods discussed in this chapter. You'll learn how to suit your tactics and your rifle to the terrain, the cover, the availability of water, and other local conditions. I aim to tell you how to hunt wherever this truly great game animal ranges, and I think some of the tactics will surprise you.

SAGEBRUSH

Sagebrush is essential to many mule deer. It provides indispensable forage during the harsh winter months and shelters them where no other cover is available. The first mule deer I ever killed was shot in a vast expanse of sagebrush. I was surprised, because my Eastern upbringing had taught me that deer are always found in or near trees or thickets.

Deer are found in sagebrush when they're feeding in it, passing through it, or bedding in it.

To get a shot when they are feeding or moving usually requires an early-morning vigil because wise bucks like to be in heavy cover soon after dawn.

If deer are bedding in the sagebrush, they are usually quite safe. Some folk think it's a cinch to shoot a bedded buck in the sage because he be-comes very visible when the hunter spooks him and he jumps up to run. Getting a shot is really tough to do. It's tough to walk quietly in sagebrush, even though the ground is usually soft, sandy loam. The swishing sound made by sage branches rubbing on the hunter's pants is almost impossible to avoid in thick sage, and a mule deer's outsize ears pick it up at long distances.

One way to solve the problem is to hunt on days when the wind is blowing and natural noises of moving branches mask the sounds you make. On calm days, a very careful, slow stalk may bring you close enough to a bedded animal.

To hunt this way, you must pinpoint bedding areas without spooking the deer. Use a spotting scope or good binoculars during the early morning. When the deer lie down, pinpoint the location by taking bearings on surrounding objects. If you have several sagebrush bedding areas located before the season opens, you're ahead of the game.

Many hunters simply don't believe that mule deer often spend the daylight hours lying down in waist-high sage, and therefore they pass up good hunting areas. A veteran game warden once told me that there were no fewer than 50 deer lying down on a sagebrush-covered hill. I didn't believe him, because the sage was low and thin. But when we rode into the cover, we kicked out 62 deer. Eight of them were bucks.

BUCKBRUSH

Many intermediate elevations in the West are covered by thick brush that is head-high or taller than a

Mule deer use sagebrush when they're passing through it, feeding in it, or bedding in it. (Gabby Barrus photo)

man. Oak is dominant, but mountain mahogany and serviceberry are common.

Often called "buckbrush," this vegetation may harbor deer all year, though very deep snow can drive the deer down to the valleys. Food is always present, regardless of the season. Acorns provide food from August through the following spring. Deer can paw through several inches of snow to get them. Serviceberry yields blue-black fruits in the fall, and deer browse on the twigs.

Deer are difficult to hunt in mountain brush because it is dense. The animals can scramble about almost anywhere and remain unseen. Driving the deer to standers is one method of hunting, even though the walking is tough. A driver must weave his way through the brush.

The deer seldom run straightaway in this brush, and they may sneak through or outflank the drivers. In most cases, the deer refuse to leave the cover. If they come out at all, they usually do so at the top of the drainage. If the brushy hillside falls away into a rugged ravine, however, the deer may try to bottom out and escape into it. You should place your standers accordingly.

This habitat is ideal for the lone hunter who is willing to spend time pussyfooting along in search of feeding deer. In much of this cover, there are natural avenues that are wide enough to allow reasonably silent walking. Deer make the trails, but there are usually so many of these runways that it is difficult to choose the ones that are heavily used.

Openings of an acre or less may be used as feeding places. Though there may be adequate forage in the brush itself, deer always seek variety. Watch the openings, and if deer pellets are fresh and frequent, sit for your buck early and late.

If a bluff or ledge overlooks a large expanse of this brush, use it for a vantage point. Glassing may turn up a big buck.

QUAKING ASPEN

The trails on the sidehill converged into one main runway. I sat concealed in a deadfall where I could watch the convergence. Twenty minutes after I sat down, a handsome buck sauntered along the runway, and my arrow took him squarely. I was hunting the aspens during hot, dry weather.

A stand of quaking aspens is a haven for deer, and many hunters are aware of it. So competition can be keen in a good area near any decent road. But there are many stands, most of them at elevations of 7,500 to 8,500 feet, and scouting usually turns up good spots.

If the leafy cover on the forest floor is wet, the hunter can sneak along and stillhunt to his heart's content. But if the woods are dry, it's either take a stand and wait or stay at home. Even on deer and cattle trails, the hunter makes too much noise if it's very dry.

Most aspen forests are relatively open, but here mule deer travel on trails almost exclusively. The trails are fine avenues for hunters who are trying to move quietly. In aspen forests where cattle graze, the trails are well used and wide, and they almost always lead to water holes. Deer travel on these cattle trails, too, so deer are accustomed to noises made by walking steers. I've sometimes managed to walk right up to a deer simply by using cattle trails.

Deer like to bed down just under the ridge line in an aspen forest. They have a good view of the slope, and if there's a thicket of serviceberries or evergreens for concealment, that's where they will be.

A spooked deer is a tough target among the tree trunks, and a spooked buck usually keeps right on going. You can forget about the legend that most mule deer stop to look back. A good pair of binoculars helps when you're trying to spot antlers, and a low-power riflescope is a must for its light-gathering capability.

RIVER BOTTOMS

Of all the habitats utilized by mule deer, bottomlands are perhaps the toughest to hunt. In many of these areas, tamarisk grows in dense thickets. This shrub isn't native, but it has frequently replaced valuable shrubs and trees, especially willow. Tamarisk provides little if any food for deer, but a dense tamarisk thicket makes a fine, sheltered bedding area for them. If tamarisk isn't present, the rich soil and abundant water of the bottoms engenders dense native growth. In these places, it's almost impossible for a lone stalker to fill his license. He would have to bull his way through the growth, and that's almost impossible to do without spooking the deer.

Deer that live in these streamside thickets behave a lot like whitetails, and some whitetail-hunting techniques work well. The deer usually move out to adjacent farmlands to find suitable feed. This occurs during darkness or during the early morning and late afternoon. Hunting in the evening isn't usually productive if there has been heavy pressure. The deer seldom leave the dense cover until legal shooting hours are over.

In the bottoms, however, mule deer use well-defined trails, and a hunter in a tree stand at a well-chosen spot overlooking a much-used trail has a good chance to score. You may also get a shot from a stand on a riverside bluff where you can look down into the cover. You must be on stand well before first light.

Float-trip hunting also works well in some places. Half of a party of hunters gets out of the boat at the upper end of a densely wooded bottom. The other hunters quietly float downstream to the lower end. The two groups then walk toward each other to stir up the deer. Obviously, everyone must be very careful when shooting in the dense vegetation. Some

hunters make it an iron-bound rule not to shoot straight ahead under any circumstances.

Another way is to float downstream slowly and glass each ledge and bluff. A big buck may be bedded just under the rim. If you spot one, don't go ashore where he can see you. Float out of sight, and then go ashore. In many states, it is illegal to shoot from a boat.

DESERT

This is the harshest of the eight habitats. Water and forage are scarce, and the deer must travel a great deal to water and feed.

Most arid Western lowlands are "cold deserts." The four seasons are well defined, and snow often falls. Mesquite, greasewood, and saltbush are common here.

The deer often travel two miles daily to water, but ambushing bucks near water is difficult since they

Of all eight types of mule-deer habitat, desert is harshest. Deer move mostly at night. (Gabby Barrus photo)

Pinyon-juniper forest: example of habitat that results from dragging area with chain between bulldozers.

commonly drink only at night. The openness of the desert environment apparently causes deer to move about mostly during the dark hours.

In many desert regions, rock outcroppings and ridges loom above the flats. If water is reasonably close, mule deer prefer these high places for bedding. The bucks like to shade up just under the crest of a high place where the visibility is good. North slopes are usually best for hunting since they provide more shade. The best way to hunt these ridges is to glass carefully from below. If a buck is spotted, make a careful stalk so that you approach from above. If no deer are seen with binoculars, the ridge should be hunted only if fresh tracks are found near water holes.

Arroyos and washes that cut through desert will shelter the deer. Vegetation growing in low places shades out the hot sun, even though most washes are dry in the fall. If two or more men are hunting in a wash, one walks in the bottom and lags slightly behind to flush deer out for hunters on the rims. Solo hunters often stay high and toss rocks into the brush below. Flushed deer don't always stay in the bottom. Many angle upslope to get out of the wash.

Since much of this desert terrain is administered by the Bureau of Land Management, its local officers can supply information on water holes.

PINYON-JUNIPER

Scrub evergreens carpet millions of acres in the West. This is the juniper-pinyon pine association, common at lower elevations. Often simply called "the cedars," this vegetation harbors many mule deer.

The cedars are tough to hunt. Loose shale is common underfoot, and the cover is thick, so it's difficult to move quietly. Another factor favors the deer. The lowest branches are almost always dead and bare, so bedded deer easily see a hunter before a hunter can spot the low-lying animals. It's almost impossible to locate a bedded deer without spooking it. But the cedars are higher than sagebrush, so the hunter seldom sees the fleeing animal, though he often hears it.

There are few distinct deer trails in the cedars, and the shale layer makes it difficult to find fresh tracks. So it's important to scout around and listen to local people until you have a good idea of where the deer are using.

There is little deer forage in the cedars; the animals must leave the trees to feed. Small sagebrush draws and openings usually are scattered throughout the forest and are favored feeding spots. Old burns are good places too, because of the lush vegetation that springs up.

Land managers often "chain" otherwise barren areas to engender forage. A huge ship's anchor chain is dragged between two bulldozers, and the trees between them are uprooted and windrowed. The cleared site is then seeded with forage plants favored by deer.

To hunt chainings and other clearings, watch the edges for feeding deer. It's usually an early-morning tactic. Good areas close to roads get plenty of pressure. Try to locate a small hidden clearing.

There is little water in a cedar forest, so deer must make frequent trips to the few water holes that are available. Early morning and dusk are the best times to take a stand near water. In many places, however, good water holes are well known among local hunters, and they get a lot of pressure. If you can find a hidden water source that deer favor, you have a real treasure.

HEAVY TIMBER

Although much of the West is arid, the upper elevations normally receive abundant moisture. When mountains thrust up 10,000 feet and higher, storm clouds linger and deposit substantial precipitation on the upper slopes.

Trees grow well in this environment. Lodgepole pines and Douglas firs share the habitat with Engelmann spruce and alpine fir. The dense tree growth makes hunting difficult, and hunters must work the cover methodically.

Heavy, over-mature forests provide little feed for mule deer. Sunlight seldom reaches the ground because of the canopy overhead, and the forest floor is virtually barren. Because of this, the areas that do support low browse plants are heavily utilized.

Burned-over areas are especially productive. The heavy forest growth has been replaced by succulent forms of vegetation, and deer come from miles around to feed. Some burns are essential to the welfare of the local deer. When a burn area grows up into heavy timber again, a vital part of the habitat is lost, and the herds must move out.

Old burns and other clearings must be hunted early and late in the day—the normal feeding periods. If possible, hunt burned areas during the first minutes of daylight. Wary deer seldom linger in the open when the sun climbs.

Other productive areas are adjacent slopes that are brushy and devoid of heavy timber. Since the sun shines most on southern slopes, they are often dry and brushy. Deer feed heavily on some of these slopes.

Glassing the brushy slopes in the morning or taking a stand near a burn and then stillhunting in the timber during the middle of the day often works out. Remember, however, that perhaps not all deer will move into the timber to bed down. Some may spend the day loafing on the brushy slopes, if the vegetation is thick enough to provide security.

Few forests are of uniform density. There are pockets of very heavy timber and some densely grown drainages. Where windstorms have caused localized damage, blowdowns may cover several acres. Deer seek out such places for bedding and shelter.

OPEN FOREST

The open forest is composed mostly of ponderosa or lodgepole pines or both. This kind of timber is usually just below the level of the spruces and firs.

Visibility is good in this habitat, and that is both an advantage and a disadvantage. The deer are easy to see, but so is the hunter. The sparse trees provide little cover, and stalking is difficult.

Within the open timber, small hideaways provide shelter and bedding areas for mule deer. These can be small thickets of young pines, brushy ravines, blowdowns, or other dense spots. Areas that support a mix of shrubs, hardwoods, and pine trees should always be hunted thoroughly since deer prefer to frequent them for food and cover.

Since much of the open area between the trees is covered with grass, the deer spend little time feeding there. Mule deer are browsers, and they favor twigs and soft tips of various shrubs. Feeding areas may be a long distance from bedding locations because of the scarcity of preferred foods. And the animals may be out in the open longer because of their need to travel from one place to another.

During the middle of the day, approach every patch of brush or thicket with caution. Try to angle toward them so that spooked deer will be in sight after they flush. In this habitat, you're likely to get a running shot because of the open ground.

Experienced hunters will use spotting scopes or binoculars to locate distant animals. When a herd is spotted, note the general direction. Choose an interception point if that is possible. Deer traveling along the contour of a ridge will likely stay on the contour until the ridge drops off or joins a larger one. In this case, a good method would be to follow the contour far ahead of the deer and place yourself for a shot from above.

When cover is sparse, deer often bed down in small creek bottoms or brushy washes that meander through the forest. Flushing deer from these places is difficult. One way is to throw rocks into the tangles and hope that a buck will bust out. If the drainage is large and difficult to cover from one spot, two or more hunters should work it.

This habitat involves a great deal of long-distance observation. Binoculars are a must, and a scope-sighted rifle is essential. Long shots are the rule, so a flat-shooting rifle is a big help.

Treacherous High-Country Hunting

Jim Carmichel

The crosshairs lurched away from the aiming point on the buck's chest as a sharp jolt of pain tore through my left arm. Dropping the rifle from my shoulder, I jerked the tight sling from around the cramping arm and flexed the elbow until the muscle spasm relaxed. Then I quickly looped the sling back around my arm, brought the rifle to my shoulder, and settled the crosshairs back on the deer's chest.

He was watching me intently, facing me dead-on with his head low and ears focused at me in the customary pose of a buck mule deer trying to make up his mind. For five minutes, perhaps a bit less, I'd sat on the stony hillside above him with my Ruger M-77 .280 aimed at his chest. He was big, and his high and heavy antlers were festooned with strips of dried velvet. Normally, I would have fired at such a trophy as soon as I could get my rifle into action. And ordinarily he would have shifted into high gear just at the sight of me. But the same force that kept me from shooting also kept him from running.

That force was another deer lying half hidden in a sparse clump of evergreen scrub. I couldn't see anything but its hindquarters, but I had a notion it might be an even better trophy than the buck standing guard. From what I could see, the mystery deer was too big to be a doe, and besides we were above doe country. This was old-buck territory, the top of Sheep Mountain. And the way the visible buck was acting made me suspect that he was probably guarding a patriarch.

This was all guesswork, nothing more than a hunch. But trophy hunting calls for guessing and playing hunches, and turning down big bucks in the hope of finding an even bigger one. The buck I could see was a fine trophy in every way, and in another moment he might be gone. The buck in the bush might not be so good.

As these thoughts were nagging at me, the deer turned his head for a moment and looked at his pal. The partly hidden deer was moving. He was standing up. I figured that there would only be a moment to choose between the two and get off a shot. I thought the deer would get to his feet and look at his chum. He'd then follow the other deer's gaze up to me, and in the next second they'd both be off and running.

But it didn't happen that way. The second buck just stood there. I could see his back, his side, and most of his legs, but not his head. All I could do was wait. My arm began to cramp again.

My pal Fred Huntington and I were hunting in the Greys River area of southwestern Wyoming. Our outfitter and guide, Bud Callahan, operates the Box-Y Ranch and runs one of the slickest outfitting operations I know of. Fred, who is the founder and president of the RCBS-OMARK reloading tool company is a relentless hunter. Six months earlier we had hunted together in the African rain forests, and each of us had taken a bongo. Though we have hunted together on four continents for some mighty exotic species, the lure of the big buck is as strong as ever. Nearly every autumn finds us in the high country looking for trophy mule deer.

I had hunted pronghorn with Callahan the season before, and I had been so impressed with his guiding, the beauty of the Greys River country, and the abundance of game that I had booked a hunt for Fred and myself the following season.

Box-Y hunters stay at the ranch in warm, comfort-

Our party rides along crest of Sheep Mountain, seemingly improbable deer habitat. Minutes later, we spotted my trophy.

able bunkhouses. Since the ranch is in the middle of prime game country, hunters don't have far to go. But Callahan keeps horseback time to a minimum by trucking his riding stock close to the area to be hunted each day. By doing so, hours of uneventful horseback riding are reduced to a half-hour truck ride. You mount up before daybreak and make the final ride into the area chosen for the day's hunt.

On the morning of our first day, the sun kissed the peaks just as we topped out on the mountain we would be hunting. Stopping to let my horse catch his breath, I twisted in the saddle and surveyed the incredible panorama.

Not too many miles to the west, the Salt River Mountains glimmered like burnished copper. To the east soared the Wind River Mountains and Gannett Peak thrusting to an elevation of nearly 14,000 feet. Beyond the foothills of the Wyoming Range where we were hunting lay the sites of old Fort Bonneville and the Rocky Mountain Fur Company, where

mountain men had held the famous Green River rendezvous in 1835. To the north stretched the Snake River Range, the Gros Ventre Mountains, and the glistening tip of the Grand Teton.

Our hunting party had split here, and our California friends and their guides circled to the south. Fred and his guide and Bud and I had planned to hunt the upper part of the mountain by keeping on the ridge crests and glassing the meadows and draws below. The first time we looked over a precipice, four does and two smallish bucks broke out of cover 200 yards below and pogo-sticked single file around the hillside.

For the next three hours, we didn't see anything worthwhile. But just as we were settling down for lunch, Bud caught sight of a fair buck at the edge of a timber boundary some 300 yards below us.

The boundary was on the backbone on a steep slope, and with luck the deer might be pushed out for an open shot. Fred's guide took off on foot and circled behind the backbone, and Fred got into a solid shooting position with his rifle rested along a stubby pine. I stood just behind Fred with my camera ready, hoping to get a picture of the action. But the action never happened. After our tense wait, the guide appeared from the timber. The deer had been there all right, he told us. But as he moved up behind, the deer turned and ran the other way, refusing to cross open ground.

Later, stretching in the sun after lunch, I studied the sheer rock face of a mountain a few miles to the north.

"That's Sheep Mountain," Bud said.

"Do you ever hunt there?" I asked.

"Not often. It's very tough to climb, but there are some good bucks there. Since it's so rough, most hunters leave it alone. That's why the bucks get old and big."

"Interesting," I said, and then thought no more about it.

That evening at dinner Bud brought up the subject of Sheep Mountain again.

"There's a way to take a horse up from the backside," he said. "A Basque shepherd told me about it. It's rough, but we can give it a try."

"I'm game," I answered. "How about you, Fred?"

"Count me out for tomorrow," he said. "I'm going to take the day off."

"In that case I'd like to go along," said Ozzie Davis, a widely known international hunter from Heywood, California.

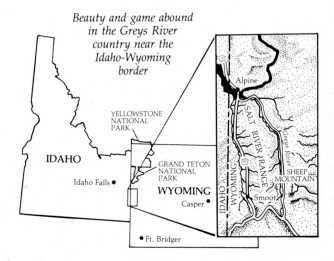

Beauty and game abound in the Greys River country near the Idaho-Wyoming border

I'm glassing slopes of mountain from edge of typical steep cliff. Even after you spot a fine buck, it may be impossible to get close.

"That settles it," I said. "Tomorrow it's Sheep Mountain."

Next morning we were at the base of the mountain waiting for enough light to begin the climb. As we had ridden toward the mountain, an eerie chorus of coyote calls had drifted out of the darkness.

Guide, on the left, and Ozzie Davis, on right, have just spotted a good prospect. Bud Callahan is checking with spotting scope.

Ordinarily I like to hear coyotes call, but this was different, mournful, as if to warn us away. If I had known the danger that awaited above, I would have heeded their warning.

As the darkness dissolved into gray gloom, we started up the mountain. The trail was easy enough at the start, winding around the lower slope, but after a while it narrowed and steepened in frequent switchbacks. At one point the trail, no wider than a horse's hoof and notched into the mountainside, crossed a steep rock slide. The footing was treacherous. Fist-size rocks rolled like ball bearings under the feet of our horses.

We were almost across the slide and had only one sharp switchback to go when Ozzie's horse slipped and fell to its front knees. Twice it struggled to regain its footing, but each time more loose stones gave way and it fell again. Growing panicky, the animal lurched wildly, lost its footing altogether, and fell back toward me and my horse.

The trail was so steep that Ozzie's horse was a full horse's height above me though only a few feet ahead. When the horse started its backward fall, it was actually falling down on me and my horse. I headed out of the saddle, but it was too late. Trying desperately to avoid the oncoming body, my horse reared on its hind legs. The trail gave way, and my horse toppled over in a twisting, rearward somersault. Somewhere in midair, I cleared the saddle and landed on my feet on the downhill side of the trail under the falling horse. Instinctively, I hit the ground running, trying to get out from under.

I must have been moving fast, because I felt only the upside-down animal brush against my shoulder as I got clear. But now a new and even greater danger loomed. I was running down the 45° slope so fast I couldn't stop. And I was running out of space in a hurry. Just a few yards ahead, the slope disappeared into empty space. It was the sheer edge of a cliff!

Digging in the heels of my boots, I threw myself backward in a hard fall. When I hit the ground I clawed at it and felt myself slide to a stop only feet from the edge of disaster. For long moments, rolling rocks kept pummeling me, and I remember a brief but terrible thought that the horse might be falling toward me. But when I raised my head to look, the horse was on its feet and apparently O.K.

After I collected my hat and made sure the horse wasn't hurt, my only concern was for my rifle. Miraculously it wasn't even scratched, thanks no doubt to the hard, molded-plastic Koplin scabbard I was using. Ozzie hadn't been so lucky. Though his horse was O.K., his custom rifle was a shambles.

From there on to the top of the mountain, the trail got easier. Bud had been right about the deer on Sheep Mountain. The crest was a long, swaybacked ridge, and as soon as we got to the top we spotted four bucks at the other end of the crest. They were all good four-pointers (per side, Western count), and they ambled along with apparently no concern over our presence. Their behavior was confirmation that there had been little or no hunting on the mountain.

A careful glassing of the backside of the mountain disclosed but one solitary buck. He was a long way off, and Bud got out his spotting scope for a better look at his rack. Bud shrugged and gave me the thumbs-down sign.

What had started out as a sunny day changed rapidly as a weather front moved in. Low clouds scudded over the mountain, and heavy thunderheads rose on the horizon. The air turned chilly, and we huddled in the lee of the ridge as we glassed the clumps of trees and scrub.

After an hour or so, we mounted up and made our way along the crest of the mountain. As we went over the highest point, the crest took a turn to the west and ran by a stand of timber. Since it was a time of day deer like to lie up, it looked like a good place for a short drive. Bud told Ozzie and me to ride around the timber and take shooting positions while he and the guide rode into the trees to push the deer ahead. Bud and the guide agreed to wait 15 minutes before beginning the drive. That would give Ozzie and me time to get into position.

But before we had even made our way to the trees, the guide came rushing after us and signaled for us to follow. When we got back to the place where we had split up, Bud was off his horse and waiting with his spotting scope in his hand. As soon as we dismounted he described the situation. He and the guide had spotted two bucks about 300 yards below the crest. They were both bedded

I pose with my mule deer soon after the kill. One of the hunt's biggest challenges was to negotiate terrain between where I shot and where the big muley fell.

down in a small thicket. One had good antlers, but the other's head hadn't been seen.

As Ozzie and I pulled the rifles from our scabbards, it occurred to me that we hadn't agreed on who would have the first shot. After his rifle got banged up, Ozzie had traded rifles with Bud, but we had forgotten to toss a coin for first shot. I couldn't find a coin in my pockets, and neither could the others. I crouched and sorted through some pea-size rocks. Then, showing my closed hand to Ozzie, I said, "I have either one or two stones in my hand. Take a guess."

"Two."

I opened my hand to reveal a single gravel. I had the first shot.

Crouching low and keeping behind the crown of the hillside, we made our way to the cover of some evergreen scrub. In a similar stand of scrub on the opposite side of a deep cleft, I could see one deer lying down with his head up. One foreleg was tucked under his body and the other stretched out in front. It was a big-bodied deer and had a good rack. A few feet away, on the uphill side of him, I saw the rump of the other, but that was all.

Though the patch of scrub gave us good cover, it was impossible as a shooting site. When I got into a sitting position, the crown of the rise was so high that it blocked out any sight of the deer. I had to get closer to the brow of the crest for a clear shot. But that meant I would have to cross open ground. The buck would surely spot me.

Since I couldn't get a clear shot any other way, it was a have-to-risk. And even if the bucks broke and ran, they would have to cross 200 yards of open ground before getting to the next cover. I would have a running shot in any event.

Crouching low, I moved quickly to the brow of the crest and hastily settled into a sitting position with the rifle's sling looped tightly over my left arm.

The buck saw me and jumped up but didn't run.

This standoff I described at the beginning of this chapter lasted several minutes. By then the others had gathered around me.

Suddenly the hidden buck took a step forward. I got a shadowed look at one side of his antlers. It was wide and high. But I could see only one side. What if the other side was deformed or even missing?

As if to settle my doubts, the buck looked back over his shoulder and gave me a clear look at the other half of his rack. It was a perfect match, and the rack was better than the other buck's. Bud gave a low whistle of appreciation.

I wanted to shoot, but now the deer's body was mostly obscured by brush. The shoulder area was clear, and as I settled the crosshairs on the open spot behind the shoulder, I whispered that I was going to fire.

"Not yet," Bud whispered back. "Wait until he's in the open."

For a moment I heeded his advice, but the situation reminded me too much of a chance I'd had for a fine elk several years before. The bull had been partly hidden behind a tree. And though I had a good shot at the vital area, I decided to wait until he was in the open. Then he turned and ran straightaway and I never got a shot.

The .280 cracked, and the deer was down even before I heard the sound of the bullet hitting. A moment later, the deer was back on his feet. But before he could take a step, he was dead and rolling down the mountain.

The mountainside where the deer had fallen was so steep and treacherous that it took the better part of an hour to cover the 300 yards. Several times I had to back up and try another route when the rocks were too sheer to negotiate. When you go after big bucks on Sheep Mountain, you must take your chances.

Old Crooked Horn

by Lew Littleton
as told to Jim Zumbo

The big mule-deer buck was mad. He wheeled, lowered his head, and charged Vaughn Wilkins, who was atop a green broke colt.

The sight of that big, mean buck charging head-on toward Vaughn was more than his nervous colt could stand. Vaughn was plumb scared, too. The big buck we called Crooked Horn knocked sunflowers every which way as he came flying along.

The colt spun around and bolted, and I don't think Vaughn tried too hard to stop him. The buck kept up the attack and chased Vaughn and his colt into thick timber at the edge of the patch. Finally Crooked Horn backed off and disappeared into the brush.

It was opening morning of Utah's deer season. Nine of us had just ridden horseback through the sunflower patch, where we knew Crooked Horn hung out. We saw his fresh tracks but couldn't jump him. That's when Vaughn volunteered to really bust up the sunflower patch on his colt.

We were pretty confident the buck was in the area, because he had laid claim to the 300-acre abandoned farm field about a month before the season. I had seen him several times in the area, and I couldn't wait for deer season to open.

Vaughn's strategy was simple. We would scatter outside the tall sunflowers and take up positions while he tried to jump the wary buck. He left his gun with one of the boys because he couldn't shoot off his green broke colt, and if he dismounted quickly, he wouldn't be able to see the buck because of the high sunflowers.

As luck would have it, Vaughn jumped Crooked Horn far up the patch and out of our sight. The chase was on as Vaughn scrambled after the buck, trying to haze him down the field toward us. Finally, Crooked Horn had been crowded too close by Vaughn and his colt. The deer made a quick 180° turn and headed straight for the startled horse and rider.

The drama was over by the time we rode up the field, except for the dust that was still billowing around. Vaughn was walking through the weeds, looking for his hat, which had flown off during the melee.

"You missed quite a ride," Vaughn said. "If I was in a rodeo, I'd have won top prize. No way was I going to leave that saddle while that crazy buck was around."

"Too bad you didn't have your rifle," someone said.

"Yeah," Vaughn answered. "That buck was so close he'd have had powder burns if I could've hit him from that buckin' colt."

Vaughn found his hat, beat the dust off it, and climbed back on his horse, still shaking his head in disbelief.

We combed the sunflowers the rest of the day, but couldn't turn up the buck. The story was the same the rest of the season. We hunted hard and long, but couldn't find a trace of him. The big buck had simply disappeared.

Two days after the season ended, I saw Crooked Horn back in the sunflower patch. The big deer grazed along as if he knew he was safe. For the time being, he was, but I'd be after him next year.

The first time I ever laid eyes on Crooked Horn, he was drinking from a sandbar along the Green River late one summer. One of his antlers had a natural five-point spread, but the other grew straight sideways from his head at a 90° angle. It was about 35 inches long and had five points sticking out at regular intervals. Because the horn was so freakish, I judged that the outside spread was more than 45 inches.

I should explain my credentials to have estimated the buck's antlers at such an impressive width. I was born and raised on a ranch on the Leota Bottoms, next to the Ute Indian Reservation in northeast Utah. I've been a hunter all my life, and I've killed my share of huge bucks. I knew the river bottoms as well as anyone, and learned where the big bucks lived. This buck, which I named Crooked Horn, was not only the weirdest deer I'd ever seen, but also, as I'd soon learn, the smartest.

As soon as I saw him, I thought about the big-buck contests that scored deer by the widest antler spread. A lot of sporting-goods stores in Utah gave away expensive prizes for the biggest buck. A 40-inch outside spread was usually required to be considered in the contests. I knew Crooked Horn would be way up in the running, and probably the first-place winner. I could picture myself winning one of the four-wheel-drive vehicles that were top prizes, or at least a new Winchester rifle.

Between ranch chores, I spent all the time I could studying Crooked Horn's habits and the places he frequented. I noted that he shied away from heavy timber, squawbush, and other places that impeded his travel. His wide antlers simply couldn't fit through those tight spots. He bedded down in patches of sunflowers, young willows, or other areas that had pliable plants but still offered concealment.

The closer deer season approached, the bigger Crooked Horn looked. His antlers seemed even wider when he scraped off the velvet.

I watched for him all day and dreamed of him all night. I was so excited and confident I'd get him that I signed up in big-buck contests from Vernal, Utah, to Las Vegas, Nevada.

A group of us, all friends, had hunted together for years. Each season the boys would gather before the opener and tell tall tales at the ranch house. This year, I was nervous as an alley cat, and couldn't seem to get into the merriment and festive mood. I wanted to take Crooked Horn very badly and didn't tell the boys about him. Somehow, I had to get away from the group so that I could hunt alone. There were some crack shots in our party; each of the men had plenty of big-buck racks nailed to his barn. Any of them could easily enough bust Crooked Horn.

I couldn't sleep a wink the night before the opener. I tossed and turned and listened to the horses as they snorted and whinnied in the corral. The broncs knew what was coming up in the morning. We'd been working them hard, riding back and forth through the thickets along the river.

Long before first light, we gathered and planned our hunt. I think some of the boys grew suspicious of me, because I never made any suggestions or volunteered any information about our strategies. That was unusual, because I was more or less the leader of the group.

To hunt the river bottoms, the most successful method is to make drives on horseback. Because I was most familiar with the area, the men depended on me to plan the drives. I was pretty sure I knew where Crooked Horn was, so we hunted in another area. That old buck was going to be my trophy.

Hunting was fair that day. Several of the boys killed nice bucks. I hadn't planned on it, but I had a good chance at a big buck and passed it up. The deer would have been an easy shot, but Crooked Horn was foremost in my mind. The boys knew for sure then that something was fishy. It wasn't like me to let a big buck go by. Some of them guessed I was waiting for a special deer to show.

"Why didn't you kill that big five-point?" one of them asked as they gathered around. "Lew, you ain't been actin' right. You've got something up your sleeve."

"All right, fellers," I said. "Guess I'll tell you, although I'll admit I wasn't going to. There's an unbelievable buck in the bottoms. He's the biggest I've ever seen in my life, and I kind of wanted a crack at him alone. His rack is freak, and I'm sure it'll go almost four foot wide, outside spread."

"Holy mackerel," someone said. "That buck will win a Jeep in one of the Salt Lake City big-buck contests."

"I'm sure of it," I admitted, "so let's go get him. I know where he is."

I felt a little better after the confession. It had been tough holding my secret in, especially because we were all pals.

We figured a plan for morning. Crooked Horn had been feeding in a meadow, so I planned to cut his tracks and find out for sure where he was. It would be easy to locate him, because he had tracks unlike any other I'd ever seen. Because he couldn't get into the softer ground of the thickets on account of his wide antlers, he spent most of his time on the sand along the river. The sand wore his hoofs in such a way there was no missing them. They didn't wear and break off like normal hoofs, but were longer and flat-sided.

Sure enough, the buck's tracks were where I expected them the next morning, and they were fresh.

Our party spread out and worked through the brush. I cheated a little and stayed on the outside because I knew Crooked Horn wouldn't go far into the brush—not with those handicaps on his head.

A couple of little two-points jumped, but we let them go. Crooked Horn's tracks led us to the river. The ornery cuss had crossed it, but we couldn't follow him. The water was too deep for our horses. We rode back to our pickup trucks and loaded the horses, then drove to the little Indian settlement of Ouray, where we could cross the river at the bridge. Then we cut back to where Crooked Horn should have climbed out of the water.

The buck hadn't come up onto the shore at all. He'd just waded along the river and walked out onto a small island that was thick with trees and bordered by a grove of young willows. I checked and double-checked, and I was positive he was still on the island, unless he had swum off into deep water, but I doubted it. I was excited, more excited than I'd been on my very first hunt years ago. It looked as though we had the big buck cornered.

Old Crooked Horn had been crowded too closely by horse and rider. The deer turned quickly and charged. (Leon Parson art)

71

Right off the bat, I knew Crooked Horn had to be in those young willows. We tied the horses on the mainland and left Colin, who was one of the best riflemen around, to watch a game trail that the buck might use if we jumped him. The rest of us went back to the upper end of the island and made the drive afoot.

I've got to hand it to that buck—he stayed tight until we were almost on top of him. And when he made his break, he was fast and smooth. Crooked Horn tore down the trail, traveling at a full head of steam, and headed straight for Colin. Colin couldn't shoot, because we were in the line of fire behind the buck, so he figured he could jump on his horse and outrun the deer. Besides, he had to get off that trail pronto. The buck was bearing down on him, showing no fear whatsoever. Colin jumped into the brush to where he had hidden his horse and tried to mount him.

Maybe the horse saw the wildly racing deer, or maybe he sensed Colin's excitement. Anyway, he shied away, and Colin couldn't get into the stirrups and swing up fast enough. By the time he got up, all he could see was Crooked Horn as he crashed into the timber with his head turned sideways and the freak horn lying back alongside the buck's ribs. Colin and his horse gave the deer a good chase, but they never saw him again.

We gathered our horses and rode over to meet Colin. He was sick! The biggest buck he had ever seen could have been his if he'd stayed along the trail and shot instead of going for his horse. Crooked Horn had whisked by him only about eight feet away.

"What a buck!" Colin said as if he were in a daze. "What a buck! You were right, Lew. That's the biggest buck in Utah."

For the rest of the season, we searched for the big buck and his tracks. But we couldn't find him. He was lying low. The season closed without a trace of him. I worried that he might have been killed by poachers or other hunters, but I saw him soon after the season was over. I was mighty glad he was still alive.

The following year he gave us the slip after Vaughn chased him around the sunflower patch.

A year or so later, the U.S. Bureau of Sport Fisheries and Wildlife came into the area and started buying up land along the river to establish the Ouray National Wildlife Refuge. The government closed the grounds to hunting. We had only a 50-50 chance of finding Crooked Horn, because much of the river-bottom area where he lived was off-limits.

I had been seeing the buck in the same patch of brush. His freakish horn looked even longer than before. When the season opened, the boys and I searched for the deer, but we couldn't find his sign in the area that was still open to hunting. The sunflower patch was in the open hunting zone, but it had rained hard the night before the opener, obliterating the tracks. We decided to hunt elsewhere, and

we left Crooked Horn in peace.

Ralph Chew, an old-timer who hadn't been hunting with us before, had heard all the stories about Crooked Horn. By now the tales were getting to be awful big stories. He decided to try for the phantom buck.

Ralph strapped his sleeping bag on his back along with some grub and proceeded to look for Crooked Horn's tracks. He finally found them in the sunflower patch and even got a glimpse of the deer.

Seeing the tracks was enough for Ralph. The hunter took to the trail like a bloodhound, going slow and easy, stalking, stopping to listen, then moving on. When night came, Ralph rolled out his sleeping bag alongside the fresh tracks.

By first light, he took to the tracks again. Shortly after following the tracks in the gray time before dawn, Ralph discovered that Crooked Horn had bedded down only 100 yards from where he had slept. The old-timer was elated because he was hot on the trail, but that elation turned to consternation when Ralph saw that the wise old buck had left his bed and had gone to Ralph's bed. Crooked Horn was following him!

Ralph started backtracking, but so did Crooked Horn. No matter how hard he tried, Ralph couldn't spot the buck.

That night, Ralph came into my ranch. He tossed his sweaty hat on the couch and plopped into a rocker.

"That's the wisest old buck I've ever seen," he confessed. "Any deer that smart deserves to live forever. I'm giving him up, Lew."

Before Ralph went out the door, he turned and grinned. "In a way, I'd sure love to set fire to that danged dried-up sunflower patch," he said. "Then that old buck wouldn't have a sanctuary to hide in. But then again, I'm glad those sunflowers are there."

The boys and I hunted Crooked Horn through that season after Ralph gave up, but we never saw the buck. As always, his tracks were there to taunt us as we searched in vain.

Before another hunting season came along, the federal government had bought up almost all of the ground along the river for the refuge, including the Leota Bottoms, where the sunflower patch was. The area was closed to hunting, and Crooked Horn wouldn't have to worry about us anymore.

The last time I saw the great buck was in late November a couple of years later. He had a harem of does, and I hoped that he would pass on all his wonderful qualities to his fawns.

As I watched him, I couldn't help but rejoice that he had stayed alive. I took off my hat and tipped it to him, and then rode away on the dusty trail. I pulled my mackinaw up around my neck and put the spurs to my horse. I turned for one last look, but Crooked Horn was gone. Chuckling a bit to myself, I knew he'd be headed for the old sunflower patch.

My Life as a Guide

Bruce Brady

By crouching low and keeping well to the right of the trail, I was able to ease up the ridge without being seen by any deer that might be feeding on the mountainside to the south. A couple of hundred yards above me was a rocky knoll from which I planned to glass the opposing hillside and check the game trails that crossed a saddle still higher up.

Fifty yards from the top, I paused to catch my breath. Below, outfitter Jim Rigoli and a hunter named Steve stood with the horses. They glassed a distant ridge for game. The sun was clearing the mountain to the east now, and the ridges above were bathed in sunlight. It would be another clear, warm day in the Rockies.

When I reached the knoll, I dropped to my knees and removed my hat before checking the little flat that lay ahead. Slowly I peered around a rock, and there—150 yards away—grazed a buck with dark and heavy antlers. A doe fed a few yards behind him. Bringing my binoculars into focus, I counted four long points on each beam.

Shafts of sunlight were rapidly working down the sides of the mountain, and I realized the buck wouldn't be there long. It was a strange feeling not to be clicking off the safety on my old .270 Winchester. I carefully inched back behind the rock and dropped down the ridge until I was certain the buck wouldn't see me when I stood erect. I frantically waved my hat to attract the attention of Jim and Steve down below.

At last they looked up and caught sight of my arms extended upward to indicate a big buck. Quickly they stepped into their saddles and started

I explain to a fellow guide how we'll make a drive to push deer past standers that we've positioned on ridge.

up the twisting trail. I met them 100 yards from the top.

"You got one spotted?" Steve asked with a grin as he stepped down.

"You bet," I replied. "He's the one you came out here to get. A big four-pointer about 150 yards from the top."

Steve pulled his .280 Remington Model 700 out of the boot.

73

"I'll stay here with the horses," Jim said.

A few feet from the top, I stepped aside and whispered to Steve that the buck was grazing ahead, slightly below our position. I suggested he hold dead on the animal's shoulder. He chambered a cartridge and peered around the rock.

I waited behind him. Slowly he turned and said, "Brady, there's no buck out there."

"What?" I exclaimed, crawling up beside him. "He's got to be there somewhere."

I looked, and, sure enough, the buck and doe had vanished. I was certain they hadn't seen me, and the wind was right. What had spooked them? My heart sank when I saw the disappointment etched across Steve's face. Then I saw three orange-clad hunters, high on the ridge above us, making a drive off the top. Our buck must have seen them and ducked into the brush.

"Relax, Steve," I said. "Those fellas up there don't know it, but they're going to drive that buck right to us."

We watched as they weaved their way through the oak-covered hillside above us.

"Keep your eye peeled. It won't be long now," I said confidently.

I was beginning to think our buck had broken across the ridge and was by now safely hidden in the spruce timber below. I glassed every break in the brush I could see.

Then Steve said, "There he is in that little opening." His rifle roared, the bolt clacked, and it roared again.

"I got him," Steve said. "I saw him go down."

"Well, just in case he's not down for good, you stay here and watch the spot you last saw him and I'll go down and check," I said. "He may come out high-balling, so be ready."

I climbed down and found that Steve's buck had taken the 150-grain bullet right through the boiler room. It was a fine deer, and Steve was justly proud. I, too, was proud, for I'd been his guide.

This happened one fall several years ago while I was working as a wrangler and assistant guide for Jim Rigoli, a Colorado outfitter. I'd met Rigoli the previous summer, and we'd hunted bear together. As it turned out, he was one man shy for his fall deer hunt. Since I'd hunted his area several times before, he offered me the job. I'd never worked as a paid hand with a hunting outfit, so I decided then and there to sign on.

Rigoli had sold a successful roofing business in New Jersey and moved his wife, Betty, and his daughter, Sharon, to Colorado. They bought Buckskin Ranch on Main Elk Creek, a few miles north of New Castle, and Jim began taking hunters for deer, elk, and black bear.

Colorado hunting wasn't new to him. He had hunted the Colorado mountains for years and was a hunting pal of the late Bob Thomson of Glenwood Springs, another Colorado outfitter.

Rigoli hunted the Colorado Flattops in White River National Forest and nearby holdings of the Bureau of Land Management. Game populations are good in this area, and his hunters did well. He has since sold his outfit and returned to New Jersey.

The fall I worked for Rigoli, his brother Jerry came out from New Jersey to lend a hand in camp. Garrett Mathes, Dick Donaghy, and I served as wranglers and assistant guides. Marge Smith, the cook, completed the outfit.

During the summer and early fall, I worked into top shape with weights and a running program. I wanted to be ready for whatever came my way.

On the afternoon I arrived, Jim was stacking hay. "Put your gear in the lodge," he said, "then saddle a horse and help Sharon catch those dude horses in the lower pasture down by the creek."

We rounded up the 20 head of horses and brought them to the corral. After that, we worked getting the tack in order for each of the 10 hunters we'd have for the first five days of the season. Another 10 clients would arrive for a second five-day hunt.

Hunters at Buckskin Ranch were accommodated in a comfortable and rustic lodge. They slept two to a room. The lodge offered hot showers, a huge fireplace, and plenty of good food. Breakfast and supper were both served in the lodge. Lunches were prepared each morning for hunters to tuck into their saddlebags.

"The guys hunt harder when they know they'll come in each night to a hot shower, a big meal, and a warm bed," Jim said.

Sometimes tents were used if hunting conditions dictated a move away from the ranch.

At breakfast, Jim told me he insisted that every hunter's rifle be checked for zero as soon as he arrived at the ranch. Hunters would be arriving all day, and it was my job to take them to the bench and see that their rifles were properly sighted.

"I don't want any misses to occur because a guy's rifle ain't right," Jim snapped. "If they hesitate to shoot, don't take any bull. You shoot their rifles and see that they're zeroed."

During the course of the day, I checked every rifle. I found that several weren't hitting where they were aimed, but by supper I was satisfied the rifles would do their part. While I worked at the rifle range, Garrett and Dick had been shoeing horses and doing a host of other chores that had to be finished that day.

Our hunters came from all across the country. After supper, while the hunters talked and visited, Jim called his hands together and reviewed our various jobs and responsibilities. My duties, besides wrangling stock—which included the saddling, feeding, and watering of horses—covered chipping in as a guide, gutter, packer, and skinner. Later, other tasks were to come my way.

That's me on the lead horse as I guide my hunters toward top of range. Duties like this are enjoyable; some aren't.

Jim went over the first day's hunt in detail, explaining that Dick and Garrett would take most of the hunters eastward in four-wheel-drive vehicles, while he and I, and one hunter, would hunt westward on horseback. The weather was unseasonably warm, and he expected to find game still very high.

"Okay," Jim said finally, chewing on a cigar, "don't any of you guys for any reason ever leave a hunter on horseback on the mountain alone. Take matches, a length of rope, your knives, and any other gear you think you or your hunters may need. Make conversation with these guys, answer their questions, be accommodating, and do all you can to get them the buck they're out here to find. Do no shooting yourselves, except to keep a badly wounded animal from escaping. Do all of you have your licenses?"

We nodded.

"That's it," Jim said, grinning. "I'll get you fellas up an hour before the hunters roll out so you can tend the stock and do the chores."

Garrett and I shared a room, and he was asleep when the light went out. I had trouble going to sleep. I always do the night before opening day. I tossed and turned and checked my watch four times during the night with a flashlight. I was awake when Rigoli came and flicked on our light and whispered, "Let's go."

The hunters were eating breakfast when we arrived back at the lodge. It was a crystal clear night with only a hint of frost on the ground. Soon Garrett and Dick pulled out with two loads of hunters in the vehicles. They would hunt the mountains above the ranch, making short drives and working the rims and pockets of timber.

Rigoli, a hunter named Jim, and I rode our horses northward along Elk Creek for a mile or so. Then as day broke, we followed a long trail on a ridge to the west. A number of years before, I had hunted the same area with friends. It's big country with rugged oak ridges and juniper canyons. There are pockets of spruce and pine and enough rimrock to satisfy the biggest old bucks.

We had just turned up a switchback when I saw a buck in the aspens on the opposite hillside. I whistled a warning to my pals up ahead and checked the animal with my glasses. The hunter quickly stepped down and slid his rifle out of the scabbard.

"Pretty good buck," I said softly. "Four on a side."

The deer was about 300 yards out and was feeding in a small stand of aspens, their trunks stark white in the early sun.

"Do you want him?" I whispered.

"I don't know," he replied, looking at the buck through his 2×-to-7× variable scope. "What do you think?"

"How big a buck are you after?" I asked.

"As big as I can get," he said. "This is my first Western hunt. Would you shoot him?"

I glanced at Rigoli, but his expression told me nothing. He, too, waited for my answer.

"Well, I have a couple of larger heads mounted," I said, "but if I'd never killed one. . . ."

"Do you think we might find a better one in the next five days, Brady?" he asked.

"I think there is a good chance we will," I said.

"Then I'll pass him," our hunter said with a nod.

We mounted up and left the buck standing there, and I wondered if I had said the right things. We hunted the rest of the morning, and though we saw a number of does, we saw no bucks. That afternoon I tied my horse and zigzagged on foot across a mountainside thick with oak brush. Rigoli and the hunter stayed together and watched from the next ridge for any bucks I might stir up. I kicked two bucks out of their beds, one small and the other not so small, but my partners didn't spot either. They did see one huge buck ascend the mountainside just 50 yards above me, stand silhouetted against the sky, and wait for me to pass by before dropping back into the brush. He was too far to chance a shot. We hunted hard until dark, then picked our way down the mountain by starlight.

After supper that night, I overheard our hunter remark, "Well, I had a chance to take a good four-pointer early. Then we hunted all day long and didn't get a crack at another buck, a bear, a mountain lion, or anything."

I soon came to realize that hunters on their first trip West have a misconception about how much game they will encounter. For years, these guys have looked at hundreds of pictures of huge bucks in outdoor publications. Many of these photos are taken in areas where all game is protected. But when the hunter comes to the mountains, he expects to find many big bucks as well as a generous supply of lions and bears. Actually, it's much more likely that he will see squirrels, grouse, and average-size bucks.

During that first day, Garrett, Dick, and their hunters saw a number of bucks, one of which was an old mossyhorn. They took several shots but killed no deer. The highlight of the day for Garrett's crew came when they rounded a hill and came face

During a break, I point out a mule deer on a distant ridge. Finding a deer for your hunter is one thing, but getting him close enough to shoot is usually a tougher propostion.

I follow outfitter and client along ridge. This hunter turned down a muley buck the first day, later took another.

to face with six Rocky Mountain bighorn rams standing no more than 50 yards up the trail.

After supper, Jim called us together, and we reviewed the events of the day. Finally, it was decided we would load up and hunt eastward on the second day. The plan was to station the hunters atop ridges with good vantage points. Then the guides would stomp timber and try to push game out.

It was nearly noon when the drive was completed. Some bucks were jumped and some shots taken, but no one connected. I hiked back to collect the standers. One hunter said he'd left his binoculars and asked me to retrieve them for him.

"They're right over that hill," he said, pointing to a ridge a quarter mile away. "You can't miss 'em, Brady. They're on a log."

I climbed the ridge and was amazed to see a stand of timber with as many fallen trees as upright ones. It took me over three-quarters of an hour to locate the glasses.

During the afternoon, we hunted the beaver-pond country of East Elk Creek, but again took no bucks.

When we returned to the ranch that night, we learned that Sharon had saddled a horse, ridden up Main Elk Creek, and shot a nice buck through the neck with her little .243. She gutted the buck, got a packhorse, and packed the buck out herself. There weren't many words of congratulation from the paying hunters. I had to smile when I saw the expressions on some of their faces.

That night there was less talk in the lodge, and the guys turned in earlier. I was tired, too. Despite my old boots, I was getting blisters on my heels from the walking I had done. At our meeting that night, it was decided we'd all take horses and the whole outfit would hunt the mountains to the west the next day.

Despite my comfortable old boots, I find I'm getting blisters from all the walking I need to do. It feels good to sit back and rest my bones while devouring lunch sandwiches.

The next morning after breakfast, Garrett, Dick, and I saddled up, adjusted all the stirrups, and gave the hunters a brief lesson in horsemanship. Before we left the ranch, Jim cautioned the guides and wranglers to pay close attention to all riders, regardless of experience they claimed. I understood why later that morning when I turned in the saddle and saw a hunter behind me riding with one rein dragging in the dust and both hands locked tight to the horn.

It was on that third day Steve collected his big buck. Later in the afternoon I was called upon to anchor a buck that had been gut-shot and would have escaped if I hadn't stopped him.

It was a day full of action, and six good bucks were tagged. One hunter insisted on field-dressing his own buck, while Dick, Garrett, and I gutted the others. The guys pitched in, and we dragged the deer to spots easily reached with the packhorses. The man I guided on opening day was glad he had passed up the first buck because he got a big four-pointer that day.

With hunter and buck I helped him get, I pose feeling release from the pressure of trying to find game.

Jim rode back to the ranch, and he and Sharon returned with a string of packhorses. It was well after dark by the time we got off the mountain, hung all the deer, and tended the stock. It was another starlit night. Across the way, the lights were glowing in the lodge, and I could hear the hunters laughing and recapping the day's events.

After supper, one hunter came up to me and whispered that he'd somehow lost his rifle, which he had borrowed from a friend back home. On the ride off the mountain, the rifle had spilled out of his saddle scabbard, and he didn't miss it until his horse was unsaddled at the corral. Luckily, we found it on the trail the next morning.

The following day, we hunted to the west again. Just at daybreak, I spotted a nice four-pointer feeding atop a narrow bench 250 yards away. The two hunters tossed a coin for the shot. While I tied the horses, the winner dropped into a sitting position and brought his .300 Magnum to bear. I had my glasses on the buck and didn't notice that my hunter was crawling the stock of his rifle. At the report, he hollered. I thought it was just because he had missed the buck. Actually, the recoil had driven the rim of his scope into his eyebrow, cutting him to the bone. Blood spurted out of the gash.

"I'm cut!" he said, mopping the blood away from his eyes.

"Forget it!" I shouted. "Shoot again!"

He fired again, then again, and the buck went down as it topped the last ridge. I shook his hand and told him to apply hard pressure to the cut while I dug a bandage out of my saddlebags.

Then, while my hunters rode up and around the bowl-shaped ridge, I cut straight through the brush on foot and gutted the deer. We shot some pictures and talked. We decided that I would drag the buck downhill to a dry wash where I could pack him out later. My hunters would take my horse and backtrack the trail and meet me below on a bare knob.

I was soaked with sweat when I finally got down, and my hunters should have been waiting. They weren't there. Rigoli's warning about never leaving any hunters on horseback alone came quickly to mind. I gave a shout, but no one answered. I waited nervously for several minutes, then took off uphill on foot. I was almost to the spot where the shot was taken when I heard the hunters yelling my name in the distance. They had gotten off the trail and ridden southward.

That afternoon, my other hunter joined Dick's crew while we packed the buck back to the ranch.

Dick and Garrett also put their hunters on deer. They missed three, wounded one, and planned to take up his trail the next morning. One hunter fell and broke the stock of his rifle. Another was pulled out of the saddle by a low-hanging limb he failed to rein his horse around. He wasn't hurt, but he lost his eyeglasses in the spill.

At supper, a hunter asked me to try to find his long-john bottoms. Seems he'd gotten hot, taken them off, then lost them somewhere on the moun-

As deer come in, I need to take up my skinning knife. I remain in camp for this chore while others are out looking for deer. This was one of my busiest days.

tain. Another spoke up and said he'd lost his hunting knife. Someone else explained he'd lost a shirt his wife had given him as an anniversary present. By that time, everyone was laughing.

The first five-day hunt was drawing to a close, and as skinner for the outfit, I had my work hanging from the meat pole. So on the fifth day, as Garrett and Dick took the hunters who hadn't connected, I remained in camp and worked with my skinning knife. Late that afternoon, I took a pickup truck and delivered the meat to a processing plant in Silt, where it would be cut, wrapped, frozen, and shipped to the hunters' homes. I also delivered capes and horns to a local taxidermist and assisted the hunters in selecting their trophy forms. It got to be one of my busiest days.

That evening we learned one of the hunters had missed a shot at a good buck. He laughed at himself for missing. I asked him if he had enjoyed his hunt even though he didn't get his buck.

"I had a ball, but I'll tell you, Brady, I can't wait to get into those polyester pants and patent-leather shoes and hunt me up some bright lights!"

The second hunt began as busy as the first. We shuttled the hunters to and from the Grand Junction airport, rifles were checked on the range, and the hunters briefed. Stirrups were adjusted and a hundred chores done.

We were hoping for a good snow to put game on the move, but the weather stayed mild. Still, we were able to locate a good number of bucks. Perhaps the most memorable thing about the second hunt

was that one hunter fired 28 shots at six different bucks at ranges of 60 to 300 yards and never drew blood.

Another hunter wandered off one afternoon while we were making a drive and "got turned around," as he later put it. We found him an hour after dark.

There was one injury. Dick Donaghy fell and cracked some ribs. That put him out of action, but Garrett and I managed to take up the slack. We made it through in good shape.

Serving as a wrangler and assistant guide for an outfitter was a revelation to me. Previously, I had always been a "dude," and I'll admit I gave little thought to how everything was done as a hunt progressed. I discovered that everyone working with a hunting outfit goes at a fever pitch and must be prepared to tackle any assignment that comes his way, regardless of his experience or personal preference. I came to realize that running a Western horseback hunt is a very complex operation and involves a large investment in time, equipment, and money. I learned that all those connected with legitimate operations earn every cent they are paid.

Most hunters in the West for the first time are not prepared for the rigors and hard work of a mountain hunt. Almost to the man, they overestimate their strength and endurance. The first few days of rough country and high altitude take a heavy toll. Muscles ache, feet blister, bodies rebel, and shooting is not what it should be. Spirits sag, and thoughts turn homeward. By the end of a hunt, most guys are just working into good shape and getting hard. What a difference it would make if they shaped up beforehand at home and practiced with their rifles.

I learned that a guide suffers for his hunters, and not just physically. I came to know that succeeding is tremendously important to a guide and that it is an awesome responsibility.

The last day of the season, I hunted with a young man from the state of Washington. He was in top shape and was a willing hunter. He had taken a week of his annual two-week vacation to come to Colorado and pound the mountains for a mule-deer buck. He was a good guy as well, and I wanted badly to find a decent deer for him.

About mid-morning I located a big buck, bedded down. The shot was a long one—few riflemen could have made it. He missed. We hunted hard the rest of the day, and I tried everything I knew to produce another buck. When the stars tumbled out, we headed for camp empty-handed.

I guess Bill could sense my disappointment.

"Well, Brady," he said as we picked our way down a long ridge, "you gave it all you had, and that's what counts. Besides, I learned a lot, made some good friends, and saw some beautiful country. Next year I'll get a good buck. Next year for sure."

I felt better. 🦌

PART 4

GUNS, SCOPES, AND AMMO

The Hunting Rifle

Jim Carmichel

I know some Tennessee hill farmers who think a varmint rifle is something you keep ready to hand in anticipation of a visit from the revenuers. From their point of view, that may be quite correct, but most of us find it useful to know what we're talking about when it comes to firearms. In this chapter, I aim to do away with some of the widespread mistakes and myths and furnish all the information you really need to choose and use a centerfire hunting rifle.

Let's start with rifling, the spiraling lands and grooves in the barrel wall that distinguish rifles from smoothbores.

RIFLING AND BARRELS

No one knows for sure who invented rifling or even where the concept of a rotating projectile was first put to use. We do know, however, that the rifled barrel existed as early as 1560, because examples dating to that time survive. Some historians maintain that rifles could have been built even earlier because the principle of rotational stability was well known and had long been put to use by applying a certain amount of pitch to arrow fletching.

Even though the inventor remains unnamed, there is no denying the fact that when he cut those twisting grooves into a gun barrel, he completely redirected the course of firearms design.

A rifle is, by definition, a firearm with twisting grooves cut into the inside of the barrel that cause the fired projectile to rotate around its directional axis. This spinning causes the bullet to become a gyroscope and, in the manner of gyroscopes, to main-

RIFLING

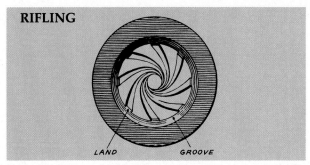

LAND   GROOVE

Raised lands cut into the bullet and impart spin as the bullet moves down the rifled barrel.

tain a stable, point-on attitude while at the same time resisting external forces. We see this principle at work when a child spins a top. As long as the top is spinning, it remains stable on its axis and will even return to a stable attitude after it has been disturbed.

A modern, high-velocity rifle bullet may be spinning as fast as a quarter of a million r.p.m.'s when it leaves the muzzle and maintains a high percentage of this rotational speed throughout flight.

Though a modern rifle barrel seems to be a simple fixture, it's really one of the greatest marvels of machine-age technology. The drilling of a straight, small-diameter hole through a bar of tough steel is difficult enough, but cutting evenly spaced twisting grooves to microscopic uniformity borders on the fantastic. Yet, thousands of very accurate rifle barrels are manufactured every day. The rifling in some is cut in the traditional way with a small hooklike blade that scrapes away whisper-thin ribbons of steel, one at a time, until each groove is cut to its final depth. A more modern way, the so-called "button" process, rifles a barrel by pushing or pulling a slug of tungsten carbide through the bore. The button literally presses rifling grooves into the barrel's walls. Another system forms the barrel by hammering a tube of steel around a bar which impresses the rifling.

Modern rifle barrels are made of tough, abrasion-resistant steels specially alloyed for durability. One popular barrel steel, commonly referred to as "chrome-moly," includes carbon, chromium, manganese, and molybdenum. Some target barrels are even made of stainless steel.

The rifling in a barrel is made of a series of lands and grooves. The lands are the "ridges" and the grooves are the "valleys." Usually, there are four or six of each but there may be two, three, five, seven, eight, or even more. The bore diameter is the width between the tops of opposing lands and the groove diameter is the width across the bottoms of opposing grooves. A typical .30-caliber barrel has a bore diameter of .300 inch and a groove diameter of .308. This shows that the grooves are each .004 deep.

Most American rifling is of the modified Enfield type with square-topped lands and radiused groove bottoms. In American rifles, the grooves are wider

than the lands—about three times as wide in the standard Springfield-type.

The bullets used in a given barrel should exactly match the *groove* diameter. Standard .30-caliber bullets for standard .30-caliber barrels have a diameter of .308. Each land cuts into the bullet to a depth of .004, giving the rifling a good grip on the bullet and causing it to spin as it travels through the barrel. Other calibers have varying groove depths.

One of the least-understood aspects of barrel making is the "rate of twist," or the speed of rotation the barrel gives the bullet. Since different sizes and weights of bullets require different rotational speeds for best accuracy, rifle barrels are made with different angles or "pitch" of rifling. This is expressed in inches per one complete turn of the bullet. A .30/06 barrel, for instance, usually imparts a twist of one turn in each 10 inches of barrel length. Smaller, faster bullets such as those used in a .222 Remington do best with one turn in 14 or 16 inches. As a rule of thumb, bullets that are long and heavy in proportion to their diameter require a faster rate of twist to be properly stabilized.

The length of a rifle's barrel may play a significant role in determining muzzle velocity, but, contrary to popular belief, it has a surprisingly small effect on accuracy. Long rifle barrels provide target shooters a longer sight radius, which aids in accurate aiming, and the extra weight gives a steadier hold. In terms of accuracy potential, however, a 20-inch barrel may be as accurate as one 10 inches longer.

Barrel length is an important velocity determinant with some high-intensity cartridges that are loaded with slow-burning powders. A barrel length of 24, 26, or even 28 inches may be needed to effectively consume the powder and generate top velocity. Cartridges of this type are those that have a large case capacity in relation to their bullet size, such as the .270, 7-mm. Remington magnum, and .300 Winchester Magnum. Rounds that have a relatively low case capacity compared to bullet size, such as the .30/30 or .35 Remington, are loaded with faster-burning powder.

The advertised velocities of most large-capacity

HOW BARREL LENGTH AFFECTS VELOCITY			
CALIBER	BULLET WEIGHT (grains)	BARREL LENGTH	MUZZLE VELOCITY (f.p.s.)
.243	100	26	2,969
.243	100	24	2,919
.243	100	22	2,856
.264 Win. Mag.	140	26	3,151
.264 Win. Mag.	140	24	3,086
.264 Win. Mag.	140	22	2,024
.270 Win.	130	24	3,140
.270 Win.	130	22	2,070
.270 Win.	130	20	2,990
.30/06	180	24	2,700
.30/06	180	22	2,675
.30/06	180	20	2,640

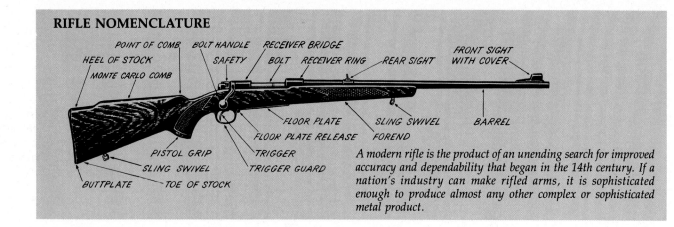

RIFLE NOMENCLATURE

POINT OF COMB · BOLT HANDLE · RECEIVER BRIDGE · FRONT SIGHT WITH COVER
HEEL OF STOCK · SAFETY · BOLT · RECEIVER RING · REAR SIGHT
MONTE CARLO COMB
PISTOL GRIP
SLING SWIVEL
BUTTPLATE · TOE OF STOCK
TRIGGER
TRIGGER GUARD
FLOOR PLATE
FLOOR PLATE RELEASE · FOREND
SLING SWIVEL · BARREL

A modern rifle is the product of an unending search for improved accuracy and dependability that began in the 14th century. If a nation's industry can make rifled arms, it is sophisticated enough to produce almost any other complex or sophisticated metal product.

cases are achieved by using a 26- to 28-inch barrel. To estimate the approximate velocity in a shorter barrel, deduct 35 f.p.s. (feet per second) for every inch less of barrel length from the advertised figure. Actual tests with various calibers have given the results shown in the accompanying table.

ACTION TYPES

Rifles are almost universally named for the action type. "Automatic," "bolt action," "pump," and "single shot" are really generic terms for wide assortments of specialized mechanisms.

One of the simplest, and least expensive, mechanisms is the "break action" single shot, which is characterized by a hinge that pivots the barrel away from the firing mechanism for loading and spent-case extraction. These were quite common during the later part of the last century but are now available in only a few makes and models. Paradoxically, some break-action single shots are finely made and quite expensive. Its first cousin, the break-action double-barreled rifle, is the most expensive type of rifle. Double rifles have been made in virtually all calibers, but they are usually chambered for large calibers used to stop dangerous African game.

The next category is the fixed-barrel single shot, which may be hammerless or have an external hammer. With this type, the barrel is rigidly attached to the receiver frame with the breechblock being movable for loading and extraction. This type includes wide variations in design from the little Stevens .22 Favorite to the powerful Ruger Number 1. Often used as the basis for fine target and varmint rifles, some of these actions have a stiffness that makes them second only to bolt actions in accuracy.

Though the bolt-action design is considered a modern rifle mechanism, it is actually one of the oldest, dating back to Von Dreyse's design of the 1830's. The advantage of the bolt gun is that it combines magazine feed with great strength, reliability, and unsurpassed accuracy. Bolt-action rifles are produced by more manufacturers, and come in more variations, than any other type.

The lever-action rifle has been the all-American

favorite since 1873 and remains as popular as ever. It is reliable and accurate enough for most kinds of hunting, and it offers a lot of firepower. Though some lever designs are only moderately strong and are therefore used only with moderate-pressure cartridges, some, such as the Savage M99, are quite strong.

The so-called "automatic" sporting rifle is actually a semi-automatic; true automatics are machine guns. As the M1 Garand rifle of World War II, and later the M14, have proven, auto-loading rifles can be remarkably strong, reliable, and accurate. This, combined with their high rate of fire, the highest of any sporting type, makes them popular with woods hunters.

Pump-action rifles have been with us since Colt produced its Lightening slide action of 1884. They have never enjoyed more than moderate appeal, mainly to hunters who also favor the use of pump-action shotguns.

Any sporting rifle is judged on three basic criteria: strength, reliability, and accuracy.

Of these, strength is the most important because

RIFLE ACTIONS

BOLT ACTION
SINGLE SHOT
SEMI-AUTOMATIC
PUMP ACTION
LEVER ACTION

Most modern rifle actions fall into five types, but there are others—for instance, the over/under or side-by-side break-action double-barrel rifle that is built like a shotgun.

any rifle must be strong enough, with an extra safety margin, to handle the high pressures generated by smokeless-powder cartridges. Strength is the result of good steel, adequate mass of material, and rigid interlocking of parts.

Reliability generally results with rifles that utilize a minimum of moving parts and a minimum of small, delicate parts. Complex mechanisms, no matter how well they are built, are generally more apt to fail than simple designs.

Accuracy is the result of a combination of good ammo with a uniform barrel and a stiff, solid-locking, non-flexing action. Bolt-action rifles excel in this respect because they are simple, lock solidly, and are stiff. The rigid, one-piece stock helps.

STOCKS

A rifle's stock is one of its most distinguishing and attractive features. It also plays a major role in how the rifle is handled and aimed, how it recoils, and how accurately it shoots.

Walnut has long been a favorite material because it is strong, dense, and moderately light in weight, carves and finishes well, and has pleasing color and texture. Other popular woods for stocks are birch and maple. Sometimes these are stained to look like walnut. Occasionally, laminated woods are used for rifle stocks, especially when extra strength and warp resistance are desirable. In recent years synthetic materials such as nylon and fiberglass have been used. Fiberglass is very desirable in some stocks because it combines light weight with high strength and warp resistance.

Rifle stocks are made in a wide variety of shapes and styles, and the basic type is determined mainly by the purpose for which the rifle is intended. Hunting rifles, for example, have simple, cleanly shaped stocks that allow the rifle to be comfortably held and aimed under a variety of shooting conditions. A varmint rifle, which is usually fired from a rest, often has a wide fore-end, which facilitates shooting over a sandbag rest. Target-rifle stocks may have thumbhole grips, adjustable combs, and specially shaped fore-ends, all of which aid in holding and aiming.

The principal dimensions of any stock are the length of pull (measured from the trigger to the center of the buttplate), drop at comb (measured from the centerline of the bore to the top of the comb), and the drop at heel (measured from centerline of the bore to the top of butt).

Length of pull is important because it largely determines how comfortable a rifle feels when mounted on the shoulder. Drop at comb is especially important because it determines how well the eye is aligned with the sights when the cheek is pressed to the comb. Most shooters can adapt to a length of pull anywhere from 12 to 15 inches. Drop at comb is much more critical. A quarter of an inch often makes the difference between an easy-to-aim rifle and one that is difficult to aim. This is especially

important when telescopic sights are used. The so-called Monte Carlo comb is only one way combs are raised in order to permit more comfortable aiming with a scope.

SIGHTS

Though rifle sights seem to come in almost endless variety, there are only three basic kinds: optical, or telescopic, which usually, but not always, magnify the image of the target; aperture, or peep, which are aimed by looking through a hole in the rear sight; and the open sights, which are aimed by aligning the front sight in a rear notch.

Open sights are simple, rugged, light in weight, low in cost, and easy to use. They can be aimed very quickly, and for this reason are used on heavy, big-bore express rifles for close-range shots at dangerous game. The disadvantages of open sights include lack of precision. They are difficult to aim precisely at long distances, and they usually have only rudimentary or no provision for adjustment. Open sights are sometimes difficult to use because the eye must shift focus to three separate elements: rear sight, front sight, and target.

Peep or aperture sights are an improvement over open sights because the eye simply looks through, not at, the rear sight. This means the eye need only focus on two elements. Peep sights usually are mounted on solid bases, which provide for fast, precise sight adjustments for different ranges. A fine marksman can aim peep sights with an accuracy of one-half inch, or even better, at 100 yards. Aperture sights are used in Olympic rifle competition. The disadvantages are increased cost and slightly greater weight.

Telescopic sights offer the advantage of placing the target and crosshairs on the same focal plane. Both are seen with equal clarity. The magnification allows the shooter to see the target in better detail and thereby place the shot more accurately. Without high-magnification telescopic sights, long-range hits on tiny targets would be virtually impossible.

The magnification, or power, of telescopic sights is expressed as $2\times$, $4\times$, $6\times$, and so forth, meaning the image appears twice, four times, six times as large as it does with the unaided eye.

The disadvantages of telescopic sights are increased weight, cost, bulk, and fragility.

Express sights are quick to use and are therefore favored for dangerous game. The peep is more accurate. Many Americans use V-notch sights, a good compromise.

The aiming element in a telescopic sight is called the reticle and may be a crosshair, a dot, a post, or a combination of these.

The golden rule for adjusting open or peep sights is to move the *rear* aperture or notched blade in the direction you want to move the point of impact. For example, if the bullet is hitting to the left of where you aim, simply move the rear sight to the right. Peep sights, both target and hunting type, usually have a calibrated scale which shows you how far to shift the sight for a given point-of-impact correction. These calibrations are almost always in minutes-of-angle or a fraction thereof (one-half or one-quarter). A minute-of-angle is almost exactly one inch wide at 100 yards, two inches at 200, and so on. If, say, your rifle is six inches low at 100 yards, you raise the aperture six minute-of-angle calibrations on the scale. It's quite simple.

Open rear sights usually have no scale, but it is still easy to make fairly accurate adjustments. First measure the distance between the front and rear sights. This is the sight radius. This radius, in inches, is divided into the distance, also in inches, at which you are shooting. Let's say your rifle has an 18-inch sight radius and you are shooting at 1,200 inches (100 yards). Since 18 goes into 1,200 some 66.6 times, you know that every movement of the rear sight will be multiplied 66.6 times on the target. In other words, a rear-sight correction of $1/10$ inch will move the point of impact 6.6 inches out there on the target.

TRIGGERS

A trigger's weight of pull is the pressure required to release the sear and fire the rifle. This is expressed in pounds and is easily measured by attaching a simple scale to the trigger and reading the pounds needed to release the sear. A trigger weight of three to $3^{1}/2$ pounds is a good all-round weight for hunting, varmint shooting, and some types of target shooting. Some specialized rifles, however, such as benchrest rifles, have triggers that release with only a few ounces of pressure. Most hunting rifles leave the factory set at five to 10 pounds.

Most good-quality bolt-action rifles made today have trigger mechanisms that can be adjusted for weight of pull, creep (the amount a trigger moves before firing), and backlash (the movement after firing). Ideally, the trigger should not move perceptibly when pressure is applied. It should break cleanly with no travel afterward. Trigger movement tends to disturb your aim.

Trigger adjustments should be made with care because what seems to be a finely adjusted trigger may also be dangerous. When the weight of pull is set too light, for example, the sear may sometimes accidently release when the rifle is jarred. Likewise, the creep adjustment usually determines the amount of sear engagement. When it is adjusted so fine that the sear edges have only a few thousandths of an inch of contact, the rifle may fire when the bolt is violently closed. This is a very dangerous state of affairs.

Nearly all modern rifle triggers are of the single-stage type, meaning that the sear begins to release when the trigger pull begins. Some rifles, especially military rifles, have a two-stage trigger, which may move half an inch or so before beginning to disengage the sear. This is a safety feature designed to help avoid accidental discharge during combat. Interestingly, though, some highly specialized target rifles also have double-stage triggers that aid in precise trigger control.

Some rifles, especially European rifles, have double set triggers. Two triggers are mounted one ahead of the other. To operate, the shooter must pull the "setting" trigger, usually the rear one. That cocks a spring mechanism. A very light touch on the other trigger fires the rifle. Single set triggers operate in a similar way, except that the hair-trigger mechanism is cocked (set) by pushing forward on the trigger.

BULLETS

Since the invention of firearms, bullets have been made of everything from clay to steel to glass and in an almost endless assortment of shapes and sizes. Modern sporting rifles range in caliber from the little .17 up to a big .60, with nine out of every 10 rifles falling in the .22-to-.35 bracket.

A TRIGGER MECHANISM

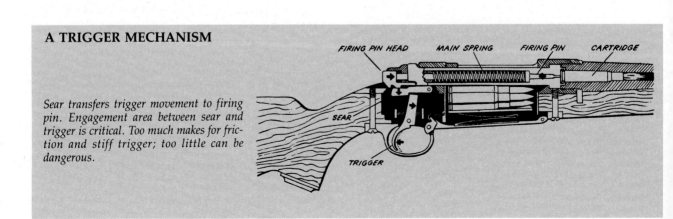

Sear transfers trigger movement to firing pin. Engagement area between sear and trigger is critical. Too much makes for friction and stiff trigger; too little can be dangerous.

FIRING PIN HEAD   MAIN SPRING   FIRING PIN   CARTRIDGE

SEAR

TRIGGER

BULLET TYPES

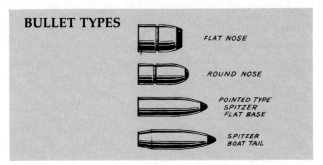

FLAT NOSE

ROUND NOSE

POINTED TYPE
SPITZER
FLAT BASE

SPITZER
BOAT TAIL

Almost all modern rifle bullets consist of a soft lead core inside a copper-alloy jacket.

Aside from the all-lead bullets used in .22 Rimfire cartridges and the lead-alloy bullets used in a handful of odd calibers, all commercial rifle ammunition is loaded with jacketed bullets. These are manufactured by swaging or pressing a cup or jacket of relatively tough metal around a soft lead core. The jacket may be made of brass, steel, nickel, copper, or an alloy of copper. Copper and certain copper alloys are excellent for bullet jackets because they are strong enough to withstand the rigorous trip through a rifled barrel and yet are soft enough not to cause a high degree of barrel wear. Copper and copper alloys also have a suitable coefficient of friction for bullet use, and their ductility makes them ideal for drawing into bullet cups. This does not mean that only copper is suitable. Mild steel is widely used as well, especially in Europe.

Other than diameter and weight, the most distinguishing characteristic of a bullet is the shape of its forward section, or nose. Bullet noses may be sharply pointed, semi-pointed, round, flat, or hollow pointed. For the most part, the shape of a bullet's nose is determined by the purpose for which it was designed. Sharply pointed, streamlined bullets, for example, retain their velocity well and are the best choice for long-range shots at game or targets. Blunt bullets, on the other hand, are designed to expand well at low velocities. So-called full-patch or full-jacketed bullets, with the jacket completely covering the nose, resist deformation while penetrating deep into the flesh and bone of large, dangerous game.

Certain bullets—those used in the popular .30/30 are a good example—have flat noses so that they can be loaded nose-against-primer in tubular-magazine rifles without danger that recoil will cause all the rounds in a loaded magazine to detonate. Some hunters believe that these flat-nosed bullets are good "brush busters." In fact, they are no more efficient at penetrating brush than any other shape.

The relationship between the diameter and weight of a bullet is called sectional density. Bullets that are quite long and heavy in relation to their diameter have a high sectional density. Other things being equal, they retain their velocity and energy better than bullets of the same diameter but lesser weight. Long, slender bullets are less affected by crosswinds, and because they retain more velocity, have a flatter trajectory.

In order to find the sectional density of a bullet, simply divide its weight, in pounds, by the square of its diameter. The formula is: S. D. = (W in grains ÷ 7,000) ÷ D^2. The higher the number, the better.

The ballistic coefficient of a bullet is a very important factor because it indicates the atmospheric drag on that particular bullet. A very streamlined bullet with a sharply pointed tip has a higher ballistic coefficient than a bullet of the same caliber and weight with a less streamlined shape. More streamlined means the bullet loses its velocity less readily, has a flatter trajectory, and is affected less by crosswinds. Determining the ballistic coefficient of a given bullet is a fairly complicated process, usually done with a computer.

The beveled heel of some bullets is commonly known as a boattail and adds an additional streamlining effect that aids long-range performance. Long-range target shooters have long used boattail bullets, and they have become more common on hunting bullets in recent years.

The accuracy of any bullet is largely determined by uniformity of construction. A bullet with an air pocket between the jacket and the core, or a jacket that is thicker on one side, is unbalanced in flight and wobbles like an out-of-balance automobile tire. Dimensions must be held to extremely close tolerances so that each bullet will fit the barrel precisely. If a bullet is over or under the desired diameter by only a few thousandths of an inch, accuracy suffers greatly. If the bullet is grossly oversize, the added friction may cause pressures to rise dangerously.

CARTRIDGE NOMENCLATURE

Rifle cartridge names are ongoing sources of confusion. Such "names" as .30/30, .30/06, .45/70/405, .220 Swift, .222 Remington are helpful in identifying the round, and sometimes they even tell us something about it. Yet English-speaking gunmakers have never used a specific system for naming their ammunition. Before the advent of smokeless powder, self-contained cartridges were identified by caliber, the weight of black powder contained, and sometimes, by the weight of the bullet. A cartridge name such as .45/70 told us that the bullet was of .45 caliber and that the case contained 70 grains of powder. If the round was billed as a .45/70/405, we also knew that the bullet weighed 405 grains. This bit of data told shooters of that era quite a bit about most cartridges and what they would do. Even so, it was often easy to confuse cartridges. Around 1885, there were three different cartridges designated .40/60. One was by Maynard, one was a Marlin, and the other was a Winchester. All differed and could not be used in the same rifle. If that wasn't confusion enough, sometimes the case length measurement was thrown in for good measure as with the .45/120/ 3½-inch Sharps.

U.S. AND METRIC CARTRIDGE DESIGNATIONS

U.S. NAME	BULLET DIAMETER (INCHES)	METRIC NAME
.22 Hornet	.223-.224	5.6×35R
.222 Remington	.224	5.7×43
.223 Remington	.224	5.7×44
6-mm. Remington	.243	6.57
.243 Winchester	.243	6.51
.250 Savage	.257	6.3×48
.257 Roberts	.257	6.3×57
.25/06 Remington	.257	6.3×63
.264 Winchester Mag.	.264	6.5×63
.270 Winchester	.277	6.9×64
.280 Rem. (7mm Rem. Express)	.284	7.63
7-mm. Mauser	.284	7.57
7-mm. Remington Mag.	.284	7×63 Rem. Mag.
.30/30 (.30 WCF)	.308	7.62×51R
.30/40 Krag	.308	7.62×59
.300 Savage	.308	7.62×47
.308 Winchester	.308	7.62×51
.30/06	.308	7.62×63
.300 H & H Mag.	.308	7.62×72
.300 Winchester Mag.	.308	7.62×66 Win. Mag.
.303 British	.311	7.7×56R
8-mm. Mauser	.319-.323	7.9×57
.32 Winchester Spec.	.321	8×51R
.338 Winchester Mag.	.338	8.58×63 Win. Mag.
.35 Remington	.358	9×49
.375 H & H Mag.	.275	9.5×72
.44 Magnum	.429	10.9×32
.45/70	.458	11.5×53
.458 Winchester Mag.	.458	11.5×63

The system became more confused each time a manufacturer marketed a new cartridge. Worse was yet to come. Smokeless powder created a whole new problem in cartridge nomenclature because the amount of smokeless powder used doesn't reflect the round's velocity or energy, at least not in black-powder terms. For a while, however, the old system was used with the new smokeless powder shells. That's how the .30/30 WCF and .30/40 Krag got their names.

But smokeless powders can be made in endless varieties, and it was soon apparent that the old naming system should be laid to rest. Then what? In 1903, the U.S. Government replaced the .30/40 Krag with a new service round, which was called the .30 Caliber of 1903, for short, .30/03. In 1906, the .30/03 was replaced with—you guessed it—the .30/06. Obviously, such a "system" was bound to get out of hand and was never really adopted.

Most modern American sporting cartridges are simply called by whatever name the originating manufacturer decided to use. The numerical prefix usually indicates only the *approximate* caliber. The .300 Savage, .300 Magnum, .30/30, .308 Winchester, and .30/06 all are so-called .30-caliber cartridges, but only the .308 truly reflects the .308 diameter of a modern .30-caliber bullet. The same confusion exists with the .222 Remington, .223 Remington, .224

Weatherby, .225 Winchester, .22/250, and .220 Swift. Each fires a .224 diameter bullet.

Europeans use a more practical but less colorful system. Under the metric system, cartridges are simply called by their metric caliber and case length. Thus the popular 7 × 57 tells us that the round is 7-mm. caliber and has a case length of 57 mm. If the cartridge has a rimmed case, the metric name is followed by a capital R, as in 6.5 × 57R.

The accompanying table lists the actual bullet diameter in inches of some of the more common calibers along with their metric designations and American designations.

PRIMERS

The primer, or self-igniting device, is the end result of several hundred years of experimentation and development. Likewise, the type of priming used is often considered the most important identifying characteristic of a modern cartridge. Today's rifle cartridges are ignited by either rimfire or centerfire priming. The rimfire ignition is almost exclusively used in short cases for .22-caliber bullets. This was not always the situation. During the last century, there was a fairly wide range of calibers using rimfire ignition. By the first part of the 1900's, the number of rimfire cartridges other than the .22's had been reduced to a few low-powered rounds from .25 to .41.

As the term implies, rimfire priming is contained in the fold of metal making up the rim of the case. The priming compound runs completely around the rim and is exploded by a firing pin striking anywhere around the rim. Though this is a simple, reliable, and inexpensive ignition system, it results in a somewhat weak case structure which cannot contain the pressures generated in a high-powered, smokeless-powder cartridge.

The heart of all modern big-game cartridges is the primer located in the center of the base end of the

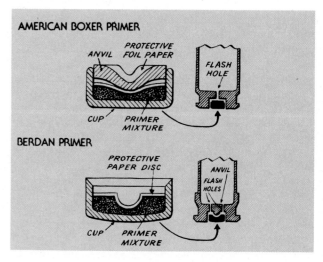

Primer mix explodes when crushed between firing pin and anvil. Resulting flame ignites main powder charge in cartridge case.

case. The primer may be nickel-plated, brass, or copper-colored. It is held in the case by a press fit. After firing, it can be removed and replaced by hand loaders.

The primers in American rifle ammo, regardless of manufacturer, are of two standard sizes: the .175-diameter Small Rifle size used in small cases such as the .22 Hornet, .222 Remington, and so on; and the .210 diameter Large Rifle size used in all other rounds from the .22/250 Remington on up through the .458 Winchester Magnum.

Another characteristic of U.S. primers is that they are of the type invented by Edward M. Boxer, a British officer. The Boxer primer is made up of three parts: the cup, the anvil, and the primer mix. When the rifle's firing pin hits the cup, it is dented inward against the anvil. Between the two is the sensitive chemical mixture that is exploded by the concussive blow. The flame of the exploding primer mixture blazes through the flashhole into the main chamber of the cartridge case.

Centerfire ammo made in Europe, paradoxically, utilizes a priming system invented by an American, Hiram Berdan, of Berdan's Sharpshooters fame during the Civil War.

The primer cup and explosive mix in the Berdan primer are similar, but the anvil is built into the primer pocket of the cartridge case rather than being housed in the cup. The anvil is an integral part of the case, and there are usually two flashholes, one on each side of the anvil. This arrangement makes the primer rather difficult to remove, and as a result, Berdan cases are hard to reload.

In days gone by, primer mixes contained compounds of mercury that caused brass cartridge cases to become brittle, or they contained chlorate compounds that deposited harmful salts in the rifle's barrel. The salts attracted corrosive moisture, which quickly ruined the bore if it was left uncleaned. Primers used in military small arms ammo during both world wars were of the corrosive type (except .30 Carbine ammo). That's why the Army had such a hang-up about proper cleaning. Modern ammo, including military small-arms rounds, is primed with non-corrosive chemicals, which greatly reduce the need for immediate and arduous cleaning. U.S. military ammo manufactured since January of 1950 has non-corrosive primers and may be considered "safe" to fire without immediate barrel cleaning afterward.

CARTRIDGE CASE

Since the invention of self-contained ammunition, cartridge cases have been made of all sorts of materials, including paper, brass, tin, zinc, copper, steel, plastic, and even solid powder. Brass remains the favorite, however, because of its desirable elasticity. When a modern high-intensity cartridge is fired, the case must be strong enough to hold tons of internal pressure. It must also expand to seal the chamber and stretch without rupturing. Nothing else does

this quite as well as brass. When a cartridge is fired, the brass case expands so that it fills the chamber, but if it has to stretch too much, it ruptures, and the blast of released gas floods back into the action, twisting steel, shattering wood, and very likely injuring the shooter. This is why rifle and ammo makers are very careful that ammunition of a given caliber fits a rifle of corresponding caliber within close tolerances. This takes us to the mysterious topic of headspace.

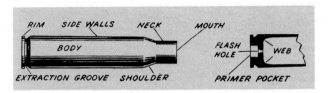

Cartridge cases are usually made of brass because brass expands when cartridge is fired. This seals chamber against gas blow-back. Otherwise, the rifle would "backfire" dangerously.

Since the brass case will stretch and swell only slightly before rupturing, it must be supported at the sides and rear by a closely fitted chamber in the rear, or breech, end of the barrel. It would be difficult and expensive to manufacture ammo and cut chambers which fit each other perfectly, and such a close fit would create feeding problems and other complications. Therefore, makers of ammunition and rifles strive for a compromise fit that allows for slight manufacturing variables while at the same time remains within what they consider to be the safe stretch limits of the brass case. American rifle and rifle ammo makers conform the shape and size of their cartridges and rifle chambers to guidelines set forth by SAAMI (Sporting Arms and Ammunition Makers Institute).

The allowable free space in a chamber, usually scant thousandths of an inch, is called headspace and is not necessarily the same for all cartridges. In fact, as we shall see later, there are different ways of measuring headspace. Whenever a chamber is longer than the allowable maximum (or the cartridge case too short) a condition of *excessive* headspace exists, which may be dangerous.

Excess headspace can be caused by hard wear or abuse, but usually is the result of faulty ammo, improper barrel fitting, or mismatched action parts. When the bolts of two otherwise identical rifles are swapped, it is likely that a condition of improper headspace will result. This is why it is especially important to have the headspace on surplus military rifles checked.

Though a rifle's chamber must be held within certain dimensions in regard to diameter, shoulder shape, and overall length, the headspace length is a linear dimension and, according to the caliber, is measured in different ways. Modern rimless calibers, for example, are measured from the face of the bolt or breech block to a "datum point" somewhere on the shoulder of the chamber. The chambers for belted Magnum cases are measured from the bolt face to the front of the belt. In fact, this system of headspacing is the purpose of the belt. It was not intended to add strength to the case.

Most rimmed calibers such as the .22 Rimfire, .30/30 WCF, etc., are headspaced only from the face of the breech to the front face of the cartridge rim.

INTERNAL BALLISTICS

Internal ballistics describe the complex sequence of events that begins when the firing pin activates the primer and ends when the bullet leaves the muzzle.

Rifle ammo is loaded to the pressure level that can be safely held by the type of rifle in which it will be fired. For example, the venerable .45/70 round could easily be loaded to velocities above the advertised 1,330 f.p.s. of factory loads, but the additional pressure might well exceed the strength of older .45/70 rifles. So the pressure level of factory .45/70 loads is held to about 18,000 Copper Units of Pressure (c.u.p.'s). By comparison, a modern high-intensity cartridge may generate over 50,000 c.u.p.'s. Naturally these can be safely fired only in strong, solid-locking rifles.

Though velocity is the result of pressure, there is no precise relationship between the two. In other words a muzzle velocity of 3,000 f.p.s. (feet per second) with a given caliber and weight of bullet does not always tell us the precise or even the approximate pressure. This is because the particular pressure generated when you fire a rifle is caused by a number of factors. One of the most important of these is the burning rate of the powder.

The pressure generated in a rifle is usually measured in one of two ways. The first is the copper-crusher system in which a precisely measured copper slug is held in a vise-like fixture built into a special test gun. When the cartridge is fired, the pressure crushes the slug, and the amount of flattening is translated into c.u.p.'s. Until recent years, this reading was expressed in pounds per square inch, but now ballistic engineers do not think this is a realistic way to translate the crusher system.

ENERGY OF POPULAR AMERICAN CARTRIDGES

CALIBER	BULLET WEIGHT (GRS)	MUZZLE ENERGY (foot-pounds)	100 YARDS	200 YARDS
.222	50	1,094	752	500
.243	80	2,077	1,619	1,249
.25/06	100	2,316	1,858	1,478
.270	130	2,790	2,300	1,883
7-mm. Rem.	150	3,221	2,667	2,196
.30 Carbine	110	967	600	383
.30/30	150	1,902	1,296	858
.30/06	180	2,913	2,468	2,077
.45/70	405	1,590	1,227	1,001
.458 Win. Mag.	500	4,989	3,999	3,174

RECOIL

We all know that a light rifle kicks more than a heavier one, all other things being equal. This is so because the additional weight absorbs more of the recoil energy. This is also why the weight of the rifle is so important when calculating the recoil *energy* of a rifle.

Though both the velocity and energy of a rifle's recoil can be calculated, it really isn't worth the bother, because the shape of a rifle's stock plays an important part in the recoil you feel.

EXTERNAL BALLISTICS

External ballistics deal with the flight of the bullet.

Once it leaves the barrel, the bullet is acted on by three major forces: gravity, the atmosphere, and wind.

Of these, surprisingly perhaps, it is the effect of the atmosphere which concerns us most. When a bullet leaves the rifle's muzzle at supersonic speeds, it slams into a wall of air. It is like diving into a pool of molasses. And the faster the bullet is going, the thicker the molasses becomes. We can offset this drag factor somewhat by using streamlined bullets, but even so, the atmospheric resistance is nothing less than tremendous.

To give you an idea of the magnitude of atmospheric resistance, or drag, consider a super-streamlined boattail, .30 caliber, 180-grain bullet leaving the muzzle at 3,200 f.p.s. At standard atmospheric pressure, the bullet would be slowed by 200 f.p.s. during the first 100 yards! If the same bullet had a round nose, it would lose 25 percent more velocity in the same 100 yards.

Gravity, as we all know, causes a bullet to fall at a given rate. In fact, if dropped from your hand, all bullets—regardless of size, shape, and weight—fall at the same speed and hit the ground at the same time. But we also know that different bullets from different caliber rifles have widely differing trajectories, some more curved than others.

Let's consider again the old .45/70 with a 300-grain bullet leaving the muzzle at 1,300 f.p.s. At 100 yards, the flat-nosed bullet has slowed to 1,060 f.p.s. and it has fallen nearly a foot below the level bore line. A .220 Swift with a pointed 55-grain bullet fired at 4,000 f.p.s. drops only about one-tenth as much as the .45/70 slug. Even though gravity has an identical pull on both bullets, their curves differ because the faster bullet covers the distance in a much shorter time.

To get an idea of how drag enters into trajectory, let's consider the flight of the flat-shooting .220 Swift bullet for a few hundred more yards. At 100 yards, the bullet has fallen 1.13 inches from the level bore line. At 200 yards, the bullet has not fallen just 1.13 more inches but an additional 3.82 inches! And between 200 and 300 yards, it drops another 7.2 inches! By the time it goes 500 yards, it has fallen over 40 inches. This is because air drag is causing the bullet to lose velocity at a rapid rate.

To get a solid grasp of these time/distance relationships, drop a bullet from a height of 40 inches. The time it takes to reach the floor is the same time it takes the .220 Swift bullet I just described to travel 500 yards.

Though the effect of wind on a bullet can be calculated mathematically, it is a rather complicated process and not practical when you're making cross-country shots at elk. Expert riflemen therefore rely on experience to tell them how much to allow for wind.

VELOCITY

English-speaking people express the speed of a rifle bullet in feet per second, meaning the distance the bullet will travel, in feet, in one second if it could continue at a steady velocity.

The velocity figure we most often use is muzzle velocity. It is the bullet's speed just as it leaves the rifle barrel. This is impressive, because it is the fastest. But muzzle velocity is misleading because bullets lose a lot of velocity during the first few feet of their flight. Some bullets lose a higher percentage of speed than others. The 100-yard velocity, and in some cases, the 200- or 300-yard velocity, gives a more realistic idea of cartridge performance.

Ballistic experts often use the time-of-flight figure when appraising bullet performance. Time of flight may be used for any distance from 50 to 1,000 yards or even farther. It is a useful comparison tool because time of flight for different bullets may vary widely, even though the bullets may start out at the same muzzle velocity.

Over the years, bullet velocities have been measured and calculated in a number of ways. Modern chronographs operate by counting the pulses emitted by a crystal when an electric current is passed through it. A bullet passing through a wire or light field starts the flow of electricity to the crystal, and when it passes through a second "gate," the current is stopped. Since the crystal always pulses—or vibrates—at a precise rate, the number of pulses counted represents a highly exact time interval. With this exact time lapse, it is easy to calculate velocity.

The energy, or kinetic force, of a bullet is what hunters usually call "knock-down power." This is expressed in foot-pounds of energy, meaning the power required to lift a given number of pounds one foot.

The foot-pound energy of any bullet is a mathematic expression determined by its weight and velocity. It can be calculated by multiplying the square of the velocity by the weight of the bullet (in grains) and dividing by 450,240 (Energy = $V^2 \times W \div 450,240$). By this calculation, we see that if we double the weight of the bullet, we double the energy level. But if we double the velocity, we quadruple the energy. This is why nearly all ballistic research of this century has been directed toward higher velocities.

The trajectory of a bullet is usually described in three ways: the absolute trajectory, the corrected (or elevated) trajectory, and the mid-range trajectory. The absolute trajectory describes the fall of the bullet when fired from a perfectly level rifle barrel. The force of gravity takes hold of the bullet the instant it leaves the muzzle, causing it to begin falling immediately. The bullet never rises above the bore line.

The downward curve of the absolute trajectory is surprisingly steep. A 180-grain spitzer (pointed) bullet fired from a .30/06 at a muzzle velocity of 2,700 f.p.s. drops 2.4 inches during the first 100 yards, eight inches more at 200 yards, and a combined total of 24.5 inches at 300 yards.

If we had to live with these curves, we would not be able to hit a distant target very well. We solve part of the problem by sighting our rifles so that the barrel is inclined slightly upward. This means the path of the bullet is somewhat *above* the line of sight for part of its flight. If the sights are correctly set, the bullet will be within a few inches, above or below, of the point of aim at all practical hunting ranges. This is corrected, or elevated, trajectory.

When the rifle is sighted this way, there is a certain point somewhere along the bullet's path where it reaches its highest point in respect to the line of sight. The height of the bullet above the line of sight at this point is called the mid-range trajectory. Most hunting calibers, when properly sighted for normal ranges, have a mid-range height of two or three inches. For extreme long range, however, such as 1,000-yard target shooting, the mid-range trajectory may be a dozen or more feet.

Each rifle should be sighted to take full advantage of the cartridge used.

The Winchester and Remington catalogs contain trajectory tables for many rifle calibers, and they also appear in several books on rifle shooting and ammunition reloading.

Another thing to remember about trajectory is that a rifle bullet hits somewhat higher in respect to point of aim when shooting at an up *or* down angle than it does when shooting over a level but equal distance.

For example, let's say your .270 Winchester rifle is loaded with 130-grain bullets and sighted to hit dead on at 200 yards. If you shoot uphill or downhill at a 45° angle, the bullet will hit some 2.5 inches high at 200 yards.

Good shooting! 🦌

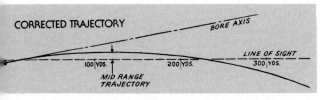

To "correct" bullet's curved flight, most rifles are sighted in so that the barrel tilts slightly upward. Bullet crosses the line of sight at about 25 yards and again at about 225 yards.

Hitting Them the Modern Way

John O. Cartier

Any rifle can be a good deer rifle if the hunter using it is a good deer hunter. This conviction of mine took on weight during many deer seasons, but I especially remember a whitetail hunt I once made in Montana.

One hunter in my group was a local citizen who turned up with an old .32 Remington Woodsmaster that had a peep sight. It turned out that this old-timer had owned the rifle for about 30 years. He wouldn't tell me how many deer he'd shot with it for fear of being quoted, but he did tell me something that's good advice.

"It ain't the rifle that makes the killing shot," he said. "It's the man behind the rifle. I know exactly what this Remington will do, and I know how to make her do it. A guy's a good shot or he ain't. The best modern rifle won't kill a deer for a man unless he knows how to use it. That's the thought you writers ought to promote instead of wasting so much ink on ballistics and such."

There's a lot of truth in that opinion, but it needs to be qualified. I discussed the statement with one of today's leading gun writers, who summed up the qualification very neatly.

"I've run into a lot of those old-timers who are excellent shots with old rifles," he told me. "These guys don't keep up with modern advances in guns, ammunition, and scopes. They have no reason to. They nail their bucks every year with their old rifles because they've had the hunting and shooting experience necessary to do the job.

"The thing is," the writer continued, "that today's average deer hunter just doesn't use his rifle except during deer season. But one way he can up his odds is to use the equipment that's best suited for the type of hunting he's going to do. Today's rifles and scopes enable the modern hunter to down deer the old-timers would have had no chance at, regardless of their hunting skill or familiarity with their guns. You get an old-timer who will cooperate with you and try modern equipment, and you'll really see his eyes light up."

I was part of such an incident on a hunt in Wyoming, though the hunt involved antelope rather than deer. My partner and I were camped with a fold-out camper along a cottonwood creek bottom. One evening the rancher who owned the property drove up to see how our hunt was going. It so happened there was a small herd of antelope grazing along a hillside above us. They were nearly 400 yards away. Neither of the two small bucks in the herd wore horns that interested my partner or myself. However, they interested the rancher very much.

"That's prime eating up there," he said. "Wish I had my rifle, I'd sneak up there and pop one of those bucks."

"No need to be sorry," I said. "Take my rifle and try dropping the buck you want. You can shoot from right here. Just lay the rifle across the hood of your truck, put the scope's crosshairs just above the animal's shoulder, and squeeze off a shot."

The guy looked at me to see if I was kidding, decided I wasn't, and then asked, "What caliber is that rifle?"

"It's a .243," I said. "It's sighted-in to hit dead-on at 250 yards. The slug will drop several inches at your range, that's why I'm telling you to hold high. But it will get there and do the job. Try for one of those bucks. You just might be surprised at what happens."

So he did. At the crack of my rifle, the rancher's antelope went down as if his legs had been kicked out from under him. The animal didn't move an inch after he hit the ground.

"That's damned hard to believe," the man said with awe. "I wouldn't have the least idea of where to hold my rifle on a target that far away."

When we analyze this incident, we arrive at a conclusion that seems contrary to the statement made by the Montana hunter with the old .32 Remington who said, "The best modern rifle won't kill a deer for a man unless he knows how to use it."

Well, my answer to that is simple. Though the

Wyoming rancher wasn't familiar with my rifle, he was more than familiar with his own firearms. He used his rifle more or less year-round for shooting coyotes, and he had used it for many years while hunting mule deer and antelope. He knew how to get a sight picture, he knew how to squeeze off a shot, and he wasn't much concerned with buck fever. In short, he knew plenty about how to use a rifle. All he had to be told was where to hold, and then he sent his bullet home with no problem.

At no time in history have rifles, ammunition, scopes, and related equipment been so reliable as they are now. The so-so deer hunter of today has the opportunity of hitting his buck the modern way with modern equipment. Let's develop this thought a bit further.

Years ago, the Model 94 .30/30 was a famous deer rifle. Winchester has sold more than 3,000,000 of them, practically all to deer hunters, since the rifle was introduced in 1894. Years ago, when you saw another deer hunter in the woods, he probably would be carrying a .30/30. How many of those rifles do you see in today's woods? Not many, and here's why:

The muzzle velocity of 170-grain factory loads for my .30/30 is 2220 feet per second, and their energy at 100 yards is 1350 foot pounds. The muzzle velocity of 100-grain factory loads for my .243 is 2960 feet per second, and the energy at 100 yards is 1620 foot pounds. Obviously the .243 slug and others comparable to it step out faster and hit with more shocking power.

Sight-in a .30/30 to hit at point of aim at 100 yards. If you have to shoot at a deer 300 yards away, your bullet will drop 29.6 inches from point of aim. My .243 slug will drop only 12.2 inches. Again it's obvious that, given the same shooting opportunity, the man firing the .243 or a comparable modern caliber is much less likely to miss than the man with the .30/30 if both men have the same shooting skill.

Going a step further we can say that the old-timer with a .30/30 would have no business shooting a deer 300 yards away because his iron sights and beer-belly bullet trajectory would give him a very bad combination of sight picture and bullet-placement estimation. The same guy shooting my .243 would have a most reasonable shot because he would be shooting a flat-trajectory bullet and he could turn my variable scope up to 9× and be presented with a very good sight picture. Also, if shooting light happened to be poor, iron sights would be difficult to line up. A scope gathers light, so it offers a far better sight picture and will allow a hunter to shoot earlier in the morning and later in the evening, especially on the dull days that are common in deer country everywhere.

MORE ON SCOPES

If the foregoing isn't enough to convince you that the modern hunter is foolish to go into deer woods without a scoped rifle, consider another important point. Most whitetails are shot in thick brush, which means the hunter must shoot through openings in the brush so his bullet won't be deflected before it gets to his buck. A scope, because of its magnification, often makes it possible for a hunter to pick a clear path for his bullet. Iron sights of any type lack this advantage.

Also, a scope has more of a built-in fail-safe system for accurate shooting than does an iron-sight setup. With iron sights, you must line up two different sighting points at different distances from the eye. With a scope you have only one sighting point, normally the intersection of the crosshairs.

I believe that many shooters, especially inexperienced deer hunters, tend to line iron sights on a deer's vital section and then look up as they pull the trigger. This tendency results in shooting high and is caused partly by buck fever and partly by the difficulty of keeping two sights lined up. You can't fall victim to this problem with a scope, because you must have the crosshairs (or post) on the buck to get a sight picture. If you look up for any reason, that sight picture is gone immediately. So, with a scope, you have either a good sight picture or none at all.

The biggest problem with using a scope is its comparatively narrow field of view. The average hunter thinks he should close his left eye as he mounts his rifle for the shot so that he can pick up his target through the lens with his right eye. This is *all wrong*.

You should get into the habit of keeping both eyes open as you shoulder your rifle. Use the same technique you use with a shotgun. In this way, you can see both the deer and his surroundings with both eyes until you get roughly on target. This tactic eliminates the problem many scope users have when they suddenly see a deer against the wide landscape, then have trouble finding him through the scope. This happens because the field of view from natural eyesight becomes abruptly narrowed.

You should get roughly on target with both eyes open before you close the left eye and lay the crosshairs exactly where you want them for the shot. The reverse is correct for left-handed riflemen. The both-eyes-open technique will greatly help the sight-picture problem that many unknowing scope users complain about.

Most hunters who have trouble finding game through a scope bring it on themselves because they never look through their scopes except during deer season. Practice makes perfect in anything we do, so it's just common sense to practice with your scope during the off season. The both-eyes-open technique can be used for dry-firing practice any time and anywhere.

A good trick I've always promoted is to get plenty of practice with a scoped .22 rifle. I use one for small-game hunting before deer season and for plinking year-round. When you get good with the .22, you won't have any problem finding game with the larger scopes used on deer rifles. Any shooting practice with any type of scope helps improve the sight-picture situation.

What scope is best? There's no specific answer, but much depends on where you hunt. If you hunt in densely wooded whitetail country where brush is thick and shots are short, you'll want a scope with a wide field of view. Most modern scopes have a very wide field of view, which is the main reason they have become so popular. The scopes of years ago had such narrow fields of view that most old-timers figured they were nearly worthless. That's all changed now.

An average modern scope of 2½× will present a view circle of 42 to 44 feet at 100 yards. A 4× covers 30 to 34 feet. As the power increases, the view-circle coverage decreases. Short-range whitetail hunters will limit their ability for quick shooting in thickets if they go beyond 4×.

However, if the same hunters mix their deer gunning with occasional trips west to mule-deer states where shots are often long, they'll be limited with their 2½-to-4× scopes because of lack of target definition at long range. One answer for these hunters is a variable scope that will adjust from, say, 2 to 7× or 3 to 9×. I have scopes on my deer rifles in both categories, so I'm set to hunt whitetails in the East or mule deer in the West with no problems concerning scope power.

There's one problem with scopes that seems to be a holdover from the old days. During those times, it was common practice to come in out of the cold and stack rifles in the corners of cabins or tents, perhaps near blazing-hot wood stoves. This habit caused no problem, because the rapid change from cold to hot temperature had little effect on iron sights. It's a different story when glass optics and mounts are involved. Too-rapid temperature changes can expand or contract scope mounts and stocks, and cause them to shift sufficiently to change the point of aim.

If I'm hunting my local area, I store my rifle away from heat sources in my house or in my locked car after I have sighted it in. If I'm on a trip, I store it in the coolest and safest place available. (Fogging, either on the inside or outside of a scope, can be caused by rapid temperature changes, too. Storing my rifle in the coolest place available also licks this problem.) And, if I'm on a trip, I always resight my rifle after I reach my destination. Often this can't be accomplished before I reach the hunting area, but I'd much rather risk spooking game than shooting at a fine buck with a rifle that doesn't shoot where I think I'm aiming it.

The serious automobile driver wouldn't think of driving with a dirty windshield, yet few hunters seem concerned with the fact that a scope's lenses can easily become dusty, water-spotted, dirty, finger-marked, or oil-smeared. Trying to aim through such neglected lenses dramatically increases the odds of missed shots. If you don't have protective caps for the ends of your scope, you should buy a pair. Keep caps on your scope at all times except when actually hunting. While in the field, I keep a few sheets of camera-lens tissue in my wallet. It takes only a moment to clean my scope's lens surfaces whenever they become dusty or dirty. Camera-lens tissues can be purchased at any photo shop, and they won't scratch a lens as will your dry shirttail or handkerchief.

WHERE TO HIT THEM

Regardless of what caliber rifle or sighting setup you use, the goal is always to put your bullet where it will make a clean kill. Since bullet placement is the critical factor, it logically follows that the biggest vital area of a deer will be the easiest to hit. The lung area is very vulnerable since lungs are filled with blood vessels and protected by only a thin rib cage. Hit a deer in the lungs with any expanding bullet of suitable caliber and he's yours. He may go a few feet or yards, but he's going to go down in the immediate area, and he's going to stay down.

As long as there are deer hunters, there will be arguments about this premise. Many veterans say a deer shot in the heart, brain, neck, or spine will drop in his tracks. This is true in most cases, but my contention is that the guy who can hit these small areas consistently has the shooting ability to make the Olympics. Shooting at deer under normal hunting conditions is too tough a job to permit hitting the smaller vital areas with any degree of success.

I long ago concluded that many hunters don't

Since the lungs make up the largest vital area and since deer that are lung-shot with modern expanding bullets are goners, your aiming for the lungs will give you the optimum record for kills over the years. Shooting offhand at 100 yards, few good riflemen can hold a one-foot group anyway. Even from a rest, a perfectly squeezed longer shot may miss the mark because of misjudged distance. A shot for the lungs that ranges high may hit the spine; foward, it may smash the shoulder; low, it may enter the heart—all capable of downing deer quickly. Odds are with the lung shooter every time.

have the shooting ability to consistently hit a deer, period, let alone in a specific area. Even among good rifle shots, there are few who can keep all their offhand shots in a one-foot circle at 100 yards or a two-foot circle at 200 yards. So what sense is there in the advice of many so-called experts who promote heart, head, spine, or neck shots? The average guy simply can't hit targets that small under hunting conditions. Why do so many hunters discount the deadliness of the lung shot? A good question, and I can only guess at the answer. It seems to me that a good many riflemen believe that if a high-powered slug hits bone it will blow up something and create sudden and violent shocking force. This may be okay if you're after dangerous big game, but it doesn't hold true when you're after deer. If you put a properly expanding slug of good construction and weight into a deer's lungs, it's a physical impossibility for him to go far. An expanding bullet will produce profuse hemorrhaging and the animal has to drown in his own blood in moments. It's as simple as that.

MORE NOTES ON CARTRIDGES AND RIFLES

If a bullet doesn't open up well, it won't do maximum damage upon entering the lung area. This is why some overgunned hunters don't like the lung shot. Their big bullets don't open up in an animal as small as a deer; they zip right through the critter while hitting little or no bone and produce a wound that may take hours to kill. The guys using heavier slugs in big-caliber rifles lose a lot of deer because their bullets go through the animals before they have a chance to kill by expanding. That just doesn't happen with calibers such as the .243, 6-mm., and .270. Regardless of caliber, if you confine your deer shooting to bullet weights in the 100- to 150-grain class, your slugs will expand in a deer's lungs. And when they expand, they kill in short order.

What about the "brush-buster" capabilities of the bigger slugs that so many veterans claim are so important, especially in whitetail woods? Well, in these modern times, there is considerable evidence that the old theory about heavy, round-nosed bullets plowing through brush to hit a deer at point of aim is pure nonsense.

Jim Carmichel, *Outdoor Life's* respected shooting editor, says the reverse is more likely to be true.

"In a nutshell, the class of cartridge usually referred to as brush-busters are, in fact, about the poorest choice for the job," he told me. "The reason the high-velocity, pointed, and lighter slugs have more stability in flight is their higher rotational speed.It follows that a heavy, slower-spinning bullet is more likely to tumble after it hits a twig or branch. You can validate the theory by experimenting with a toy top. When the top is spinning at high speed, strike it smartly and notice how it wobbles a bit but then trues itself back up. When the top's rate of spin slows, an identical blow will knock it completely out

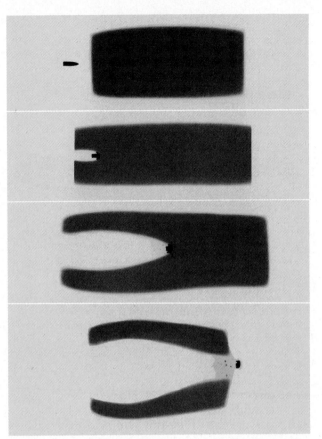

Use fast-opening bullets in the 100- to 150-grain class. In the bullet-expansion illustrations shown here, a Remington Core-Lokt pointed bullet enters gelatine and begins expanding almost immediately. The mushrooming of the lead core continues until the thickest portion of the metal jacket resists further mushrooming and helps hold the bullet together. Whether hitting bone or only flesh, this kind of bullet penetrates well, while providing good shock effect on deer size game.

of balance. The same thing can happen when a bullet of high rotational speed strikes brush. At top speed it might wobble for an instant, but then it will settle down again in a point-on direction. Slower-spinning bullets are more likely to be knocked out of kilter and begin to tumble.

"But, to be factual," Carmichel continued, "we have to conclude there is no really reliable brush cartridge or bullet. When a bullet of any sort strikes a substantial obstacle—even a twig no bigger in diameter than your finger—there is every likelihood that it will be deflected to a certain degree. The real answer, with any caliber, is to try to place your shot so your bullet has a free ride to target. The hunter who takes care to line up his shots so that the bullet has a clear right of way has a good brush rifle regardless of caliber."

I consider a bolt-action rifle to be of far safer design than other types. It is also more trouble-free. Sand or grit can get into a bolt-action and you still can ram the bolt home and get off a shot.

A friend of mine had the habit—like most of us—of carrying loose cartridges in his pockets. One time

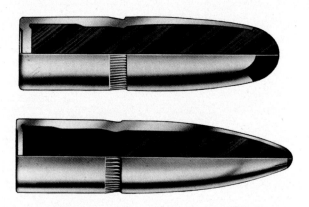

These cutaway drawings show the relationship of lead to jackets for the Remington Core-Lokt soft nose and the pointed, soft point. The greater amount of exposed lead of the soft nose is favored for short range by many hunters using rifles of .30 caliber or more because it provides maximum mushrooming and shocking power. This soft nose offers good initial wind resistance but loses velocity and energy more rapidly than the pointed bullet. The pointed bullet shoots flatter and retains energy better at longer ranges.

some dirt got into his pocket. He went deer hunting that morning, loaded his semiauto, got off one shot at a buck, then had his rifle jam when the second round failed to feed into the chamber.

Since then, he has always carried clean cartridges in a plastic bag in his pocket—a good trick for anyone. But I'll bet if he had been using a bolt-action he would have nailed that buck, or at least had a second shot. I'm partial to bolt-action rifles because I believe they're safer, more dependable, and more accurate than other designs.

After reading this far in this chapter, you certainly have reason to believe that I'm also partial to the .243 caliber. Well, I am, for several reasons. And those reasons might as well lead off my discussion of killing power.

Over a period of many years, I've been able to make two extended deer hunts each year. During one 10-year stretch, I harvested an average of two whitetails or mule deer each season. All of those animals were downed with 100-grain .243 slugs. One big mule deer managed to run off 60 yards after being hit just behind the lung area, a bad shot. One whitetail made it 30 yards before piling up; another whitetail buck struggled about 10 feet before caving in. All other deer (plus some antelope) I've taken during the 10-year period dropped in their tracks. So the main reason I shoot a .243 is that it's just plain amazingly deadly on deer. I don't have to have anybody tell me it's deadly; from plenty of personal experience, I know it's deadly.

Why is it so deadly? Because its high-velocity, rapidly expanding bullet hits and reacts with an enormous degree of shock. A 100-grain .243 bullet—or others of comparable weight and design in such calibers as the 6.5-mm., 6-mm., .264, .270, .257 Rob-

erts, .280, .284, 7-mm. Magnum, and the .30/06—begin expanding soon after contact. By the time they reach the inside of a buck, they're really blowing up. That's why they're so deadly. Quick-opening bullets hitting at high-impact velocity are by far the best for deer hunting.

These days, deer hunters often make trips to relatively distant areas for mule deer and whitetails, and long-range shooting is much more common than it was years ago.

The trouble with long-range work is that most hunters don't have the shooting experience to handle it. We all hear tales about guys who nail mule deer across canyons with 500-yard kills, but it's best to take those stories with more than several grains of salt. Consider that 500 yards is the length of five football fields placed end to end. You could hardly see a deer that far away in most terrain conditions.

Then consider how far a bullet drops from line of sight at extreme range. Even a .243, sighted-in at 200 yards—which is a fairly long range—will drop its bullet more than 40 inches out at 500 yards. In my opinion, successful 500-yard shots are pure luck unless the shot is wide-open at a stationary target. Even then, the rifleman has to be blessed with good fortune if he even hits the deer at that range, let alone puts his slug into a vital area.

Add to all this that the average hunter's range estimation can be pretty sloppy. It has to be. How much range-estimation practice have you done in your lifetime? Most of us would have to answer, "darn little." But we can help ourselves. Practice range estimation whenever you take a walk or while hunting small game. Pick a spot ahead that you guess to be 200 yards. Pace it off. You'll probably be surprised to find it's far closer to 150 yards. An estimated distance of 400 yards will be more likely to measure closer to 300. That's why you hear those stories of 500-yard kills. If the guys who made them had later paced off the range, they'd most likely find they'd been toying with the truth.

SHOOT FROM A REST

It's always best to shoot from a rest whenever possible. I can't emphasize this rule too strongly. Most of the shots I've missed at deer came about because I shot offhand. A big percentage of offhand shots are tried because the gunner shoots too rapidly. Most deer shot at from stands are unaware of the gunner, and are standing still or walking slowly. Stalking and stillhunting gunners are not so likely to get standing shots. But if they do their jobs right, they'll often have enough time to utilize a rest. So the guy who shoots too rapidly usually does so because he has some degree of buck fever. He tries to beat the shakes and wobbles by yanking off a quick shot. This results in flinching, which compounds the problem. The steadier your sight picture is on your buck, the less likely you are to try a quick shot. The best way to keep a steady sight picture is to shoot from a rest.

The standing position is the worst possible selection. The kneeling position is best for a quick shot if no rest is available.

The beauty of it is that some sort of rest is often at hand to use with the physical positions that, by themselves, are not desirable. The human body is wobbly to start with and becomes much more jumpy during the excitement of the shot. Nothing counteracts the buck-fever tendency as well as a rest.

I have yet to meet the serious deer hunter who is not occasionally subject to momentary jitters when taking a shot at a buck. The serious hunter is the one who gets a supreme thrill out of deer hunting; if there were no thrill, he wouldn't go. It follows that if there is a thrill, the hunter enjoying the excitement is subject to some degree of shakes. Veterans are able to control the malady because they don't blow their cool as easily as inexperienced hunters and because they have confidence in their shooting ability. But they're well aware that nothing quiets the nerves like shooting from a rest.

Most rests are improvised, but some can be planned. I use one that I've never seen used by another hunter. When building a blind stand in whitetail country, I often stretch a taut wire around the trees that form my blind boundaries. The wire is at rifle-resting height when I'm sitting in the blind. Regardless of the direction in which I spot a deer I can slide my rifle over the taut wire. I thereby have an immediate and soft rest.

Another good trick is to nail reasonably solid limbs or weathered boards around a blind stand at rifle-holding height.

Improvised rests can be utilized almost anywhere. In the West, you sometimes can use sagebrush for a handy rest. The trick is to place a hat or jacket on a bush, settle the rifle down on it, and touch off. Standers in whitetail country are often careful to select stands adjacent to stumps or windfalls that will make excellent rests. A reasonably solid rest can be gained most anywhere in deer country by grabbing the trunk of a small tree, then laying your rifle over your wrist. In some areas, rock outcroppings or large stones make natural rests. But keep in mind that if you shoot off a solid surface, you should pad your rifle with a cap, gloves, or other soft object. Without such padding, your rifle will recoil upward and send your bullet high.

THE RIGHT RIFLE

You may have noted that nowhere in this chapter have I gone into the subject that has drawn so much ink from gun writers: "The Right Deer Rifle—East and West." I happen to disagree with the theory that Eastern whitetail hunters should go with a light fast-pointing rifle and the Western hunter should go with a flat-shooting heavier rifle. For one thing, there are some long-range shooting opportunities in the East, and there are a lot of mule-deer shot at short ranges in the West.

In fact, North American deer are hunted in more places and over more types of terrain than any other big-game animal by far. This fact suggests that it's simply impossible to conclude that any one deer rifle is the "best" anywhere. If one rifle in one caliber was the best in a given area, most deer hunters in that area would be using a specific gun and cartridge combination. You just don't see this situation in deer woods today.

What you do see are more and more hunters going to bolt-action rifles that shoot high-velocity cartridges. This modern trend is noticeable everywhere in deer country—East, West, or in between. I think the reason is that the "brush-buster" myth has been exposed, that such supposed truths as the advantages of the semiautomatic have not proved to be realistic, and that many of today's traveling hunters want a rifle and cartridge combination that works reasonably well in both East and West.

The important point is that the ease-of-use offered by modern rifles, and the ballistics offered by modern cartridges, have significantly narrowed the advantages and disadvantages long claimed in the East-West controversy. It's a controversy that just isn't very important anymore. And one of the main reasons, one I mentioned earlier, is that any rifle can be a good deer rifle if the hunter who uses it is a good deer hunter. Go with a modern rifle shooting a modern high-velocity bullet in the 100- to 150-grain bracket, and you'll be well-armed wherever you hunt deer.

SHOTGUNS

Another subject I haven't mentioned in this chapter is the use of shotguns loaded with slugs or buckshot. I've never hunted deer with a shotgun, but I've talked with a lot of hunters in farm country who are limited by law to the use of these firearms. The serious ones tell me that the specially barreled slug guns equipped with low-power scopes are quite accurate out to 100 yards. They claim that regular-choked shotguns shooting slugs lose accuracy at about 50 yards, and that the use of buckshot ought to be outlawed.

The thing with buckshot is that it's extremely dangerous. A shotgun shooting buckshot sprays lethal balls in several flight patterns. Your chance of hitting someone are far higher with nine or more balls than with one slug. Further, you can aim a slug. Your chance of hitting a deer at point of aim with buckshot is practically zero. Nobody can tell exactly where buckshot will hit a deer.

If you want to be a serious deer hunter and you hunt where rifles are legal, don't even consider using a shotgun. Your investment in a good rifle and scope will average out to very few dollars per hunting season if you have a reasonable number of hunting years ahead of you. If you're limited by state or county laws to the use of a shotgun for your deer hunting, you'll be wise to invest in one of the specially barreled slug guns and a low-power scope.

Bad-Weather Scopes and Sights

Jim Carmichel

Iused to have horrible nightmares about a huge bear attacking me in the misty North Woods. I was armed with a powerful rifle and would have been able to save myself, except that when I tried to shoot at the snarling beast, my aim was blocked by a fogged scope. I must have read too many hunting stories about the "big one that got away" because the hunter's scope was fogged, waterlogged, frosted, or mildewed.

In the old days, it was an article of faith that a scope would fog every time a cloud crossed the sky, so outdoor writers busied themselves composing desperate-sounding articles on how hunters could bag a buck or bull even though their telescopic sights were on the fritz. Nowadays we don't see such articles, because they are as out of date as leaky scopes. In fact, this chapter may be about the last I'll have to say on the subject of bad-weather sights.

I wish that for dramatic effect I could tell a heart-rending tale of how I once leveled my rifle at the all-time biggest buck, only to find my scope rendered useless by a severe case of fogging, but it has never happened to me.

Once when I was bear hunting along the Alaskan coast, a giant wave overturned my skiff and dumped my rifle in a few feet of ocean. The salt water was tough on my rifle, but the scope remained in perfect working order.

I've carried scoped rifles to the summits of Asian mountains, across parched deserts, and through sweltering tropic swamps without once having a scope let me down. It's really not worth mentioning, but I *did* once own a German-made scope of high repute that leaked like a gutter-spout. It carried so much water that I called it my "canteen." But to be fair, it was a pre-war model, and scopes built then weren't expected to be moisture-proof. Since I knew its faults, I never mounted it on a big-game rifle.

The only times I've had a scope get even temporarily out of order were when a plug of snow blocked the lens or when big drops of water on the outside of the lens made viewing difficult. In either situation, a quick wipe set things right. All in all, dust has caused me more scope problems than rain and snow combined. But more about this later.

I'm sure the reason I've had such unblemished success with telescopic sights is that I use good-quality, modern scopes. This is not to say that all modern scopes assure trouble-free service. I get a lot of mail from shooters here and overseas complaining about scopes that went wrong at the worst possible moment. Virtually all the gripes involve off-beat brands hustled by fly-by-night operators. A good rule of thumb when buying a scope: If you never heard of the brand, you're probably better off without it. A few years ago it was considered wise to avoid Japanese makes. But today, some Japanese brands are really excellent. Others are as bad as ever.

Fogging is caused by water droplets that form inside a scope when the temperature drops. At normal temperatures, this moisture is not visible because water vapor is suspended in the warm air inside the scope. But take the scope out on a cold day, and the air inside the scope contracts and creates beads of water on the inside of the scope. Sometimes this condensation only partially coats the lenses, allowing some vision through the scope, but usually the lenses are so heavily coated that the scope is made useless.

THE FOGLESS SCOPE

Good modern scopes are filled with a dry gas, usually nitrogen. Then they are sealed so that moist air

96

cannot get inside. This is why it is vitally important that telescopic sights never be taken apart except at the factory. Since unauthorized tinkering with scopes is the major cause of fogging and most other problems, some manufacturers have begun making "one-way" scopes that can be disassembled only with special tools.

If you own a scope that is prone to fogging or leaking, my advice is simply to replace it with one of the new fog-proof models. Scopes are relatively inexpensive, so it's poor economy to try to get by with an antique.

QUICK RELEASE AND PIVOTS

Back before fog-proofing techniques were developed, a scope was considered a fair-weather friend at best. Old-timers will recall that makers of scope mounts were not as interested in designing and manufacturing mounts that were strong and simple as they were in making mounts that permitted the scope to be instantly removed. With these "quick-detachable" mounts, the hunter could jerk the bum scope out of the way and aim with the rifle's open sights.

During the last half of the 1940's, there must have been a score of various quick-detachable scope mounts on the market, all assuring the buyer that his troublesome scope could be instantly snatched out of the way and that the ever-faithful open sights would save the day. Firearms writers of that blissful era were especially fond of speculating, in print, on what iron or open sight combination went best with what scopes and mounts.

The more esoteric combinations were found on custom-made rifles that featured a neat little felt-lined compartment in the butt of the stock just under the buttplate. Access to this compartment was through a spring-loaded trap door in the buttplate, and its purpose was to house part of a "peep" sight mounted on the receiver. With the disabled scope removed, the "peep" slide was taken from the butt

Of all the methods of protecting scope lenses, I prefer "flip-up" covers. They're made for all makes and models of scopes and are operated by pressing release buttons.

and inserted into the mounted housing. In seconds, the rifle was restored to action. A hunter who owned such a rig was considered fortunate indeed. Trap-door buttplates now have become quite the rage among custom rifle makers, but I'm not sure if anyone remembers that they were often used for this purpose.

The best of the old quick-release mounts, at least the ones that survive, are the Pachmayr and Weaver pivot-type mounts and the Griffin & Howe lever-release type. The pivot mounts do not actually release the scope but allow it to swing aside so that the open sights can be seen. The G & H lever mount, which has been copied in various ways, utilizes a rail-like fixture mounted on the left side of the receiver. The scope rings straddle the rail and are held in place by lever-activated clamps. When the lever(s) is turned, the scope slides off, leaving the top of the receiver free and clear for instant iron-sight action.

When I was planning for my first African safari, I had my .458 Winchester Magnum rifle outfitted with a set of the beautifully machined G & H-type mounts made by LanDav of Falls Church, Virginia. This rifle was to be my "heavy" for use on lions, elephants, and the deadly Cape buffalo. Since I figured I would be forever getting into tight situations with dangerous game, my plan was to slip off the scope and use the open express sights if the need arose.

After several safaris, I've bagged lions, a half-dozen tuskers, and upwards of three score buffalo with this rifle, but not once have I removed the scope! And I've had my share of shooting at close quarters. There was a time or two when I might have removed the scope if I had thought of it, or had time, but when dangerous game is after you, you've something more to occupy your thoughts than taking the scope off your rifle.

I presently own three or four rifles with the G & H lever-release scope-mount system. Though I freely

Factory inspector puts Redfield scope through pressure tests to check for leaks. A leak would allow the escape of the antifogging inert gas.

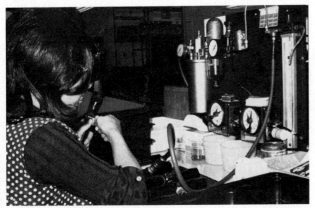

admit I never need to remove the scopes (except to show folks how it works), they're fun to have around because they are nicely made and look good on a fine rifle. Lenard Brownell, the well-known custom rifle maker, manufactures a neat-looking adaptation of the basic lever-release system that attaches to slender blocks on the top of the receiver, thus avoiding the difficult side-mounting arrangement.

Nice as it may be, the quick-release scope-mounting system is going out of style simply because we are running out of reasons to remove our scopes.

The telescopic sight has become the best all-purpose, all-weather sight you can use for every type of hunting that calls for a well-aimed shot. Be it a drizzle, downpour, or snowstorm, if you can see the target at all, you'll see it better with a scope. A few years ago, I spent some time comparing open sights, peeps, and scopes in different sorts of bad weather. In every trial, I was amazed at how quickly heavy snow or rain reduced or eliminated the usefulness of both open and peep sights. Peep sights are the worst in rain because a web of water quickly spreads across the rear-sight aperture. Snow quickly blocks open sights because a single flake of snow or bead of water is enough to block the rear notch. Of course each of these blockages can be quickly cleared away, but perhaps not in the time span it takes a deer to vanish.

LENS COVERS

Scopes can be used, even when the lenses are streaked with rain or specked with snow. This simply does not happen if protective lens covers are used. With any of the various lens-protectors available today, a scope becomes completely efficient during even the worst conditions. I prefer the "flip-up" covers such as those manufactured by the Butler Creek Company of Jackson, Wyoming. These are made for all makes and models of scopes and are operated by pressing release buttons. The spring-loaded caps jump out of the way instantly. Other types include models that fit more snugly over the lens. Do-it-yourselfers can make very effective lens protectors simply by cutting a two-inch-wide "rubberband" from a section of automobile inner-tube. Stretched around the scope, front to rear, the big rubberband tightly seals and protects both lenses and is quickly removable.

Some makes of scopes come factory-equipped with lens covers. These and other such covers do a good job of protecting lenses and keeping them free of dust during storage or traveling. But under hunting conditions, they are too slow to remove, and this is why I prefer the speedy flip-up type. The transparent plastic covers sometimes cause problems of their own making. For best results, plan on aiming through naked scope lenses.

Aside from the obvious advantage of keeping drops of water off your scope lens, covers also protect lenses from dust. Dust is a two-pronged evil: it can reduce visibility through the scope, and it can

also do permanent damage to lenses. Late one afternoon when I was hunting along the edge of the dry and dusty Kalahari Desert, a beautiful kudu bull charged out of the brush and went prancing across a fairly open space about 200 yards wide. It might have been an easy shot, but when I leveled my rifle on him, all I saw was a reddish haze of reflected sunlight. The sun, low on the horizon, was glinting off the thousands of tiny diamonds of dust accumulated on the front lens. As it turned out, I got the kudu, but only after my guide shaded the scope with his hat.

Dust can damage the coating on a lens, thus impairing its optical quality. This often happens when the lens is wiped with a handkerchief. The abrasive dust cuts the lens surface like sandpaper. Such scrubbings, if repeated often enough, cause permanent damage. The correct way to clean a lens is with alcohol and soft cotton balls, or with a soft-hair lens brush. But who's likely to have these handy when they're really needed? The best remedy, again, is lens covers.

One valid reason for having an alternate aiming system on a scoped rifle is to provide for situations in which the shooter has difficulty in finding the target through the scope. This sometimes happens, paradoxically, when the target is too close, or on moving shots, but it usually happens because the shooter is inexperienced or the scope is poorly matched to the rifle.

SEE-THROUGHS

Various "see-through" or tunneled scope mounts are available. They permit the shooter to aim with his open sights while looking *under* the scope. Usually the scope bases are pierced with see-through "tunnels" as much as an inch wide. Other models achieve the same effect by attaching to the side of the rifle rather than to the top.

This system is in some ways superior to the quick-detachable or pivot mount, especially in that the scope is permanently secured to the rifle by a simple but sturdy mount. The disadvantage is that the scope must be mounted too high for efficient aiming. Many hunters who have trouble aiming with a scope are really suffering from an excessively high mounting system or a stock with a comb that is too low.

This doesn't mean the see-through mounts made by Weaver, Kwik-site, Holden, and others can't be used. The trick is to match the system to the rifle. For example, if you are contemplating a see-through mount on a new 99 Savage lever gun, the smart move would be to buy the model with the Monte Carlo comb. This should elevate your eye enough to compensate for the additional scope height. Most makes and models of rifles can be bought in either a high-comb configuration or a Monte Carlo version. So keep this in mind when selecting your rig if you intend to use a see-through mount. It will make your shooting easier and a lot more effective.

Optics
for Hunters

Tom Gresham

Smart hunters spend a lot of time looking for game. In fact, a hunter's success usually depends on seeing the animal before it sees him. Good optics allow a big-game hunter to size up trophy heads at a distance, saving himself long stalks over rough ground. He can plan a stalk by carefully glassing the terrain between himself and a trophy, or identify a movement or a shape in thick brush.

Besides riflescopes, the main optical helpers of a big-game hunter are binoculars and spotting scopes. Binoculars can be used at any range farther than 25 yards, and a spotting scope is generally used to size up trophy heads at greater distance.

Keep in mind when you shop for optical equipment that you should always buy the best you can afford. Optics, as an optical engineer told me, is an inflexible science. Corners cut in manufacturing to cut cost invariably means lower quality.

If you understand optical terms, you'll be better equipped to intelligently compare models and choose the binoculars or spotting scopes that are best for your hunting needs. Power, relative brightness, field of view, and focusing are important.

Power is the magnification of objects being viewed. A seven-power binocular, written $7\times$, makes an object appear seven times as large as it appears without the binoculars. Binoculars used by hunters range from $6\times$ to $10\times$. Spotting scopes usually range from $15\times$ to $45\times$.

Some hunters think that high power makes binoculars better. But high powers have disadvantages too. Generally speaking, the higher the magnifica-

Optics for hunters: From left, rubber-coated spotting scope, 8 × 20 roof-prism binoculars, compact 6 × 24 Porro-prism glasses, wide angle 7 × 35 Porro prisms, 8 × 30 waterproof roof prisms, 10 ×40 roof prisms. Roof prisms are usually smaller; Porro prisms sometimes offer better dollar value.

Spotting scopes, because of high magnification, should rest on something solid. A tripod is best, but crown of hat or bean bag made from old pant leg will also work just fine.

tion, the smaller the field of view, and the dimmer the image. It's also harder to hold higher-power binoculars steady, and high power magnifies shakiness. Because it's more difficult to make high-power binoculars than medium-power ones, a pair of top-quality 10× glasses might cost much more than a pair of comparable-quality 7× glasses.

The amount of light available to your eyes is as important as the magnification of the binoculars or scope. This is partly determined by the size of the exit pupil, the circle of light you see in the eyepiece when you hold the optic a foot from your eye. The greater the diameter of the exit pupil, the better the light-gathering ability of a binocular. The diameter is determined by dividing the diameter of the objective lens (the one farthest from the eye) by the magnification. For example, a 7×35 binocular, with 7× magnification and 35-mm. objective lens, has a 5-mm. exit pupil.

Field of view is the area seen through the viewing instrument. Higher magnification generally means a narrower field of view, although wide-angle binoculars are available. A wide field of view enables a hunter to glass more country and makes it easier to keep running game in view.

Binoculars are available with central or individual focusing. A single knurled wheel between the barrels focuses central-focusing binoculars. An adjustable eyepiece on one of the barrels compensates for differences in an individual's eyes. This is the quickest and most popular focusing method.

Each eyepiece of individual-focusing binoculars must be focused separately. Although these glasses are much slower to focus, they are generally more water- and dust-resistant. In fact, some individual-focus binoculars are guaranteed waterproof.

When you select a binocular for hunting, you must balance the factors of weight, magnification, brightness, and cost. For most hunting and general use, a 7× or 8× magnification serves well. But consider special situations. The small 6× glasses I use when hunting in thick woods are invaluable. For glassing long distances over open plains or in mountains, 9× or 10× might be best. You can minimize shakiness by using some type of rest: Steady your binoculars on the saddle of your horse as you stand next to it, or sit with your elbows propped or

Cutaway shows roof-prism binoculars, sometimes costly but light and compact. (Bushnell photo)

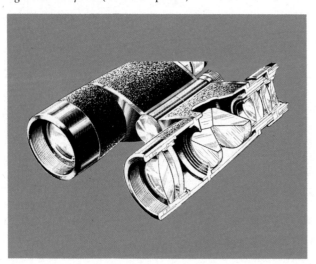

Porro-prism design corrects lens image through multiple reflections. (Bausch & Lomb photo)

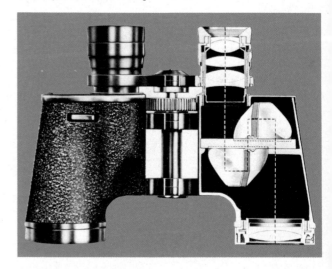

raised knees. When looking at something on or below your level, you can even lie prone.

Binoculars come in two basic designs: roof prism and Porro prism. Both kinds of prism systems turn the inverted lens image right side up so you see the correct orientation as you look through the glasses. The difference is in the way they do it, and it almost takes an optical engineer to explain. Both are capable of delivering a good, sharp image. The Porro system tends to be bulkier and heavier than the roof-prism system, but Porro-prism binoculars are also generally cheaper than roof-prism designs.

There's a great deal of overlap in size, quality, and price. If you hunt in situations where bulk and

To steady binoculars, place your thumbs under and against your cheek bones.

weight are critical, you'll probably be glad to invest extra dollars in a compact binocular, whichever prism system you choose. And if you don't mind extra ounces, you can probably save some money.

Once you decide on the design and magnification, it's time to look at some models in the store. First, buy only binoculars that have all the glass elements coated. To make sure, look for the words "all coated" or "100 percent coated" in the accompanying literature. Coating increases light transmission, and that's helpful during the game-active first and last minutes of the day.

The binoculars you choose should feel good in your hands. This is why it's important to handle them. When you've narrowed your selection down to two or three models, you can determine right in the store which is sharpest. Place a page from a magazine or newspaper (something you haven't read before) on a wall. Back away about 25 feet, and look through one model of binoculars. Move toward the page slowly, refocusing as you go. When you can first read the text type mark that place on the

floor. Do the same with each model you are considering. If all are the same magnification, the binoculars that let you read the words from the greatest distance are the sharpest.

Most people don't know how to correctly focus an optical instrument. If you just twist the focusing knob, your eyes will be changing focus while you try to get the image sharp. It then appears sharp due to the combination of your eyes changing and the binoculars focusing. This causes eyestrain as your eyes struggle to keep the image focused.

The right way to focus is to look, without the glasses, at some distant object. Then glance back through the glasses to see if the image is focused correctly. If not, continue glancing away and refocusing as your view returns to the magnified image.

Besides resting binoculars on something solid, you can steady them by placing your thumbs right under and against your cheekbones as you hold the glasses, anchoring them to your skull so that they move together.

If you wear eyeglasses, keep them on when using binoculars. Be sure to buy a binocular with retractable or fold-down eye cups for a full field of view while wearing glasses.

The Spotting Scope

A spotting scope is a specialized instrument of higher magnification than binoculars. Varmint hunters, big-game hunters, and competitive shooters use spotting scopes.

Although most scopes are available with variable-power eyepieces, the fixed-power, interchangeable eyepieces are still the most popular. The main reason is that the variables still aren't quite as sharp as the fixed powers. A 15× or 20× eyepiece is usually screwed onto the spotting scope for trying to locate big game. To check out a head that looks interesting, a more powerful lens, maybe 30× to 45×, is useful. The higher powers are hard to use when there is heat mirage or atmospheric haze.

Because of its high magnification, a spotting scope must be rested on something solid. A small tripod, although ideal, may be hard to carry into the outback. The crown of a Western hat is often used, with varying degrees of success. Borrow a trick from photographers and make a bean bag out of a discarded pant leg. Place the bag on something solid, and nestle the scope into the bag. This is as steady as a tripod and a lot easier to carry around.

Top-quality optics, the only kind worth having, don't require much maintenance. Try not to expose them to severe dust or moisture. However, good binoculars will take a lot of abuse. Clean the lenses whenever needed, but don't do it with a T-shirt. Only three things should touch the lenses of fine optical instruments: a soft camel's-hair brush, lens tissue designed for cleaning camera lenses, and air.

Keep spotting scopes in cases when not in use, but keep binoculars around your neck whenever you're hunting. Binoculars in a case never helped a hunter see anything.

PART 5

OUTDOOR LORE IMPROVES YOUR ODDS

The Complete Tree-Stand Hunter—Gun and Bow

Glenn Helgeland

One peculiarity of hunting is that a technique common and valued in one region may be totally unknown, ignored, or illegal in another. For many years, this was especially true of tree stands. They have always been popular in the South but not even legal in Michigan until 1974. They have been regarded by some as unfair because they are above game animals' normal scent and vision defenses. Yet those same people probably would hunt in mountains by climbing high and then shooting down—because that's the smart way to hunt in mountains.

The use of tree stands—especially portable ones—is now accepted in the Northeast and Midwest, but this status has come within only the past few years. Tree-stand hunting has been a much-used and often necessary technique for many years for firearm and bowhunters in the South. Vegetation there often is so thick you can't see into it unless you are up in the air. In the West, tree stands aren't as popular, because mountain geography lets you get above the game. In parts of the West, it's also often hard to find a tree large enough to place a stand, and game animals don't follow distinct trails as often as whitetail deer do in the Midwest, East, and South.

A tree stand can help your hunting in several ways:

- It can put you above the game animal's normal line of vision and scent. This is highly desirable because most expert hunters believe a game animal must have two of its three lines of defense (eyes, ears, nose) alerted before it will spook, whereas alerting only one sense may create curiosity and work to your benefit.

- Tree-stand hunting disperses your scent pattern above ground-level air currents. Since warm air rises, this keeps your scent up and spreads it over a wider range.
- Tree stands let you look down into dense vegetation and see game approaching sooner than you would from ground level.
- They let you hunt where no ground cover is available and where the artificial placing of cover would alert game.
- Tree stands can make you less noticeable to game and other hunters than a ground blind—if your tree stand is well-placed and unobtrusive. However, an overdone tree mansion can stick out like a sore thumb.
- They make wind direction less important than when you use a ground blind.
- You have more freedom in choosing hunting position. Portable stands can easily be moved until you find the best position to take game. You can also move as food sources change, such as from alfalfa to acorns. This is especially critical for bowhunters, who must get much closer to game than gun hunters.

You can use either a portable or permanent tree stand; the portable ones come in climbing and non-climbing models. Permanent tree stands have been around the longest. They can be comfortable and safe. Once erected, they don't need to be carried into the woods each time.

The best permanent-stand setup is three trees close together so you can erect a triangular frame for the platform. Wire or spike a 2 × 4-inch frame to the trees, and make the platform from one-inch lumber or plywood. Lumber is the easiest to carry and work with. You'll probably use boards for steps. Nail them to two trees so they won't swivel when you step on them. Place them close together; when you're wearing heavy clothing, you'll take only short climbing steps. Nail some scrap carpeting on the platform to quiet your movements. Add to this a chair or stool, and you can sit comfortably for hours.

Rifle hunters may want to build a wood wall or rail around the stand for security and to use as a rifle rest. Some vegetation tied around it will help camouflage it, as long as the vegetation remains fresh and doesn't look like a Christmas tree suddenly sprouted in thin air. Beware of overdoing it. Bowhunters would be better off to use for security a safety belt fastened to the tree and to their midriff. Several manufacturers make them. They're better than tying yourself in with a rope, because they have quick-release buckles that you can flip if you have problems. If you're tied in with a rope and the stand falls, you're hung up in midair. A railing would get in the way of a bow.

How large should a permanent stand be? It should be large enough to be comfortable without

PORTABLE TREE STANDS *usually should be eight to 12 feet above ground, although some hunters like to be 20 feet or more up. A stand should be about 10 to 25 yards from a trail for bowhunters, probably more for gunhunters. The right distance allows a good shot without spooking the game. Secure yourself with a safety belt so you won't fall, and sit in a position that enables you to shoot with least movement.*

NATURAL TREE STANDS *can be used if limb formations allow you to sit or stand in reasonable comfort. Use caution when climbing a tree, especially in wet weather, because bark can become extremely slippery.*

PERMANENT STANDS *can be safest and most comfortable, but their use is restricted in many states and they also can advertise good hunting spots. Three trees or limbs make a good triangular base; two trees or limbs with support boards nailed on opposite sides of each can also provide base for a platform.*

inhibiting shooting or being an eyesore in the woods. If you make it at least 2 × 2 feet, it will give you room for a seat, keep your legs from becoming cramped, and permit turning.

The fact that permanent stands are always there is comforting, but their permanence makes them less convenient, and less versatile than portable stands. You won't want to build one everywhere you want to hunt. That can be a lot of work and can get expensive. And if you don't have permanent access to land, it may be senseless to build them anyway.

Although most states allow permanent tree stands on private land, some have never allowed them anywhere. Most states have detailed regulations on what you can drive nails into and what you can do to vegetation on private and public land.

It's absolutely essential, before you take any action on tree stands, to closely check state regulations (and—if you'll hunt on federal land—federal regulations) on stand use, tree-step use, and so on.

Nails and wire left in trees could wreak havoc with a saw blade if that timber is taken to a sawmill. Oversize stands can be aesthetically unpleasing, and a permanent stand tells every other hunter that here is a good place to hunt. With more hunters becoming aware of the potential of elevated stands, why advertise the locations of your most productive hunting spots?

Of the two styles of portable stands—climbing or non-climbing—your choice depends on several conditions: personal preference, tree types in the area you hunt, your physical ability, stand weight and bulkiness, how often you will move the stand, state laws, and who owns the land.

Climbing stands should be used only on mature trees that have thick bark or on trees that have hard or thick bark at all stages of growth. Soft-bark trees—such as pines, poplars, and young maples—can suffer severe and sometimes fatal damage if the tree-gripping devices on the climbing stand bruise or cut the inner cambium layer of bark.

Trees with slick, loose, or scaly bark—such as some ash, hickory, and pines—can be tricky to climb. On loose-bark trees, bits of bark under gripping segments of the stand can pop loose and send you skidding down the tree fast. Smooth-bark trees also can be difficult to climb, since they are hard to grasp firmly with your arms and can't provide a firm grip for the tree stand. Beveled-metal gripping edges on climbing stands and hand climbers need to be sharp enough to grip the tree, but not so sharp that they cut the bark like a knife. Some stands avoid this problem by using a rubber sleeve on the support arm and leather bushings on the platform, where it butts against the tree.

Climbing can be difficult in other ways, too. For example, gripping a tree with just your arms and hands isn't easy for many persons. You can scrape and bruise your chest, arms, and hands—especially if you slip. It helps if you are in good physical condition. The average person, with experience, will find it easier to climb using a climbing tree stand. But you still must have the strength to lift your lower body, legs, and tree stand without slipping.

Some hunters can climb all afternoon and seem to slide down four feet for every three they go up. This can happen because of poor physical conditioning, or from placing your weight wrong on the stand. The gripper units of a stand need to be seated firmly against a tree trunk when you lower your feet and the stand into a gripping position. If you just lean the grippers against the bark lightly, or if you place your weight too close to the tree trunk, you have more chance of slipping. Keep your weight out from the tree as much as possible; this tactic gives more leverage on the platform and a firmer grip against the tree.

If you slip, the consequences could be far worse than bruises. An archery-shop owner I know had a customer who tried a new stand on an old telephone pole that was scarred by climbing spikes. He got all the way to the top, but then he let the unit slip. He slid all the way to the bottom with his arms and body clasped to the pole. The man had slivers in places neither he nor his doctor knew could be reached by wood.

If you have trouble holding onto a tree with your arms and hands, try a hand-climbing tool. The ones on the market work on the same principle as a tree stand.

Non-climbing tree stands came into their own when manufacturers began outfitting them with above-the-platform support arms. Earlier versions generally had a support bar under the platform to jab into the tree trunk. These earlier support arms often slipped, dropping a hunter like a stone. Later versions often had a chain to loop around the tree to hold the support arm, but this wasn't secure enough.

On the newer above-the-platform supports, chains (rubber-coated or uncoated) or straps or ropes hold the stand's upper support arms as the hunter's weight pushes the platform frame—which is notched or has a shallow V—against the tree.

When shopping for a tree stand, consider these factors:

- Types of trees in your hunting area. If there are no branches less than 30 feet from the ground, you'll need a climbing stand or climbing steps of some kind to go with a non-climbing stand. If a tree has many branches, a climbing stand just wouldn't be feasible.

  If your hunting area has plenty of almost-adequate natural tree stands, you may find a non-climbing stand works best, since you can pull it into the tree and place it in position. Sitting on a branch may be easier and may mean carrying less gear, but it's not worth it if it restricts your shooting.

- Presence of a seat. You definitely can bend

and twist more easily on your feet, but how long can you comfortably stand? Sitting on the platform can limit your shooting range, especially if you bowhunt. An attached seat is the all-around best.

- Tree-stand size. The larger they are, the more comfortable they are to stand, sit, and move on, but the heavier they'll be. The weight of portable stands, especially climbing stands, is important when carrying the stand to your hunting site and when climbing the tree. In both cases, the less the weight of the stand you use—without sacrificing strength—the better off you are. Platforms range from about 15 inches square to roughly 24 × 32 inches. Most are roughly 16 inches by 22 inches. Prices generally range from $25 to $90.
- Damage to a tree. Will the parts of the stand that contact the tree gouge or cut the bark, or will they hold firmly without doing any damage?

This may seem like a minor point, but tree damage could provoke landowner complaints, and that could attract the attention of game officers. Because of the increasing use of tree stands, they are attracting more attention from game agencies in states that have tough laws against tree damage and in states where tree stands are new or their use is booming.

Anti-hunters are taking notice, too. Jim Baker, manufacturer of the Baker climbing tree stand, got a letter from a 13-year-old girl who said she and her friends were tearing down every tree stand they could find in the woods.

Despite growing interest in tree stands, they aren't for everyone, even if geography and vegetation are suitable. If you're not in good shape, a climbing stand may be out of the question and a climb to install a non-climbing stand may be more than you care for. If you are afraid of height, stay out of trees. And if you put a stand in a limber tree, you'll soon find out whether you're susceptible to motion sickness as the tree sways on a windy day.

There are safety factors to consider. Damp weather can make any tree stand dangerous. Wet wood is slippery—tree bark, steps, and stand platform. A non-skid surface or carpeting on the platform will help. So will rough soles on your shoes.

For non-climbing stands, you may want to hook the attachment bracket or chain over a branch, as well as around the trunk, to keep it from slipping. Fasten yourself into the stand with a safety belt if you don't have a rail or wall, because you can fall asleep on a warm autumn afternoon. The safety belt will also give you something to lean against when you shoot. And it will keep you from walking right off the stand when you hit a deer and forget you're not standing on the ground. This has happened—with serious injuries.

Always use a rope to pull your tackle into the stand after you have climbed up. Don't try to climb a tree with a bow or rifle in your hands. You can carry your rifle on a sling over your shoulder, but hauling it up butt-first with a rope is safer and easier and probably will scratch up the finish less. Lower your tackle to the ground with the same rope, and swing that gear off to the side just before it touches down. This tactic will get it out of your way in case you slip and fall as you're climbing down.

If you plan to be in your tree stand for several hours, take a plastic bucket along for nature calls. Urinating on the ground would mark your location as surely as a fox marks its territory the same way. Be careful of odorous foods, too. Your elevation may help dispense scents, but there's no sense stretching your luck.

Stand location is more critical for bowhunters than for hunters who use guns. For both types of hunting, position the stand where it will get you the most and best shots.

If you're using a bow, find the intersection of two deer trails or runs. The more trails you watch, the better your chances of seeing game. Try to be 15 to

Study your stand area well enough so you'll know in advance which direction thermal currents will be flowing when the hunting gets good. If thermal currents continue to blow upward in late afternoon, then obviously you should place your stand above the trail. But what if thermals generally switch about half an hour before quitting time? Then you'll have your scent blowing toward the trail. The reverse is true for morning thermals and moving stand locations. And, naturally, when general winds overpower ground thermals, set your stand downwind of the trail or trails.

A general rule is that thermals are downward in the morning and upward in late afternoon. But hilly terrain can change that pattern, especially where sun hits one side of a valley or ridge earlier than another. And if your desired stand location is halfway up the ridge side, the thermal may be right for a while, then wrong for a while. So it's very important to scout thoroughly. Then you know and can be in the right position at the right time.

20 yards off the trail if possible, and at least eight feet high (ground level to your stand, not to eye level). You may want to go higher if you need to see down into vegetation or if vegetation is sparse and you want to get further above the game's normal line of vision. I do most of my tree-stand hunting in the late afternoon, trying to catch deer coming out to feed. In the morning, get on stand between the feeding and bedding areas before the deer return from feeding. This is more difficult than in the afternoon because you have to move in the dark, often

through heavy cover in order to get to your tree stand.

Locate your stand back from fields because you'll see game earlier in the afternoon, which will allow you to get a better shot. The game wouldn't be quite as wary as it would on the edge of a field, and you'd be more likely to see a buck. During the rut, try to set up along a line of scrapes and be there for as long as daylight and your patience allow. Scrapes, incidentally, are areas about two feet square, usually sandy, that are often located in semi-clearings or on ridgetops. A buck scrapes these areas clean and urinates in them during the rut. This action identifies him and warns other bucks. It also attracts does in heat. So the scrape is an attractant and a territorial marker. Bucks will also chew on twigs directly above the scrape as another marker. The does urinate in these scrapes, too, to leave their scent marker, which the buck can follow from the scrape to

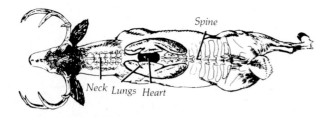

Top view of buck shows how vital organs would appear from above. Note deer's vital organs, when viewed from a tree stand, are farther back than most hunters might think.

wherever the doe waits. Bucks check their scrapes regularly, day and night, during the rutting season.

Follow the same basic principles in locating your stand when you hunt with a rifle, but get back from the trails a little farther and try to cover as much territory as possible. Consider the carrying distance of a bullet, and be extremely careful where you put your stand. Avoid long-range areas such as the edges of fields; if you're in open areas, you probably won't need a tree stand anyway. If you're in thick woods, shooting will probably be short-range, so you'll be shooting down to the ground.

Wherever you place a stand, avoid locations that would make your silhouette stand out. True, the hunting platforms of Texas can make you look like a bird on a perch, but many of them have enclosed housing to conceal you, and the thick brush may obscure the stand from below.

When bowhunting from a tree stand, camouflage yourself as well as if you were on the ground. A game animal seldom looks up, but it can—especially if there is an alarming reflection or movement. The more deer are hunted from tree stands, the more wary they seem to become of certain trees along their trails and of a threat from above.

To make sure a stand won't squeak and alarm the game, settle it in by leaning in several directions and

placing your weight on various parts of the platform when you first get into it.

Shooting from a tree stand gives a different visual perspective than shooting from the ground. To many people, game appears smaller or farther away than it really is. Just as in downhill shooting, tree-stand shooting tends to make most people shoot high. Aim lower than you think you should, and concentrate on an exact aiming point. Bowhunters often aim at "the deer," because they're excited when one comes within 20 yards of their stand instead of aiming precisely for the deer's heart and lungs. This loss of concentration tends to make shots go too high and miss entirely.

If you bowhunt, use the heaviest bow draw weight you can *handle properly*. You will be shooting down through heavy bone, such as the spine and bases of ribs, where the game animal's body depth is greater than its width. You want complete penetration for a quick, good blood trail; the heaviest equipment will help. Since trajectory isn't a factor at close ranges, suitably heavy arrows and heavy, strong broadheads are also good to use.

If you need to bend when you shoot a bow, bend only at the waist. If you simply lower your bow arm, you will heel the bow and shoot too high. All hunters should know the exact location of the vital organs of the game; their position can appear different from above. To get a lung shot from above and behind the animal, you must aim at a point of entry farther back than you would if you shot at the animal from the side.

Some hunters prefer to position a stand on the side of the tree opposite from which they expect game to approach. Then when game walks past, it presents a quartering-away angle for the shot.

To get a buck to stop in a good shooting position, you may want to place buck lure or some other scent in a spot along the trail. Put it on the side of the trail opposite your stand so the game will look away when it stops. Buck lure probably won't work unless a buck is in rut. I recommend that you never put buck lure on yourself. It draws attention directly to you. If you want to use it to lay a scent trail, put it on a scrap of cloth pinned to your boots or pants cuff and then leave it on the far side of the trail before you get into your stand.

If you use food scent, use one that's native to the area.

When you approach your stand, stay off the trail that the game uses. Your own scent can alarm them. If you're using a scent to mask your own odor, you can either alarm the game or draw it right to your tree. This is not the best shot, especially when bowhunting. Any extremely close shot is very difficult with a bow, especially when an animal is looking at you.

If you use a tree stand, respect it and its ever-present potential for accidents. When you get careless, that's when you can get hurt. But if you use tree stands right, they can improve the quality of your hunting.

Maps Can Work Wonders

John O. Cartier

A few years ago, in wild tangled country in northern Michigan, a deer hunter walked away from his camp on an overcast morning. He jumped and followed a deer in an area heavily tracked up earlier by other members of his party.

Several hours later, worn out from hiking through swamps and across ridges in deep snow, he lost the deer track and started back to camp.

He was no beginner. He had hunted deer for the better part of 20 years and knew his way around the woods. But he was in country he had never seen until that November, and he had made the grave mistake of not looking at a map at the start of his hunt. He was carrying a compass, but he had only the vaguest notion of where he was and which way to go.

He ran out of matches the first night, slept under logs after that without a fire, circling, wandering, lost in swamps and beaver ponds. He staggered out of the woods onto a road at the end of 72 terrible hours. He came out only six miles from camp, but he had traveled more than 30 miles to get there. He came very close to freezing to death, all for want of taking a good look at a map beforehand.

That ordeal serves perfectly to illustrate the most common and urgent reason deer hunters need maps if they are planning a trip in unfamiliar territory. Similar stories are read in newspapers each fall. But avoiding the trap of getting lost is far from the only reason for utilizing good maps.

Many deer hunters want detailed information on where the action is outside their home states. Letters flow in asking for information on hunting areas in many states and provinces. They also want to know how many types of maps are available. How

good are they? Who distributes them? How much do they cost? What's the latest word in maps that will benefit deer hunters?

THE OVERALL PICTURE

From my research, I was surprised to learn that many state fish-and-game departments have taken a new attitude on maps, an attitude that you'll be happy to hear about.

"Everyone seems to be map-conscious these days," one official in a Western state told me. "Our department is well aware that we haven't been able to supply the outdoorsman with the specific type of maps he needs. Frankly, we've just never had the money to publish all the maps, directories, and charts that the public wants.

"The answer is for state game-and-fish departments to cooperate with federal and private agencies in map production and distribution. We can supply hunting and fishing information—the other agencies can supply engineers, artists, and map-making facilities. The results would be maps that sportsmen would have real use for. That's the approach of many states today."

Right now there isn't any substitute for the U.S. Geological Survey quadrangles when it comes to helping the deer hunter. These maps show topography (relief features and the surface configuration) as no other map does. Some state game-land maps (hotspot areas) show the best hunting and game-concentration lands.

Private enterprise also is recognizing the ever-growing demand by outdoorsmen for accurate maps. Here's what C. Ross Anderson, President of

107

Good maps are the right tools for deer hunters who are trying to discover back-country regions that are naturals for feeding, bedding, and runway areas. The right map is practically indispensable in planning a deer drive.

AAA Engineering and Drafting Company in Salt Lake City, Utah, told me:

"After years of preparing relatively useless recreation maps for various government agencies, our company launched a private mapping program. We cooperate with every private, state, and federal agency that can supply information that answers real needs for the sportsmen. We are working very closely with park services, forest services, U.S. Geological Survey, Bureau of Land Management, state highway departments, tourist and publicity councils, chambers of commerce, snowmobile associations, and so on.

"We have produced several maps of areas in Western states. These maps are indexed to show best action areas, campsites, public lands, accommodations, boat ramps, and just about everything a sportsman wants to know. We hope to produce similar maps covering other areas of the nation. A lot of the information on these maps is excellent for deer hunters."

Another map producer, Clarkson Map Company, produces special recreation maps designed for outdoorsmen in the Midwest. The company has produced several different books of hydrographic (depth contour) lake maps covering the most popular fishing lakes in Michigan, Wisconsin, and Minnesota. Another of their productions is a book of maps covering every county in Michigan. These maps show dozens of legends including campgrounds, roads, trails, and conservation-department units. Similar books of maps cover Wisconsin and Minnesota. You can get details by writing the company at 725 Desnoyer Street, Kaukauna, Wisconsin 54130.

Government agencies are also publishing special-use maps. A good example is the U.S. Bureau of Sport Fisheries and Wildlife map of Waterfowl Pro-

duction Areas in the Midwest. That agency is responsible for the purchase and easement of 300 areas totaling 103,516 acres of wetlands in North Dakota. The areas are managed to provide the most favorable conditions for duck reproduction and to provide opportunities for hunting waterfowl, upland birds, and deer. The areas are open to free hunting and are not to be confused with refuges. You can get these maps by writing the Division of Wildlife Refuges, Federal Building, Fort Snelling, Twin Cities, Minnesota 55111.

WHY ARE GOOD MAPS SO IMPORTANT?

Maps are especially efficient in planning deer drives. I once joined a group of Wisconsin hunters who consider their topographic maps indispensable, not only for a successful hunt but also as safety tools.

Before a drive begins, they spread out a map of the area. Each hunter is shown (by landmark features on the map) where the drive will originate, where it will end, and where each posted hunter will stand. Because of the map, each member of the group knows exactly where to go and what area he should cover. The military-type planning pays off with lots of venison.

Good maps are the right tools for deer hunters who are trying to discover back-country regions that are naturals for feeding, bedding, and runway areas. Whatever your reason for getting off the beaten track, you'll find that maps are your best planning aids.

Another great advantage of carrying maps is that local people can point out hotspot locations. Many times I've had filling-station attendants, farmers, and resort operators pinpoint choice hunting areas when I pulled a map out of my pocket.

Finding an all-purpose map of a specific area is practically impossible. But several maps of the same area obtained from various sources can supply you with a wealth of valuable details.

State game commissions are obligated to put out maps that clarify deer-hunting regulations and the areas of the state to which they pertain. They are economically designed for mass distribution and they show little more than where a sportsman may hunt.

But once you select an area, you can turn to other agencies for detailed terrain information. The Bureau of Land Management, the U.S. Geological Survey, and the U.S. Forest Service are the best bets for maps showing topographic features and public ownership boundaries.

Highway-department maps emphasize all types of roads, driving distances, and locations of towns. County maps go into detail on local trails, streams, and woodlands. If you have all those maps, you have the finest information available.

FEDERAL MAPS

Topographic sheets are sold for a nominal sum by the U.S. Geological Survey. These maps are approximately 16½ × 20 inches and are drawn to scales from one-half inch to two inches per mile, depending on the character of the country charted. Bodies of water are printed in blue, man-made features in black. Features of relief (hills, mountains, and valleys) are indicated by brown contour lines. Woodlands show up in green. These maps are the best available for sportsmen who want to know the lay of the land.

Topographic maps are produced for all areas of the U.S. that have been surveyed. Begin by requesting free index maps on the states of interest. These indexes will show areas covered by quadrangular maps and prices of each. To order maps east of the Mississippi River, including Minnesota, write Branch of Distribution, U.S. Geological Survey, 1200 South Eads St., Arlington, VA 22202. For maps west of the Mississippi, including Alaska and Louisiana, write Branch of Distribution, U.S. Geological Survey, Federal Center, Denver, CO 80225.

The U.S. Forest Service publishes maps of lake and forest regions in the various national forests. Write the U.S. Forest Service, Washington, D.C. 20250 for a key map that shows areas covered. That index lists regional offices from which you can get the detailed maps that interest you.

The Bureau of Land Management (B.L.M.) is a top bet for maps showing lands open to public hunting. Most of the maps are printed in colors denoting public lands, Forest Service lands, state lands, game-and-fish department lands, national wildlife refuges, and private lands. These maps are a boon for sportsmen looking for action areas in the Midwestern and Western states that have large acreages of public-access lands.

Many of the B.L.M. maps cover entire states, but some are limited to sections of states, and these maps carry an amazing wealth of detail. They show all roads (by special symbols), from paved highways down to trails suited only for seasonal travel by four-wheel-drive vehicles. They show power lines, creeks, marshes, township boundaries, railroad tracks, and just about anything else that can be identified. One of these maps, combined with a Geological Survey map of the same area, would give a deer hunter a better picture of the land than an aerial photograph. Write the U.S. Department of Interior, Bureau of Land Management, Washington, D.C. 20240 for details and an index of available maps.

CANADIAN TOPO MAPS

To order Canadian topo maps in various scales from ¾ mile per inch to about 4 miles per inch, request instructions from the Canada Map Office, 615 Booth St., Ottawa, Ontario, Canada KIA OE9.

SPECIFIC HOTSPOT MAPS

Although a topographic and other terrain-feature map gives you a clear picture of physical characteristics, it can't give you any information on hunting hotspots. That information must come from local sources or game-and-fish officials who are close to the scene in their individual states or provinces. Some conservation departments have done a remarkable job of converting their best hunting information into maps and charts.

An official in Nebraska's Game and Parks Commission told me:

"Hunting maps are exceedingly difficult to keep up to date because of the fluctuation of prime hunting areas from year to year. But then we do publish pamphlets showing general hotspots. The pamphlets include maps of the state showing which sections harbor the highest numbers of deer. With this map, a hunter could pinpoint one of the best counties for his hunting area."

Some of the best aids to Minnesota hunters are fire-plan maps. What's a fire-plan map? It's a map drawn from aerial photos and designed primarily to aid in fire prevention and control. It shows all roads, lakes, streams, trails, railroad grades, ponds, and other details including power-transmission lines. Most of the maps cover a 36-square-mile area. The scale is two inches to one mile.

Minnesota's Departments of Natural Resources and Administration are cooperating to make these maps available to sportsmen. They cover most wooded areas of the state. You can get an index of the maps by writing: Documents Section, 140 Centennial Building, St. Paul, MN 55101.

Several excellent maps are available covering Minnesota's famous Boundary Waters Canoe Area. A map folder listing canoe routes and other useful information on the entire Superior National Forest is available free from: Supervisor, Superior National Forest, Box 338, Duluth, MN 55801.

Kansas has a good number of maps on public hunting areas. Various agencies—U.S. Army Corps of Engineers; Bureau of Reclamation; Kansas Park Authority; the Forestry, Fish and Game Commission; and others—have maps that benefit deer hunters.

The commission game-management-area maps, designed principally for hunters, cover most of the state's thirty-plus areas. They're very detailed, showing open hunting lands, roads, streams, camping areas, and so forth. The back side of these maps carries text explaining best hunting techniques, pertinent regulations, and other details that will help the sportsman enjoy himself. Many other states offer similar maps.

From the foregoing information, it's obviously a good idea to direct all your questions about maps to the Information and Education Division in the Conservation Department of the state you're interested in. If they don't have a particular map in supply, they'll know where to get it. Here's another example of what I mean:

"We keep a batch of material that falls under the heading of maps," says Joel Vance of the Missouri Department of Conservation. "Some of it is published by other organizations such as the U.S. Forest Service, the U.S. Army Corps of Engineers, and the Upper Mississippi River Conservation Commission.

"I'd say that Missouri is very well mapped from a deer hunter's standpoint. Outdoorsmen can obtain any of the maps I'm talking about by writing to: Information Department, Missouri Department of Conservation, P.O. Box 1748, Jefferson City, MO 65102."

Here's still another viewpoint from a Western state:

"Our Game and Fish Department publishes very few maps because so many good ones are available from other sources." That's the word I got from that agency's public-relations chief.

"Whenever someone asks for the best deer hunter's map available, I tell them to contact the State Highway Department," he told me. "I'm not talking about road maps. I'm referring to individual county maps that the highway people publish. These maps show remarkable detail, down to seldom-used trails and abandoned farm buildings. They're far more complete than regular highway maps. They sell for $1 or more, depending on size.

"A good bet for particular areas is the state forest maps put out by several colleges and forestry schools in the West. They contain symbols denoting public lands open to hunting, parks closed to hunting, and refuges. Lakes, roads, creeks, and boundary lines are all detailed.

"Another fine map (published by the U.S. Department of Agriculture in Missoula, Montana) shows public hunting areas in most Western states.

"In addition to those publications I'd suggest the Geological Survey and B.L.M. maps. They're hard to beat. Any state conservation agency can tell you where to get maps."

LOCAL MAPS

No matter where you go, it's a good bet that chambers of commerce, guide associations, and sporting-goods stores will have maps that show great detail on local areas. They're often extremely accurate because they cover small localities. Often they pinpoint hunting hotspots, little-known trails, and other very valuable details that are seldom included on state and federal maps. When you get into new country, always ask if such local maps are available.

HOW TO CARRY MAPS

For the sportsman who makes full use of maps and carries them on hunting trips, protecting them from wear and weather and keeping them in usable condition can be a problem. A map not taken care of has a short life. Properly protected, it will last a long time.

My maps are folded to make neat, flat packages. For instance, I fold topo maps to 7 × 11, with the name of the quadrangle exposed on both sides. Folded this way, any map is easily carried in the field in a waterproof envelope and is easily unfolded for use.

Some hunters eliminate the waterproof envelope by reinforcing their maps with a cloth backing, such as a piece of muslin sheet. Here's how to do it:

The basic trick is to glue your map to the cloth with wallpaper paste. To ensure overall contact between map and cloth, the cloth should first be stretched and tacked to a flat surface such as a plywood board. The cloth should be larger than the map to allow for trimming after the paste dries.

Small maps can be pasted in one piece. Large maps should be cut into sections to eliminate bulky folds. Start by folding the map so that it fits your pocket. Then unfold it and cut it into sections along the fold lines. Paste the sections (in their proper relationship with each other) to the cloth. Leave a space about 1/16 inch between the sections so the finished product will fold easily and compactly.

To guarantee complete contact between the map and cloth, you must wet the map—or sections of it at a time—for a moment in warm water. Then apply the wallpaper paste to the back of the map with a paint brush. Pressure by hand will ensure contact between the cloth and map. Wipe off excess paste with a damp rag. Let dry for at least one day. Then trim the edges with a pair of scissors. The reinforced map is now ready for years of use.

An outdated map may show a road that no longer exists, or it may not include new roads, trails, or other features. It's a poor idea to use maps that somebody gives you. They could have been stored away for years. Note the publishing date on any map of questionable accuracy. If it's old, order a new one from its publisher. Address information is printed on most maps.

How to Read Rubs and Scrapes

John Weiss

A minority of hunters realize that the size of a buck's scrape is a fairly accurate clue to the buck's size. A small scrape signifies a small buck. (J. Wayne Fears photo)

Sometimes, just when a hunter thinks he knows almost everything about hunting a particular species, the game does something the textbooks say it isn't supposed to do. Or, scientists come up with new information that upsets established theories upon which generations of hunters have based their strategies.

Such disruptions can make an experienced hunter feel as though he's a novice. On the other hand, pieces of disconnected information can also fit together and make sense.

Consider movement patterns of whitetail deer. Hunters have traditionally believed that whitetails spend most of their time in a 1½-square-mile home range, but at the onset of the rut bucks begin roaming over as much as a five-mile area. Well, I've known several bucks that never played by those rules.

Before Ohio's deer season one year, I spent an entire week checking out a specific buck's routine. He was a respectable six-pointer, and I knew his territory almost as well as he did. I really wanted him.

I had seen him three times before the beginning of the season, always in the same place. But as the rut came on, he became more and more erratic in his behavior.

By the time opening morning finally arrived, this hombre was acting like an idiot. When I first glimpsed him from my stand, he was moving along with a drunken swagger. He twice caromed off young maple saplings. He was drooling and wild-eyed, and his neck was almost as thick as his main torso. But there was no chance for a clear shot.

I saw the deer again the next day, at the tail end of a long line of scrapes he was tending. But that happened after full dark when the headlights of my truck panned an open oak grove. Then I saw him again the following morning, as I was hiking to my stand. This time he was loping along, heading for a gap in a dense multiflora hedgerow.

The very next morning, this loco buck was back working his scrapes again. When he eventually came to within 75 yards, I got him. But one thing bothered me.

Unlike what I had read so often about deer, this buck wasn't by any means a traveler bent upon covering long distances during his rut. He had staked out a little chunk of turf, and he'd stayed put.

Sure, he had left some scattered invitations for does; my scouting investigations revealed he checked them almost every day. But an expanded

111

home range of four or five square miles? No. If anything, he roamed no more than four or five acres. He wasn't abnormal either. His behavior was almost identical, in fact, with the restricted movement pattern of another buck I had taken in almost the same place the previous year.

My friend Larry Marchington in Athens, Georgia, has been responsible for fitting new pieces into the puzzle of the behavior of whitetails. A dedicated hunter, Larry is an animal-research biologist at the University of Georgia. He is well-known for his sophisticated radio-telemetry studies of deer. With the help of other biologists, and the assistance of several state game agencies, he catches wild deer, outfits them with collar-type radio transmitters, and then monitors their movements for many months.

This strategy has made it possible for him to plot on maps the precise home ranges of individual deer, their movement patterns, and how they interact with other deer sharing the same habitat. Larry knows just where they are all the time, and he can even sneak up closely to watch their behavior during the rut. Many of his findings have been reported in such scientific publications as the *Journal of Wildlife Management* and the *Journal of Animal Behavior*.

Hunters and outdoor writers have long believed that the statement, "Bucks travel more during the rut," meant that they travel farther distances. Instead, deer travel more in the sense that they engage in far less daytime bedding and are restless and more on their feet.

Any deer's travel tendencies, Marchington explains, depend upon deer population levels. Wherever deer are relatively sparse and fairly well dispersed, individual animals inhabiting that range typically wander farther distances during *all* months of the year. But the higher the deer population, the more inhibited or restrictive the animals become in their movements.

So, hunting is best in those areas where large numbers of deer are concentrated, even if most of those deer are does and yearlings. A hunter who tries some region where deer are prone to range much farther distances during the course of a week might never see the buck he's after. Yet in a high-deer area, with animal movements greatly restricted and confined, there is a much better chance that the buck he's after will come into view.

Another mistaken theory relates to the beginning of the rut. For generations, hunters thought that the rut is triggered by the first cold weather masses that sweep down from the North. But this has never applied in the Deep South, where even mid-winter days may be relatively warm. I used to scrape hunt for whitetails in Florida in 90° heat. Some bucks were in full rut.

Scientists have learned that it is not air temperature that triggers the rut. Instead, it's a post-autumnal equinox phenomenon. When the days begin growing noticeably shorter, a deer's behavior is changed by the decreasing amounts of daily sunlight. This results in a type of reverse-stimulation effect upon the pituitary gland. Less sunlight causes the gland's normal function of regulating body growth to cease temporarily while simultaneously spurring increases in the secretion of testosterone (the male sex hormone) and progesterone (the female sex hormone).

This hormone flow in bucks causes them to begin adhering to strict hierarchies. Naturally, the older bucks with the trophy racks are at the top of the hierarchy. The medium-size bucks with six and eight-point racks have lesser status. Spikes and forkhorns are at the bottom of the heap.

Any buck, however, reacts to these conditions in three ways. First, he wants to avoid encounters with bucks of higher ranking than he, which he does by "reading" the sign left by other bucks. Second, he wants to leave sign himself that will serve to warn or inform bucks lower on the scale than he is. And finally, he leaves yet another manner of sign to attract does that have come into heat and are receptive to being bred.

The method that bucks use to communicate their hierarchal ranking is to rub trees with their antlers. This more purposeful rubbing behavior should not be confused with the random rubbing engaged in by bucks during late summer when they are removing velvet from their racks. During second rubbing, trees and saplings sometimes may be almost totally demolished.

The rubbing behavior that takes place during the rutting season is not to polish or sharpen antler tines, strengthen neck muscles, or prepare for battles with other bucks. It's what the biologists refer to as "sign-posting," and it's done to communicate information among members of the local deer population. In other words, a rub is the identifying signal a buck leaves for other bucks. It proclaims his presence and his hierarchal ranking.

This is a tremendous breakthrough for the hunter. This information can indicate the whereabouts of trophy deer and the presence of spikebucks or forkhorns. The diameter of the tree that has been rubbed is the all-important clue.

Pay no attention to thumb-size willows, tag alders, and other small saplings. These trees were probably marked by young bucks.

Rubbed trees that range in diameter up to 2½ inches show the activity of bucks of intermediate ages. These are generally six- and eight-pointers. These deer have rather low, tight racks with slender beams and tines.

Most hunters dream of getting deer that have eight-, 10-, or 12-point typical racks, or gnarled, many-pointed nontypical antlers. These are the deer responsible for the rubs on the largest-diameter trees—usually cedars, pines, or smooth-barked saplings at least three to 4½ inches in diameter.

The hunter can take advantage of this knowledge by spending his scouting hours searching for areas in which large-diameter trees have been rubbed.

Not so many years ago, I just failed to kill the trophy of a lifetime. I had done my scouting in a large area of reclaimed strip-mine lands in Vinton County, Ohio, and I came across many huge rubs. They were along a worn trail that wandered the length of a steep ridge. Most were on trees about four inches in diameter. More than that, there were five trees along the trail averaging about six inches in diameter that had been entirely girdled. I picked out the best stand location, and on opening morning I began my vigil.

At the end of my evening watch on the second day, I was driving home and stopped at a sporting-goods store in the town of Oak Hill, where there was a deer-checking station. A game warden there described to me the largest buck he had ever seen in his life. It had been killed that morning. The deer, on certified scales, weighed 405 pounds and had 25 points on its massive, nontypical rack.

When the warden described where the deer had been killed, and showed me the location on a map,

Hunters should ignore small scrapes. These scrapes, sometimes only six or eight inches in diameter, appear to have been made only halfheartedly. Not all of the weeds and ground covering have been pawed away, and the scrapes are not so deep or muddied as to indicate the aggressive nature of a mature buck. Instead, they are invariably the work of much younger deer that have not yet reached full sexual maturity. The conclusion by biologists has been that the young deer don't really know why they are scraping, but are just beginning to feel the first instinctive compulsions to do so.

Scrapes that average 10 to 15 inches in diameter are the work of more sexually mature bucks. These deer are generally from 1½ to 3½ years old, and they usually carry six-, eight-, or 10-point racks.

I always look for scrapes with a minimum diameter of 18 inches. The hottest sign any hunter can hope to find are scrapes that are two or three feet in diameter.

Scrapes made by a mature buck will seem to have been worked thoroughly. They'll be pawed to abso-

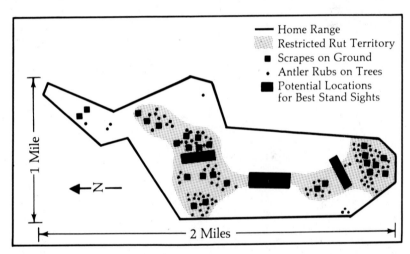

The home range of a buck was monitored with radio-tracking equipment. During rut, this buck confined his movements to a small area. Most of his scrapes were clustered, and surrounded by rubs that served as "fences" to discourage other bucks. The map's rectangular areas show potentially excellent stand sites.

— Home Range
░ Restricted Rut Territory
■ Scrapes on Ground
• Antler Rubs on Trees
▮ Potential Locations for Best Stand Sights

1 Mile
←—N—
2 Miles

my jaw sank. It was only about 500 yards from where I had my stand. The deer was not taken by another hunter, which I wouldn't have minded so much, but was killed on the highway by a truck. And it's line of travel, as it was attempting to cross the road, was straight in the direction of the ridge where I was waiting.

A few other major breakthroughs that are certain to benefit hunters relate to finding scrapes. These are generally circular or elliptical in shape, where the ground has been repeatedly pawed to bare soil. When the earth has been cleared of leaves, forest duff, and other debris, a buck hunches up his back and urinates. The urine runs down his hind legs and over his tarsal glands, located at the hock, and imparts musk scent to the scrape. It's this secretion that attracts does in heat.

Most hunters are aware of this, and diligently strive to find scrapes during preseason scouting. What most hunters don't know is that it's possible to examine the dimensions of a scrape and determine the size of the buck that made it.

lutely bare ground, without as much as a single blade of grass sticking up anywhere around. There will also probably be one or two clearly defined hoofprints in the scrape. Tom Townsend, a biologist with Ohio State University's School of Natural Resources, believes that this is still another type of whitetail marking signal, but so far no one is certain about its purpose or function.

There are also likely to be tine marks in the scrape, where a buck has dragged his rack through the dirt. Carefully examine these and note the distance between the individual tine drags as well as the width of each drag furrow itself. If five inches or more separate the tine drags, with each furrow three quarters of an inch or more in width, you can be sure there is a large deer in the area.

One scrape I remember was absolutely incredible. This was in Gallia County, in southeastern Ohio, and I think the deer that made it was the trophy killed by Ed Parkins, a local farmer. The buck weighed an estimated 300 pounds and carried a heavy, 12-point rack. Anyway, the buck began mak-

Scientific studies indicate that rubs on tree trunks of thumb diameter are usually made by young bucks.

Slightly older bucks, from 2½ to 3½ years old, rub their antlers on trees from 2 to 3½ inches thick.

ing one scrape about three feet in diameter. Then a few days later he apparently began making a second scrape. It was about five feet away from the first and about 20 inches in diameter. This double-scraping characteristic of trophy deer is not unusual. Then the deer began work on a third scrape, this one right between the first two. By the time this sex-crazed buck was finished with his mating invitations, the ground had been pawed into a mammoth scrape. It was shaped somewhat like a football and measured four feet wide by seven feet long.

When you're trying to determine where to put a stand, don't rely on rubs. Larry Marchington's radio-tracking experiments have shown that bucks don't return to specific trees they have rubbed, unless by coincidence. The rubs serve only as cues to other bucks that may happen through the area. Once they've been made, they are no longer useful to the animal that made them. A hunter should scout first, very quickly, for rubs on large-diameter trees, only to ensure he is in an area containing big bucks. Then he should refine the search for scrapes and trails to determine the best place for a stand.

Bucks sometimes return to their scrapes. But how frequently? Scientists say that it depends upon two factors:

1. The population density of deer in the vicinity (and therefore how far individual animals customarily travel).

2. As a result of this saturation level, how much of a buck's time is preoccupied with the does that he encounters.

If the local deer population is relatively small, and the animals are fairly well dispersed, a buck may have his mating invitations strung out quite a distance. It may take him as long as three days to make his rounds. Yet in an area of highly concentrated deer, with their movements restricted, a buck may inspect each of his scrapes as often as three times a day.

I like to spend about a week on my preseason scouting, but I don't spend all of this covering new ground. I like to return every day to check previous scrapes I've found and to determine which ones are being tended regularly. Scrapes that look old indicate one of two things. Either the rut is drawing to a close and the deer are reverting to their former patterns of feeding, bedding, and moving, or the buck that made the scrapes was taken by another hunter.

When the does are in heat, they are attracted to the scent deposited by bucks on their scrapes. A doe's behavior, then, is to leave her own scent in the scrape as a message to the buck that she is in the area and is waiting for him. Radio-telemetry studies have shown that a doe, about 90 percent of the time, will stay somewhere within 200 yards of a scrape she has deposited scent upon. When a buck returns to the scrape, he puts his nose tight to the ground, makes grunting noises as he follows the scent trail, and in most cases finds the waiting doe in a very few minutes.

After they mate, the doe goes about her business and eventually conceives. The buck returns to continue monitoring his scrapes to find still other does. Sometimes a buck may return very late, or the waiting doe may be spooked out of the region. When the buck finally returns and finds the scent, he will trail it endlessly until he finds the doe. This explains why a few bucks travel far distances during the rut, but it is the exception rather than the rule.

In areas where deer populations are high, a buck may impregnate 30 or more does during the brief 2½ week-long rut. The rutting activity is so energetic that a three-year-old buck that weighs 225 pounds in early October may well be down to 160 pounds by the end of December. In frigid climates, bucks may not be able to regain their lost body weight in time to sustain themselves through the coming of heavy snows and the consequent scarcity of food.

Bucks that rub trunks 3 to 4½ inches in diameter are likely to have racks with 8, 10, or 12 points.

Scrapes may be found almost anywhere, but the biggest bucks will make them mostly in higher elevations, such as along ridges, knolls, and terraced hillside benches. In the absence of high elevations, scout the grown-over logging roads and fire trails, fencelines, small clearings, and especially along the edges of woodlots that suddenly yield to open meadows, fields, and clearcuts.

According to the Marchington research, 86 percent of all scrapes are made beneath some form of overhanging tree branch. Several times I have seen bucks pawing their scrapes, and I have noticed that they frequently stand high on their hind legs to lick the overhead branch. This is followed by slashing at it, and breaking it in places with their antlers.

The scouting hunter, however, must do much more than just find a couple of scrapes and sit down and wait. The radio-telemetry studies have shown that a sexually mature buck will make as many as 27 to 35 scrapes during his rut. These scrapes usually are made in clusters.

In a one-acre area, for example, there may be anywhere from three to six scrapes. Several hundred yards away, you might find an incidental scrape or two. Still another 100 yards away may be another three-to-six-scrape cluster pockmarking an acre of ground. Each cluster of scrapes usually is surrounded by numerous rubs on trees. These are intended to warn other bucks away from the scrapes. A mature buck will make an average of 105 rubs on trees during his rut.

The dedicated hunter should carry a topo map with him when he does his scouting, systematically covering the terrain and marking the locations of all scrapes, rubs, and trails he finds. Soon a pattern should begin to emerge that will show how the deer made his scrapes (most home ranges, scrape patterns, and travel tendencies are linear-shaped), the sequence he is likely to use in checking them, the routes he generally takes, and which scrapes are vis-ited regularly. Once this pattern shapes up, the hunter can then determine where his stand should be.

The accompanying sketch of one of the radio-tracking maps Larry Marchington made shows the locations of all of the scrapes and rubs one buck made. It's easy to see how this buck began restricting, rather than expanding, his movements to a core area within his home range at the onset of the rut. It's also apparent that there are a couple of random scrapes the hunter would probably discount and establish a stand site overlooking a series of scrapes or trails leading to and from them.

There are a few other tips hunters should keep in mind. Remember the increased activity of deer during the rutting season. Unlike their activities at other times of the year, when they are on the move mostly during the early-morning or late-afternoon hours, rutting bucks may come by a hunter's stand any time of day and under any weather conditions. An eight-pointer I killed a few years back came to me at noon, in the middle of a rainstorm that was pelting me so hard that at first I had trouble seeing him through my scope.

When the rut is in progress, stay on your stand as long as possible. When the rut concludes (most do not coincide with hunting seasons), then go back to three-hour morning and three-hour evening watches and spend the midday hours napping or planning drives to roust the deer from their beds.

Also hunt the crossroads. Once you've found a trail littered with scrapes, follow it until it intersects another trail. This doubles your chances of seeing deer. Once I found a narrow gap through thick cactus and thornbrush on a south-Texas ranch where five deer trails crossed. Three of those trails were speckled with rubs and scrapes of different sizes. The rancher who now owns the land claims that he and his two sons hunt (one at a time) from a tower stand overlooking that crossing. Every year, all three fill their tags at that location.

Many hunters, after seeing smaller bucks, leave the area and go scouting elsewhere. They figure that if there were trophy deer around, they would have driven the younger bucks away. I don't buy this. According to the latest scientific reports, bucks are not territorial. Their hierarchical rank concerns them, and in any area there may well be several different age classes of bucks sharing the same habitat. Two bucks may fight if they encounter each other and if it's not immediately clear which one has the higher ranking. When the dispute is resolved, they go back and co-exist within the same range and strive to avoid future encounters with each other.

There is still quite a lot to be learned about the rutting behavior of whitetails. But modern research has eliminated much of the mystery, supposition, and speculation about it. This is not to say that it has made hunting whitetails easy or its success guaranteed. But hunters who most often take home trophies are the ones who have learned the new scrape savvy.

Gearing Up for the Vigil

John Weiss

It's only the first hour of ample shooting light, and already you're almost frozen and can't stop shivering.

Your hunt began with a bone-chilling predawn hike to your stand, with only the dim glow of a narrow flashlight beam pointing the way. As the dry snow crunched underfoot, you knew the day was sure to remain miserably cold.

Now you're perched 10 feet above the ground on a tiny square of plywood and your enthusiasm is rapidly diminishing. Each new gust of biting wind somehow manages to rake through your clothing and gnaw at your innermost fiber.

Nothing is moving. At least, not here. Yet shots continue to ring out in the distance with exasperating frequency, allowing gremlins of doubt to toy with the high level of confidence you once had in your choice of stand. With each additional burst of gunfire, it is clear to you that in this area of abundant deer, you alone have chosen to hunt a vacant spot.

Finally, you climb down out of that blasted tree and try to restore some semblance of circulation to your numb feet and hope that maybe you'll see something by prowling around a bit.

In another state, another deer hunter's vigil is substantially different. The weather is torrid, and this hunter's clothing is sopping wet from perspiration. Beads of sweat dribble annoyingly down his forehead and sting his eyes. Mosquitoes are performing the worst bloodletting he's ever experienced, and that seems to be the only animal activity in the vicinity. Eventually, he abandons his ground-level blind.

What both hunters have in common is that they did not allow the odds to build in their favor. Stand hunting involves a mathematical principle known as "geometric progression." In other words, when a hunter has done his scouting properly and has situated his stand in an area of known deer activity, the longer he remains at that stand without seeing a buck, the better his chances become.

But it's no simple matter to wait patiently for long hours, all the while remaining keenly alert. If you intend to do so, you'll need basic creature comforts plus a generous dose of mental discipline. These things are as essential to the end reward as being able to proficiently handle a firearm or bow.

Staying warm involves not only suitable clothing but also preparing your body for the task at hand. If you're tired from lack of rest, unaccustomed to physical exercise, or on a diet, you can expect to "freeze out" in short order. Your metabolism isn't ready for the assault of cold weather.

The right approach is to gradually get into shape before the season. Then, during the season, go to bed early rather than playing poker with hunting pals late into the night. Also, temporarily forget about your diet. Eat hearty meals that—if your doctor will allow—have high concentrations of protein and salt. Protein is the body's furnace fuel for producing heat, while a higher than usual salt intake increases blood flow to the extremities, thereby helping to keep your hands and feet warm.

When your body metabolism is ready, help it do the job by making wise clothing choices. Begin with cotton undergarments and wool/cotton long johns to absorb skin moisture. Then add still more layers: wool trousers and shirts, a down-filled vest, and one or more medium-weight wool or down jackets. These layers trap body heat more effectively than a single, heavy outer coat.

If you have a long hike to your stand, that can cause perspiring, even in cold weather, and later chilling. So stow your outermost jacket in a daypack and put it on when you reach your destination. Another option that's growing in popularity is a one-piece, insulated snowmobile suit combined with the layering method of other garments beneath.

Only two types of footwear are worth considering

for cold-weather stand hunting: boot pacs with felt liners and Air Force pilot air-insulated boots. You can find the Air Force boots at Army/Navy surplus stores. Whichever you choose, wear cotton socks against your skin and one or two pairs of wool socks over them. Be sure your boots are not tight.

When it comes to gloves, again the choice is limited. Some savvy stand hunters swear by heavy mittens that consist of an outer shell, inner wool liners, and a trigger-finger slot. Others prefer the super-warm gloves favored by snowmobilers. To protect my face in bitter cold weather, I even wear a knitted ski mask.

When you sit down on your tree-stand platform or in your blind, you compress the insulation that covers your posterior, allowing coldness to quickly seep in. Solve this problem in advance by cementing a square of thick-pile carpeting to the tree-stand seat. In a blind, do not sit on the cold ground. Instead, use a boat cushion or Hot Seat placed on a folding campstool. Another combination that many hunters use to ease long hours of waiting is a light-weight aluminum lawn chair plus padded cushion.

OK, now what about sticking it out in hot weather? That also requires physical comfort if you're to remain alert and prepared for action. Porous, open-weave clothing will give perspiration a chance to evaporate, thereby producing a cooling effect. On sunny days, keep your eyes shaded. Squinting in bright light makes you tired. Incidentally, the same is true in cold weather when you must look at glaring snow. Of course, the warm-weather hunter will want to use liberal applications of insect repellent to keep pesky bugs at bay. But he should hide its odor with a good masking scent.

To prepare for warm-weather hunting, you should substantially reduce your preseason daily food intake to slow down your system's production of body heat. At the same time, try to reduce fatigue and dehydration by consuming plenty of liquids that contain sodium, calcium, and potassium salts. Popular examples of these drinks are orange juice, Tang, and Gatorade.

If you expect to wait patiently and enthusiastically for long hours under any conditions, you must be able to maintain the utmost confidence in your chosen hunting area. Keep telling yourself that your buck is likely to come slinking along at any moment.

It's extremely important to ignore shots that ring out in the distance. The great majority of these, especially lengthy barrages, do not signify a trophy buck meeting its maker. Sometimes they're fired by hunters checking the accuracy of their rifles before leaving camp. At other times they're wasted, hurried attempts at deer that are hightailing it over distant ridges.

Once, I heard more than a dozen shots come from

Attitude is a key ingredient in hunting from a stand. You've got to believe that your buck can come along anytime.

a hollow about half a mile away. Because I hadn't seen a thing in hours, I unwisely left my stand to investigate, certain that I'd discover deer stampeding all over. Imagine my disgust (with myself) when I eventually came upon three hunters amusing themselves during a midday break by shooting at rats in an old dump near their camp!

Prime times to see deer are the first three hours after daybreak and the last three hours before dark. But few hunters know that deer also get up briefly around noon to feed and drink. Another factor to consider is that sometime during midmorning, most other stand hunters become restless and begin walking around. Their action greatly increases the chances that they'll push bedded deer in your direction. During the rut, keep in mind that amorous bucks—and does in estrus—may be on the move almost anytime.

So try to remain on stand all day. If the air is bitter cold or scorching hot or you're simply tired, at least stay put until 1 p.m. Then return to your camp or your car for a nap during the least favorable afternoon hours. Resume your stand later in the day.

Contrary to popular belief, you need not remain so continually motionless on stand that you seem to have been carved from granite. In fact, trying to maintain such a stance greatly contributes to the possibility of drowsiness.

To stretch and relieve cramped muscles, I frequently alternate between sitting, standing, kneeling, and squatting positions. The important thing is to make these movements in very slow motion and only after you've thoroughly panned the surrounding terrain and assured yourself that no deer are in the immediate vicinity.

Doing isometric exercises also is helpful. By tensing opposing muscles, you can—in effect—stretch them without actually moving them. Begin with your toes, and gradually work all the way up to your forehead.

Another method of staying alert is to occasionally do some deep-breathing exercises. By inhaling cool

air, you flood your circulatory system with oxygen, which is a tonic that revitalizes tired muscles. When you feel yourself dozing off, try the long-haul trucker's trick of exercising your eyes. Without moving your head, strain to look way up to the left, then far down to the right.

Every stand hunter should have a quart-size plastic bottle for urinating. That way, he doesn't saturate his area with man-scent. He also should have various food items. In cold weather, a thermos bottle filled with broth or soup goes a long way in brightening a frustrated hunter's outlook. These liquids are far more nutritious and heat-producing than tea or coffee, which have few calories.

Bring along two or three sandwiches packed in noiseless wrappers such as paper towels. American cheese or peanut butter are good sandwich choices because they leave no spicy odors. An assortment of hard candies will provide additional fuel for your furnace while raising your spirits and keeping your mind occupied.

In warm weather, use the cold beverages mentioned earlier or a low-calorie hot beverage such as tea or bouillon. For other foods, stick with those that are low in protein (to minimize the production of body heat) yet high in calories (to increase stamina). Examples are hard candies, chocolate bars, raisins, dates, figs, and nuts.

In trying to remain alert, think about almost anything other than the slow hours dragging along. As a writer, I often use stand time to work out story angles in my mind. Teachers can mentally plan classroom lectures. Businessmen can think about sales techniques or upcoming board meetings. Other people can ponder the Christmas shopping lists they'll have to contend with when the deer season is over. Many times during the day, wildlife species such as squirrels or songbirds are sure to happen by, providing intermittent entertainment.

But what if other hunters occasionally pass close by? You needn't begin feeling pessimistic. Far from hindering your chances of success, they may help. They'll keep deer circulating that otherwise might remain bedded. And the same deer, in skirting these moving hunters, may very well use one of the trails you're watching.

All in all, waiting on stand is one of deer hunting's greatest paradoxes. On the one hand, sitting still seems to require no skill at all, but in reality it certainly does. First, the stand hunter must consider the weighty decision of *where* to sit. Then, to ensure that this preliminary effort eventually pays off, he must know *how* to patiently and comfortably keep up the vigil.

If you're lucky, your buck will come along early on the very first morning. But perhaps you won't see that buck for several days. Sooner or later, though, it *will* come along. And when that handsome deer materializes, you will know that your wait has been worthwhile.

In a situation like this, you needn't remain as still as a statue. But make motions at a snail's pace.

Sense about Scents

Dwight Schuh

The last deer finally disappeared into a ravine, where the herd would bed for the day. I'd watched them do this before and had figured out their routine. Today a fine old buck would meet his Waterloo.

My one problem could be the wind. I'd followed the only feasible route into this area, and a steady breeze was drifting from my position toward the deer. But that didn't seem as critical as it could have been. The animals were a long way off—more than half a mile, according to my topographic map. Even in this open country, it seemed impossible that they could smell me from so far away. I'd just circle downwind before stalking closer.

I set out confidently, but I had gone scarcely 200 yards when deer streamed from the ravine and paraded single file across the open sage flat. They couldn't possibly have seen or heard me. They must have smelled me. I was flabbergasted.

This and the experiences of other hunters have raised many questions about big-game animals' noses. Every hunter has witnessed the scenting power of big game. In order to deal with it, hunters have devised all kinds of powerful potions to counteract human odor, and they've tried to fool an animal's keen sense of smell by using food and sex scents to draw game into shooting range.

But do these things work? Would skunk essence have been powerful enough to mask my scent from those deer in the ravine? And can you attract deer with bottled apples?

Loren Butler of Stevensville, Montana, has spent more than 25 years trying to answer such questions. He's formed some strong—and strong smelling, according to some hunters—opinions on the olfactory abilities of big game and on the value of scent products.

Butler began his work with scents in the 1950s when he started bowhunting. Having to get close to game, especially with his crude homemade equipment of that day, he learned that human odor was a major obstacle to getting a good shot. With great anticipation, he ordered a few of the then available masking scents, designed to cover up human odor. To his disappointment, they didn't work.

One day in a college botany class in the early 1960s, a friend made a fragrant wildflower perfume. Butler began to make hunting scents with the same process by building a steam-distillation system to extract pure scents from pine and other native plants. That early beginning developed into a full-time business called Mountain Scent and Bugle Manufacturing. Now Butler makes masking, repellent, and attractor scents, and he builds specialized equipment for testing scents in the field. With his radio-controlled testing gear, he can experiment on wild animals in the field to accurately gauge such factors as how fast scents travel, how violently animals react to different smells, and at what distances game can detect a given amount of odor.

First, consider some of Butler's findings about masking scents. No hunter would question the significance of human scent in hunting. In most cases, when a deer hears or sees you, it will investigate until it confirms your presence through one of its other senses. But if it smells you, it doesn't wait for secondary confirmation. It takes off immediately. As Butler puts it, sense of smell is an animal's only independent means of alarm. That's why odor is such a challenge for hunters.

Sweat causes the major problem for hunters. Sweat itself is odorless, but as soon as it surfaces on the skin, bacteria start to work on it, and bacterial action is what creates odor. That's one reason Butler questions the value of chlorophyll tablets, which, if ingested over a period of time, are supposed to eliminate human odor. The point is that odor doesn't come from within your skin but is created on the surface.

Odor is a physical thing, Butler said, made up of free-floating molecules. It has mass and can be measured. Picture it as invisible smoke. That mental picture makes it clear why you want to stay downwind of animals. If wind is blowing from game toward you, they simply can't smell you. The idea that a deer or elk has a nose keen enough to smell you from the upwind side is a myth.

To test the flow of scent in a given area, Butler suggests using a small smoke bomb. You'll see that natural features dissipate smoke, and they do the same to scents. A hedge may throw it straight into the air, and it will scatter more quickly over trees and broken topography than over open ground. On that hunt mentioned earlier, I found that in treeless country, body odor will travel intact at least half a mile or more. If you're hunting in a tree stand, you may find that your tree creates a vortex on the off-wind side that sucks your scent right to an animal.

Obviously, the first step in preventing an animal's smelling you is to understand wind currents and to

The hunter who gets this close to deer has learned how to overcome the animal's extraordinary sense of smell.

use them to your advantage. Unfortunately, that's not always possible. Particularly in the mountains, wind direction constantly shifts, and that's the real fly in the downwind ointment. Wind unreliability is what makes cover-up (masking) scents so valuable.

The idea behind a masking scent is to flood an area with an odor that's natural to it and strong enough to drown out your own odor. Under some conditions, that does indeed work, but Butler thinks many hunters overrate the value of this principle because they judge scents from a human point of view. Skunk smell, for example, is so noxious that, for humans it appears to drown out all other smells. But this is not necessarily true for animals. As Butler said, "Compared to animals, we're odor 'blind.' Human noses have about 10 million olfactory receptors. Most big-game animals have several hundred million."

In the late 1960s, Butler ran experiments on 122 hounds and retrievers. He found that these dogs could recognize their owners by smell at ranges of 225 to 310 yards. He said the noses of dogs and most big game are comparable, which is something he's tested hundreds of times under field conditions. In one test, he puts 10 to 15 drops of sweat in a sealed container and conceals it on the west side of a field where wind is blowing from the west. He waits until a herd of animals comes into the field then opens the container by remote radio control as he watches from a distance. That amount of sweat, a fraction of what would build up on your clothes during a day of hunting, consistently spooks deer and elk out to 300 yards.

Animals' noses not only pick up minute odors at long ranges but also are sensitive enough to sort out various smells, too.

"With the right apparatus, you can block several frequencies of radio waves," Butler said, "but there are channels within that range you can't block. It's the same with scents. Animals can smell through strong scents, because some smells have different chemistry ranges. Skunk scent, for example, can block odors within its chemistry range, but it can't block all odors. These are the smells a deer notices, even when you're covered with skunk scent."

Does all this mean that masking scents don't work? No, it simply demonstrates that they're not a panacea for odor and that they certainly must be used correctly.

Remember that body odor is cumulative. So the longer you go without a bath, the stronger you smell, just as a bonfire that grows bigger and bigger puts out more smoke than the match that was used to light it. Obviously, the bonfire smoke will carry farther before dissipating than will the wisp of smoke from the match, and the same can be said for accumulated body odor. At some point you'll begin to stink enough so that no kind of scent will mask your odor. That point varies in time, depending on how much you're sweating. In his testing with dogs, Butler had hound owners get as clean as possible, then apply good masking scent. For the first

two or three hours, during which the owners did no exercising to work up a sweat, hounds had to get within 20 to 30 feet to smell their owners. After four hours, that distance increased to 50 to 70 feet. From that time on, distance increased rapidly until dogs could smell their owners out to 300 yards.

From that evidence, the message should be clear. Keep clean. Butler recommends washing each day with a nonperfumed, nonallergenic soap, which you can buy in drugstores, and wearing clean clothes. Odor builds up on clothing just as it does on skin.

If you must hike hard to your hunting area, Butler suggests that you take clean shorts and a T-shirt, along with a baking soda-and-water solution in a wineskin. When you reach your destination and have cooled off, rinse your body with the soda solution and change clothes. Seal the clothing you've taken off in a plastic bag.

"It's hard to say how effective this is," Butler said, "because it all depends on how much you sweat. But it could work for up to four hours or more."

Only when you've decreased body odor to the lowest possible level will a cover-up scent work well. Masking scents, of course, do nothing to change your smell. They simply dilute your body's natural odor. When you choose a masking scent, ask yourself, "Does it smell natural?" The scent itself can be your undoing if it smells foreign to game.

Loren Butler here installs remote control devices that let him release scents when animals venture close to equipment. Assembly below allows Butler to release any of six different scents by remote control.

Scents with an off odor such as that of alcohol or disinfectant may do more harm than good. On a field trip to Utah, Butler told people his natural scents wouldn't spook deer. One skeptic said, "I don't believe it. Show me." Butler poured 30 bottles of scent around a salt lick, and that evening deer walked over it to get salt. Later he sprinkled two ounces of a disinfectant-smelling scent around the lick, and deer abandoned the area.

Butler suggests using your nose to judge a scent. If it smells like what it's supposed to smell like, then it'll probably work. Butler's company and other manufacturers make scents from the pure extracts of native plants such as pine, juniper, sage, cedar, and hemlock. He believes these will work, but he warns that the less attention you draw to yourself, the better your chances will be.

"If you're hunting antelope in a region with no pine trees, pine scent obviously shouldn't be your first choice," he said. "I doubt that it'll spook game, but it may make them curious, which will draw their attention to you."

Butler said the best way to wear a masking scent is to put several drops on your hunting clothes and seal the clothes in a plastic bag for a couple of hours until fumes pervade the cloth. Cloth fibers retain scent much better than skin. Scent applied this way will last the better part of a day.

What about attractor scents? We've all seen ads for apple, grape, or other good-smelling scents that are supposed to attract deer. Are they better than masking scents?

Not in Butler's opinion. Over a period of years, Butler has carried out 487 field tests that involved 11,452 deer in an attempt to develop an effective scent for live-trapping deer. He's found that from January through April, when deer have depleted body fat and were on a near-starvation diet, animals indeed would come to attractor scents. During that period, anywhere from 17 to 28 percent of deer in an area came to scent stations. But from May through December, less than two percent came in, and most of these were yearlings. Butler believes a small number of animals will wander in to investigate smell, simply out of curiosity.

Why don't food lures work during the summer and fall, when they'd be of value to hunters? According to Butler, deer and elk use their noses primarily for social interaction and defense, but not to find food. During summer and fall, their food is abundant.

That isn't to say that food scents never work. For some animals, such as bears, they do. Butler has developed a rotten-meat extract for use in live-trapping bears. Tests in Canada, Idaho, and Colorado have shown it to be very effective. That's because bears, as scavengers, locate food by smell.

"Scavengers are easy to attract because they make their living with their noses," Butler said. "But that's not true with hoofed game."

Are buck scents, such as so-called doe-in-heat lures, any more effective than food scents? Not in Butler's opinion.

"There's simply no way to synthesize vaginal secretions from deer," Butler said. "No one knows what they're made of. The only way to get effective doe scents is from live doe deer, but that's impractical because it occurs in such minute amounts.

"Some products on the market do seem to attract deer out of curiosity. Hunters have given me some good reports," said Butler. "But I've tested many of the so-called buck lures with poor results. I've put these scents up-wind of feeding areas at night and through infrared equipment have watched 50 bucks totally ignore them. Here again, 2 or 3 percent of all animals will check out anything, but I just haven't found any attractor scent that consistently works."

If Loren Butler's observations smell a little foul to you, take his advice and try different scents for yourself. He said testing any scent is easy because deer have only two kinds of responses—conditioned and instinctive. If they run from the smell of human sweat, that's conditioned. If they run to smell a doe in heat, that's instinctive. The point is that reasoning plays no part in their actions, so your testing can be straightforward, and the results are reliable.

Butler suggests sealing a test scent, such as a sweaty T-shirt, in a plastic bag. Stake it down where animals will feed, and string fine-wire fishing line from the bag to an observation point several hundred yards away. When animals get downwind of the bag, pull the line to open the bag. You can do the same thing by tying bottles to fence posts or trees and pulling out cork stoppers with long lines.

"You can almost predict when deer downwind will react." Butler said. "You can test any scent this way."

You also can judge the effectiveness of masking scents by using your dog. Leave him at a friend's house for a day. Tell the friend not to pet him or give him any food, only water. When he's starved for food and affection, get in a hiding place and have the neighbor lead him downwind of you. He'll respond with excitement the instant he smells you. From such tests you can gauge the value of your cover-up scent.

"These tests are fun and can help you learn," Butler said. "There's no sense in handicapping yourself in the field with a scent that just doesn't work."

Information about Butler's hunting products and equipment for wildlife-management agencies is available from: Mountain Scent Research, P.O. Box 545, Stevensville, MT, 59870.

Maybe your tests will bear out Loren Butler's findings; maybe they won't. One way or the other, the fact is that game animals have an extraordinary sense of smell, and to hunt most efficiently you must deal with that reality. Loren Butler offers no miracle solutions to the problems of smell, but at the very least his findings should help you decide what to use. 🦌

Day Pack and Survival Kit

J. Wayne Fears

Almost every survey conducted to determine why people hunt finds that "the pleasure of being afield" is the number one answer. Yet, how many hunters actually go afield—that is, beyond sight of a road? The game managers and the conservation officers say that there are three main reasons why a high percentage of hunters never get very far afield: the need to get back to the car for coffee or lunch, fear of a change in the weather, and fear of getting lost.

A good day pack and survival kit can eliminate many of the reasons that a hunter doesn't penetrate the backcountry for a full day afield, where game is more plentiful.

The confidence and independence that come with a day pack and survival kit will make you more comfortable during long hours stalking or in a tree stand. You'll be able to spend more time hunting and less time thinking about getting lost or returning to your car.

THE DAY PACK

A hunter's day pack enables him to spend more hours afield than any other piece of equipment. When properly outfitted, it can also serve as a survival kit in an emergency.

Day packs, whether used in hunting grouse, squirrel, rabbit, or deer, will vary somewhat in contents according to personal needs and taste. I'll tell you about the deer-hunting day pack I use, and you can use it as a guide in selecting your day pack and equipment:

1. This day pack is Blaze Orange, small, and made of coated-nylon pack cloth. It has one large inside pocket, two outside pockets,

At 14 pounds, this day pack carries everything you are likely to need for a day afield.

and padded shoulder straps. It stores easily. And the cost is low—about $15. When bowhunting, or squirrel or duck hunting, I would use a camouflage pack.

2. Since much deer hunting is done by stalking, an extra pair of wool socks is good to have at midday. A change also helps during wet weather.

3. The safe way to get a deer out of the woods is with a drag rope. This rope can also be used to lift equipment in and out of a tree stand. And as a survival tool, it is invaluable in making an emergency shelter.

4. A good pair of shooting gloves.

5. A clear-vinyl rain suit lets the Blaze Orange of your hunting jacket show through.

6. A small camera.

10. Binoculars.

11. A topographical map.

12. A sportsman's signal kit. The one I use contains two aerial flares, an orange smoke signal, fire-starter kit, and signal mirror.

13. A first-aid kit. The kit shown is lightweight and includes water-purification tablets.

14. Extra ammunition.

15. A bright-red distress marker. Besides being an excellent ground-to-air marker, it can be used to make an emergency shelter.

16. Waterproof matches in the pack and in your pocket.

17. A police whistle. The sound carries farther and lasts longer than your voice.

18. The Wallet Survival Guide.

19. Indian Buck Lure, for covering human scent and working buck scrapes.

20. Knife-sharpening stone.

21, 22, 23. High-energy trail food or lunch in a paper bag. Keep some aside in case you get lost.

24. Extra boot laces.

Most survival experts and seasoned guides suggest that even if you carry a well-equipped day pack or survival kit, you should always carry a knife, waterproof matches, map, compass, whistle, and space blanket on you. These basics will see you through if you become separated from your pack or kit.

THE SURVIVAL KIT

The hunter's survival kit can be used with the day pack to give you an edge on almost any unexpected event. When you leave your tree stand to trail game or explore another area, you can take the small kit and leave your day pack at the stand. If you become lost, you'll have everything necessary for making

Numbers keyed to accompanying text, here are 24 items I carry when deer hunting.

7. A flashlight can help you get into the woods earlier and leave later. I feel safer walking into the woods before daylight with my flashlight than I do walking in after daylight. Most hunters know that deer don't carry flashlights. A flashlight is also a good signaling device.

8. Toilet tissue has several uses. It's a good fire starter. And when you're trailing a wounded deer, small pieces of the tissue dropped at each blood sign makes following the trail easier. It also helps you find your way back when you concentrate on trailing wounded game so much that you lose your bearings.

9. A canteen of water or insulated bottle of coffee.

The survival kit fits on your belt so that you always have it with you.

shelter, signaling, starting a fire, securing food, purifying water, navigating, and giving first aid.

According to the National Rifle Association, a hunter in a survival crisis is generally faced with a short term danger—usually less than 72 hours. Searches can take time, however, and a lost hunter should plan for the worst, conserving energy and improving his conditions until help arrives. Stay in one location to assist searchers with visual and audible signals. This includes ground-to-air signals.

With these needs in mind, the following survival kit was developed:

1. The kit bag is an army-surplus, individual first-aid pouch. It's sturdy and fits on a belt easily or in a day pack, backpack, glove compartment, or tacklebox.
2. A Blaze-Orange smoke signal is an excellent daytime signaling device to use with ground-to-air signals.

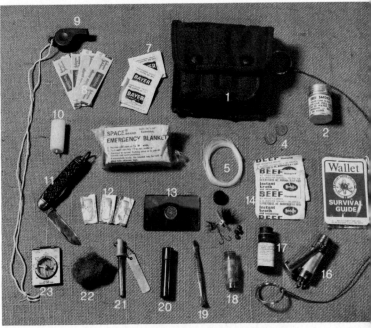

If you get lost, this 23-item survival kit will meet almost all your needs.

GROUND-TO-AIR SIGNALS

I	*NEED DOCTOR-EMERGENCY*
II	*NEED MEDICAL SUPPLIES*
F	*NEED FOOD AND WATER*
X	*UNABLE TO TRAVEL*
↑	*AM TRAVELING IN THIS DIRECTION*
K	*WHICH DIRECTION SHOULD I GO?*
☐	*NEED MAP AND COMPASS*
V	*NEED GUN AND AMMO*
Y	*YES*
N	*NO*
JL	*DO NOT UNDERSTAND MESSAGE*
LL	*ALL WELL*

To signal rescue aircraft, set up these symbols on open patches of ground using large tree branches.

3. A wire saw, which coils for storing, can be used to cut poles for shelter or firewood, or for helping quarter large game.
4. Many lost hunters have come to a pay phone beside a road or closed lodge and had no change for a call. Carry enough change for a call.
5. 20-pound-test line can be used to make shelters, mend clothes, make snares, and catch fish.
6. The emergency space blanket, when folded, is the size of a cigarette pack. It can be made into a lean-to.

7. Aspirin.
8. Band-Aids.
9. A police whistle.
10. A candle stub is an excellent fire starter.
11. A scout-type pocket knife.
12. Antiseptic.
13. A signal mirror.
14. Beef broth has some food value and makes wild food taste better.
15. The Wallet Survival Guide.
16. Waterproof matches.
17. Water-purification tablets.
18. A small tackle box can be made by winding several feet of six-pound-test line on a plastic bottle. Hold with tape. Place small hooks, split-shot, bluegill popping bug, and small dry fly inside.
19. Tweezers.
20. Lip protection.
21. Metal match, which can be used as a backup fire-starter.
22. Size 000 steel wool works with the metal match to get tinder started, even when wet.
23. A backup compass carried in your pocket.

You can find smaller and larger survival kits, but this one can serve most of your needs. For snow-country, add a collapsible aluminum cup or folded piece of aluminum foil for melting snow for water. Even with a survival kit, don't neglect to learn survival techniques, how to signal, and how to use a map and compass. A hunter with a survival kit full of items he doesn't know how to use can be a hunter in trouble. And always tell someone who is staying behind, where you are going and when you plan to return. 🦌

Bucks of the Madness Moon

Norm Nelson

During the rut, bucks lose much of their normal caution. You can take advantage of the annual frenzy to put meat on the table and antlers over the mantel. (Bill McRae photo)

The last thing I expected to hear in the silent forest glade was the loud exclamation from my Uncle Ralph about 100 yards out of sight. Ralph, bless him, is one of the few forest hunters I've known who habitually whisper when hunting. Most people have no idea how well their voices will carry, even in dense timber.

I froze facing that direction, my thumb on the rifle safety. We were making a quiet, stillhunting sweep for Roosevelt elk, working on parallel courses downhill to Old Man Pass in Washington's southern Cascades. Nothing showed up. Ralph's one-syllable shout apparently wasn't a signal that a good bull was coming my way.

After pausing for several minutes, I continued on to our road rendezvous. Ralph was waiting, eyes big as saucers, to tell me why he'd shouted. As he'd mooched along in the timber, a blacktail doe wandered about 20 yards in front of him. Right behind her came a three-point buck blacktail. The buck stopped, puzzled out Ralph, and then walked toward him. We were between the split deer seasons, when only elk are legal, or Ralph would have collected the easiest buck of his life.

The buck stopped, sized up the man some more, and then kept coming. Suddenly Ralph realized that the now-close blacktail's spinal hair was erect and his ears were laid back—both signs that mean battle stations. Ralph thrust his rifle barrel, bayonet-fashion, at the buck and yelled, "Git!" That was the muffled shout I'd heard at a distance.

Did the buck flee in panic at the human voice? Heck, no. He stopped, eyeballed my uncle rather coolly, and then slowly returned to the waiting doe. Once, the buck stopped to look back. His body language almost said, "Buddy, if I didn't mind keeping this lady waiting, I'd come back and clean your clock for you."

Admittedly, this is an extreme case of a buck feeling his oats during the rutting season. Ralph, who stuttered with lingering astonishment when telling me the story, had never seen anything like it in his 50-plus years of hunting and his lifetime career as a federal forester.

But deer lore is full of stories that involve even more aggressive buck behavior. In my files I found a clipping of an event that, if my margin note is correct, occurred in the fall of 1975 in Maryland. A husband and wife driving along a highway spotted a handsome eight-point whitetail by the roadside. Fearing that the deer would be hit by a car if it tried to cross, the couple stopped and walked back to shoo the buck into the woods. That was a *big* mistake. The buck promptly charged and gored the would-be Samaritan husband. When the wife

pitched in, the buck nailed her, too, badly lacerating her legs.

Another motorist saw the ruckus and pulled over. He tried to interpose his Volkswagen between the two injured people and the angry, prodding buck. Another motorist pulled up and jumped out of his car. He tried to grab the buck's antlers and almost got himself killed. With the scoreboard now reading Buck-4, People-0, a *fifth* motorist arrived. He happened to be a hunter (and this was deer season), and he promptly shot the buck.

A state trooper who arrived later was quoted as saying, "Had it not been for the fellow with a shotgun, someone would have been killed." Frankly, I'm surprised someone wasn't. The multiple javelins of buck antlers, thrust by 150 to 200 pounds of very muscular animal, are some of the deadliest weapons nature ever devised.

Although all deer hunters know that deer breed in late fall or early winter, there are lots of misconceptions. Weather alone doesn't "bring on the rut," as so many cold-climate hunters devoutly believe. It takes two to tango, and the doe goes into her half of

the act—the estrus or heat period—when the changing angle of the autumn sun triggers a hormonal response. According to researchers, does penned in a windowless building with a single strong light source came into heat when the light's angle was gradually changed to imitate sun declension in the fall. That's not surprising. Plant growth is turned off or on, fall or spring, by the same "light switch."

Plenty of deer observers, however, including those with a lifetime of hunting experience, believe that a temperature drop heightens the existing sex drive in bucks. In central and northern tiers of states, bucks think sex from September on, even though few does are ready to breed that early. In the Northern states, the estrus peak is in November. This time frame gets progressively later farther south.

When the rut overlaps hunting season, it's a godsend to deer hunters. Normally, a buck has it all over his human adversary. The buck knows the country; the hunter often does not. The buck is primarily nocturnal; the hunter is required by law to operate in daytime. The buck usually spends daylight hours bedded in well-chosen thickets, rimrocks, swamps, or other places that are difficult for hunters to approach undetected. The buck's normal lifestyle and outlook is one that can be described as thoughtful paranoia.

All this changes during the peak of rutting activity. The old, loner muley bucks come down from the high country to mate with the does. The invisibly bedded whitetail buck suddenly starts spending some daylight hours restlessly roaming the now-expanded area that he considers his prospecting country. And the buck gets very reckless in his pursuit of does in heat.

The weirdest case I know of concerning how obsessed a buck can get in the rut happened years ago at our family's northern-Minnesota hunting camp. My father had in hand a .243 that I'd been using all summer as a crow rifle. The trigger was set mighty light for precision varminting. Dad spotted a big whitetail intently nosing out a fresh set of doe tracks. Thanks to the too-light trigger and a gloved hand, Dad managed to fire right over the deer's back at about 50 yards.

Get this: Despite the blast of a high-intensity rifle and the racket of a supersonic bullet whizzing within inches of his ears, the sex-struck buck *never lifted his head*. He continued to cold-nose that doe track.

Again, that is an extreme example. But I got one buck whose preoccupation with sex was almost as severe. As I hiked down a logging road, the whitetail suddenly materialized about 100 yards ahead, nose to the ground on a doe track. He crossed into the woods on the other side before I could shoot. Ordinarily, a whitetail buck about to cross an opening like that stops, looks, listens, and then smokes across so fast that he appears to be 10 inches high and 20 feet long. This buck was so spellbound by the doe tracks he was following that he wouldn't have noticed the Wabash Cannonball coming down the logging road. I simply dogtrotted to where he'd entered the timber and peeked past a big spruce. A few yards into the forest, the buck was standing, alert at last and looking back in my direction. No doubt he heard the soft thud of my rubber shoepacks on the run. But out of curiosity, he dallied to see what I was, which made him the easiest big whitetail I ever bagged.

A rutting buck's curiosity can be overwhelming. One October, my brother and I were banging away with hammer and nails, building a tree stand before deer season opened. I got up into the new stand and sent Al off some distance so I could check visibility from the structure. As he walked off into the marsh grass and cattails, I spotted a sudden motion out of the corner of my eye. Sneaking past my tree stand was a huge whitetail buck, head low, stalking Al the way a cat stalks a bird.

My guess is that the buck heard the hammering and was curious about whether this racket was a buck duel in progress or a claim-jumper buck whacking a sapling. Why he followed Al's human-scented footsteps, I have no idea. But it's no wonder some Indian tribes called November the Madness Moon.

As a youngster, I was hunting October partridge at the family hunting camp when I heard an irregular whacking in the woods. Wondering if someone with an ax was cutting our timber, I headed that way. When I reached the spot that the sounds had been coming from, I glimpsed a buck bounding into thicker brush. The noise that I'd heard was the one-sided war games this rascal had been playing with an aspen sapling. He had battered the tree almost to shreds, and it was barely standing. Suddenly the screaming snort of a disturbed whitetail sounded behind me. I turned to see the buck's flag as he bounded away.

While I'd stood marveling at the single-minded destruction visited on the sapling, the buck had circled downwind to get sure scent identification of me. His track scuff in the frost-whitened leaves revealed that he'd been only about 30 yards away as he circled me in the brush. Of course, that was foolishly close range for him. My assumption is that he took the risk in the hope that I was a willing doe. If I'd been a rival buck, there would have been a showdown.

Rutting whitetails are territorial and aggressive, particularly in areas with plenty of bucks. Battles are fairly common, although the fights usually aren't 15-rounders. A mismatched pair produce no fight—the smaller buck almost invariably gives up when confronted by a superior rival. But a pair of evenly matched whitetails engage in savage combat. One battleground I found during the rut was a circle roughly 30 to 40 feet in diameter in a gray-alder swamp. Gray-alder brush is almost impossible for a grown man to snap off with his hands, yet every alder clump in that area was broken off at ground level. The dirt was churned up like the soil in a cultivated garden. A long search revealed no dead deer or locked-antler bucks.

Studying the site, I estimated that it would have taken me a solid hour with ax and brush hook to do that kind of number on that much alder brush. My guess is that a pair of big bucks duked it out here for at least two hours, smashing brush with their sharp hoofs as they strained against each other's antlers. Both must have taken an awful beating because there was an incredible amount of deer hair lying about. However, the chewed-up black swamp soil concealed any dried blood, if indeed any was shed.

Actual killings are rare (at least among unconfined deer) unless two bucks lock antlers for keeps and starve or one of the combatants suffers a broken neck. A defeated buck would rather give way than die fighting, but he may take some real punishment on the way out. A friend of mine shot a big whitetail whose skinned rump was a mass of small hemorrhages. This was during the peak of the November rut. We reasoned that the severe, multiple lacerations could come only from another buck's antler tines. Getting hit by a car would not have caused that many small, deep, semipuncture bruises. Because this buck was a sizable eight-pointer, I spent the rest of the season dreaming of running into the buck that had been big enough to whip him.

Most buck-deer equivalents of Shoot-Out at the OK Corral are generally thought of by hunters as applying only to whitetails. However, mule-deer bucks occasionally do some combat. Many of these fights don't amount to much more than a ritualized, lackadaisical antler-clashing. Through spotting scope or binoculars, I've seen this several times among muleys. None of these sparring matches got hot or heavy, nor did they last more than half a minute before the lesser buck gave way.

However, each of these half-hearted, short duels I've personally seen did not involve any does in sight. Had there been, I might well have had the spotting-scope equivalent of a ringside seat at a really serious battle. Deer authorities report that although savage fights among muleys are much rarer than among the hair-triggered whitetails, such duels do occur, sometimes with injuries and bloodshed. But as the great naturalist Ernest Thompson Seton pointed out long ago, fatalities among mule-deer combatants seem to be very rare. Aside from the seemingly milder temperament of the muley, his wide-branching antler structure may not be as formidable a killing weapon as the more compact, javelin-cluster tines of the whitetail. A muley's antlers diverge from his body axis. But a whitetail's rack aims right where he looks and lunges, and thus may well be the deadlier armament. Even so, a pair of big-antlered, well-matched mule-deer bucks could put up a fearful fight if the spirit moved them, and occasionally it does.

Where muley and whitetail ranges overlap, as they do in much of the West, some observers think the more aggressive whitetail is expanding its territory at the expense of the muley. In bygone years, backcountry ranchers in Washington's Okanogan region used to shoot whitetails out of season under the belief that this "saved" the easier-to-hunt mule deer from being aced out by the expanding whitetail population of northeastern Washington. I hope this vigilante-style wildlife "management" no longer prevails. Both species are great game animals. The only thing more enjoyable than hunting either muleys or whitetails is to hunt where both species overlap.

But how can you take advantage of the rut? First, book your hunting to overlap the peak of the rut in your area. This assumes that your state's season is late enough or long enough to take in the rut. Southern deer may hit a peak in late December and early January, Northern deer in mid-November. Because rut timing varies as a function of both geography and climate, get the word on the rut's usual peak in your region from state wildlife managers.

Second, understand that rutting behavior generally involves heightened activity along with some unusual boldness. Truly senseless behavior, such as that buck ignoring my father's close-range shot, is rare. You still have to be on the ball as a hunter to capitalize on any rut-inspired chances that a buck gives you. That buck I surprised on the logging road was careless but still took off in a flash when he spotted me. Only the fact that I was psychologically and physically ready for a very quick shot put him on the meat pole.

Third, watch the weather. A noticeable cooling trend seems to step up bucks' rutting activities somewhat. If the weather turns unseasonably warm, the rut may slow down.

Fourth, if both the calendar and the weather say, "This is it," hunt hard! Hit the woods early, and carry enough food to make a whole day of it. The peak of the rut is well worth investing all the daylight you've got. Although midday is usually slow for deer hunting, all bets are off when sex-hungry bucks roam the woods. They can show up anytime.

Fifth, hunt likely places. Whitetail cover with plenty of buck scrapes on the ground is as good as any. Radio-tracking studies show that bucks habitually return to their scrapes (not sapling rubs). Stump-sitting near a good scrape or two and a well-traveled deer trail is worth lots of patience. With muleys and blacktails, work country where doe herds hang out. When the rut's on, big bucks will join them or will be bedded not far away.

Sixth, don't get caught by surprise. Rutting bucks sometimes show up in unlikely ways. My son, in his youth, was on stand when he heard the loud, leaf-shuffling approach of a heavy-footed hunter. Pete let down his guard and relaxed, but the noisy visitor was a large, swollen-necked buck. That buck may have been careless, but he regained his wits fast enough to hightail it out of there before my son could grab his rifle and get off a shot. Pete still kicks himself for letting that one get away.

What about antler rattling? So far, my very limited rattling attempts haven't worked. But during the rut, the technique can pay off when an area holds enough bucks to make them feisty about their territories and their chances with the does. The tactics cited by successful antler-bangers are: pick a spot offering some cover plus visibility; be prepared for bucks either sneaking in warily or coming in with a snort and a rush; and wear plenty of Blaze Orange to prevent a mishap in case you rattle up an excited hunter.

Photographer-naturalist Leonard Lee Rue III tells a great story in *The Deer of North America*, published by the Outdoor Life Book Club. Some friends were visiting Pennsylvanian John Miller in the fall and commented on the unusual number of deer they'd seen on their trip. Miller said that this was due to the rut. "What's that?" his visitors asked. He explained that it's the breeding period. A lady visitor thought this over and commented, "If you're going to get into a rut, I think that's the best kind."

PART 6

IN SEARCH OF BIG TROPHIES

Trophy Buck . . . or Only Fair-to-Middling?

Erwin A. Bauer

If you hunt whitetail deer, the odds are that you have never killed an honest-to-goodness trophy animal. A good buck or two, yes, maybe several, but that genuine, bragging-size trophy is still out there somewhere in the woods. Why?

There are a number of possible answers. First, you may be hunting where really big bucks do not exist. There are such places. But more than likely you have been shooting the first legal buck that comes along because you don't want to risk being skunked. Or maybe you have made the same mistake that many of us make.

One day out hunting, you suddenly glimpse the absolutely, positively, biggest buck in the whole state. He is moving away fast. In a sudden rush of excitement, you shoot him. But when you examine the antlers, you are disappointed. The deer you shot is a dandy, but he has a mediocre or average rack at best. What *looked* like the deer of a lifetime when you first spotted it, wasn't at all.

Now it's time to look ahead. Whitetail populations are high almost everywhere. This is *your* year. No shooting the first deer that appears in your sights. This time it's a big buster or nothing. The only trouble is that you may not know that super deer if and when you see it. So let's pause here for a minute and take a test.

Assume you are sitting motionless in a blind in good whitetail country. You are alert; your rifle is accurately sighted-in. There is movement some 50 or 75 yards away. A buck appears, but he doesn't expose himself fully. Now examine the six photographs on pages 132 and 133. They show six differ-

A whitetail buck won't give you much time for evaluating his rack. Can you decide fast under pressure?

ent whitetails as they would appear to a hunter—long distance or partly obscured. I photographed them all in southern Texas.

Quickly—without using a magnifying glass—rate these bucks according to size of antlers. Mark them with a pencil from No. 1 (the best) to No. 6. The answers to this photo quiz appear later on in this chapter. Score yourself, too, or rather, score your ability to judge antlers. If you get all six right, you're an expert already and require no further study. If you're less than expert, maybe I can give you some help.

Even though I now live in elk and bighorn-sheep country and must travel far to hunt and photograph whitetails, I do so quite often simply because they are magnificent game animals. The size of whitetail

deer and their antlers varies greatly from place to place. Bucks in some regions can reach maximum antler size when only about $4\frac{1}{2}$ or $5\frac{1}{2}$ years old; elsewhere, the greatest antler mass occurs at $6\frac{1}{2}$ or $7\frac{1}{2}$ years of age.

What is a trophy whitetail? One man's standards may differ greatly from another's, but let's use the Boone and Crockett Club's system of scoring, which divides deer into two categories: typical and non-typical. Typical heads are those with symmetrical or almost symmetrical antlers. Most bucks by far have typical heads. Nontypical animals are those with an abnormal number or arrangement of points, usually unsymmetrical or even bizarre in shape. Just the same, a nontypical head can be a very impressive rack.

Using the Boone and Crockett Club's measurement system, a deer's antlers are rated according to the length of the main beams, the length of all normal points, the greatest inside spread between the right and left antlers, and the circumference of the main beams at several places. All these measurements are made in inches to the closest one-eighth of an inch. The total of all measurements is the preliminary score. But deductions are made from that score for any differences between the basic measurements of the right antler and those of the left antler. Few hunters realize that the score is reduced if the spread of the deer's rack is wider than the length of the longer main beam.

In the typical category, deductions are made for abnormal points. A nontypical rack is scored in exactly the same way, except that abnormal points increase the score rather than reduce it.

In order for a trophy to be listed in the current record book, and be officially regarded as a trophy

rack, a typical rack must score 170 after deductions. A nontypical rack must score 195 to qualify.

Considering that records have been kept for a long time, the odds of shooting a typical whitetail that scores 170, in any hunting season, are about two or three in a million, so let's settle on a more practical minimum figure and agree that a score of 150 by the Boone and Crockett system indicates an outstanding whitetail trophy. That usually means a buck with at least 10 points, five per side, symmetrical in shape, with an inside spread of 20 inches or more and long, heavy beams that measure more than five inches in circumference near the head. Every deer of this loose description will not necessarily score 150, but then many will exceed it. Let's say this is the kind of rack—nothing smaller—you are looking for in the field this fall. This 150 minimum is for a typical rack or one that has only a few nontypical characteristics.

Now for the first complication: No other horned

Try to estimate relative antler scores of each of these six bucks. Then compare your estimates with the author's noted in captions of photos of the same deer on pages 134 and 135.

or antlered species is as difficult to judge on the hoof as the whitetail. By contrast, it's often possible to study a bighorn ram or a billy goat or a caribou from every angle for a long time through a spotting scope. Very few whitetails give a hunter that much time for an evaluation. Many are gone in an instant. In addition, there is the pressure factor. My out-door-writing friend Byron Dalrymple once stated the situation this way: "Antler size is directly pro-portional to the hunter's adrenaline flow."

A hunter must use any and every small advan-tage available to him. He must remain calm and go into the field determined to see any deer before it sees him. Long before opening day, a hunter must have convinced himself that he will *not* get buck fe-ver or abandon his determination to take a trophy buck. From two unusual books currently available (*Great Whitetails of North America* and *Big Rack*), we know that an overwhelming percentage of the larg-est bucks ever taken in North America were shot

by hunters who played the waiting game. They shot from some kind of stand. The odds against jumpshooting or stillhunting a buck in the trophy category are astronomical. Hunt from a stand if you want a chance at a great deer.

Long before opening day, it is important to take every opportunity to learn exactly what a trophy whitetail looks like. Thumb through back issues of *Outdoor Life* magazine for some of the records and near-records that have been pictured. Study the photos that accompany this chapter. Visit trophy rooms and museums. Study big whitetail racks, and learn how to judge them. When unalarmed but alert and facing toward you, a buck measures 15 to 18 inches from ear tip to ear tip, if both ears are cocked slightly upward. The average healthy buck is 15 inches thick through the body from side to side. If the antlers extend several inches beyond the ear tips or the body on both sides, you are looking at a fine specimen.

C

E

F

Still, there are a few other rules of thumb to remember and consider. After checking for spread, look at antler height, which is also the length of the tines. On a trophy head, at least some points visible from the front view should be as long as the ears or longer.

Now at last it is open season, and you are on stand. A buck appears. From that instant onward, focus your undivided attention on the deer's rack. That is the cardinal rule you *must* follow. Forget other deer in the vicinity. Wait as motionless as a granite block for the deer to look in your direction. No side or rear view can possibly reveal what you need to see.

First check for antler width and height. Next count the points. You want to see 10 or more. Notice the thickness and color of the antlers. As a general rule, the darker they are, the better, although this is not 100 percent reliable. Thickness (heaviness) of antler beams is the only dimension that is a little easier to determine from a side view of the buck. Heavy beams are important in scoring.

Look so intently, so carefully for details in the brief moments you normally have, that there is no time for buck fever. I repeat: *forget body size. Look only at the antlers.* It is as simple as that.

Then, if that buck out there seems to measure up to our 150 minimum score, squeeze off a shot.

When I was taking photographs for this chapter and hunting in south Texas, I managed to follow my own rules for evaluating a deer's rack. I admit that they're hard to follow, but here's how it happened.

It began just after dawn at The Senderos, an average-size ranch. It was quiet and cold; a platinum frost glittered in those first rays of a weak, late-December sun. I crouched motionless and tense behind a high clump of prickly pear. Thirty feet behind me, Hefner Appling struck two heavy antlers to-

gether and violently shook a dry mesquite sapling. The annual whitetail rut was on, and my friend was trying to rattle up a buck for me. No, he was trying to rattle up a certain buck that had been making scrapes in the area for a week or so. The whitetail was a sleek 12-pointer. Almost immediately, there was a response to the rattling.

Without hesitation, a big buck came running downwind from my left. He made a circle, and I heard him breaking brush right where I was looking. Then, there he stood, barely 50 feet away, staring past me, through me, toward Hefner and the source of the rattling. It was a point-blank shot. I raised the rifle slowly.

The buck became suspicious and turned his head ever so slightly so that I could see the rack from the front. I lowered the rifle. In that split second, I saw that he was not the deer we wanted, though he was pretty good—10 points.

A few minutes later, Hefner said, "I'm glad you held your fire. The deer we're after came up behind me very quietly. He's older and smarter than the one you saw. We'll take that into consideration when we try for him again tomorrow."

The 12-pointer that Hefner Appling tried to rattle up for me vanished.

"I suppose," Hefner concluded, "that our deer found a girlfriend elsewhere and would be about as easy to find right now as an honest politician. Let's not waste any more time hunting for him."

So I spent the mornings and afternoons alone, on an elevated stand that overlooked a sere and thorny landscape. I could see only a tiny portion of the ranch, which is managed primarily for wildlife and hunting. Every year more and more ranches in Texas and the Southwest are put under scientific game management. At Senderos, for example, there are about 500 deer, or less than one per 20 acres, which

---

Close-ups of deer shown on pages 132 and 133 tell story. Buck A is fine eight-pointer with high horns, but rack falls far short of a 150 score. In another two years, maybe three, deer will be a terrific trophy.

Buck B also is a good buck with 11 points and older than A. He has heavier beams but less spread and height. The rack would score well below 150. I would rank this buck No. 6, the least desirable of the six.

Buck C has a splendid rack—quite wide and very symmetrical. Rack has 10 points. This was the only deer out of the six that was shot, and careful measurements resulted in Boone and Crockett score 159.

HELPFUL BOOKS ABOUT TROPHIES

For more information on whitetail trophy bucks (measuring, scoring, location, and occurrence) the following books are very worthwhile:

Records of North American Big Game, official record book for outstanding native North American big game, 8th Edition, 1981, $31.50 postpaid from Boone and Crockett Club, 205 South Patrick Street, Alexandria, VA 22314.

Big Rack and *Great Whitetails of North America*, both by Robert Rogers, Texas Hunting Services, 5058 Wingfoot, Corpus Christi, TX 78413. These describe how, when, and where the biggest whitetail bucks have been taken.

Producing Quality Whitetails, by Al Brothers and Murphy E. Ray Jr., Wildlife Services Publications, Box 2145, Laredo, TX 78041. Describes how to manage land for bigger whitetails and better hunting.

For specific information on The Senderos Ranch, write Box 311, El Campo, TX 77437.

is low indeed compared to most whitetail habitats nationwide. But half of those deer are bucks, and among the bucks are many trophy animals. During a recent hunting season, 35 hunters collected 33 bucks at Senderos, and all were eight-pointers or better. The two unsuccessful hunters had their opportunities. A similar number of does were shot by these hunters (it is legal) and by resident ranch hands. This is a remarkable score, made possible only because enough does are harvested to keep the buck-to-doe ratio approximately one to one. The range at Senderos is not overcrowded or overbrowsed. The whitetails are extremely healthy and grow rapidly.

The cover is as brittle and dense as a whitetail hunter is likely to find anywhere. I studied it for long hours, in warm sunshine and during bitter northeast winds. The longer I sat, the more deter-

mined I became to shoot a bigger whitetail than I had ever shot before. I saw my share of bucks, including a number of tempting 10-pointers. One browsed for several minutes only about 30 yards away. I watched another 10-pointer make a scrape on the ground. It seemed strange to be passing up deer that I would have dropped instantly in years past.

Suddenly, just before dusk one cold, gloomy evening, a remarkable thing happened. First a sleek eight-pointer strolled out of thick blackbrush and began to browse about 150 yards away. Directly behind him, another buck emerged and walked a thin trail toward me. Through my riflescope, I counted 12 points. The rack was fairly high. My heart was pumping wildly, and I almost squeezed the trigger.

That's when buck No. 3 suddenly materialized. Barely moving the rifle, I picked him up in the scope and waited forever for him to look in my direction. The rack wasn't quite as wide as the 12-pointer's, and there were only 10 points, but those points were long and very dark. Most of all, the heavy, forward-curving main beams caught my eye.

The third deer, I decided, had more antler mass than the two others put together. I would have liked a longer look, but all at once, the buck turned and moved off. My shot stopped him 125 yards away. My pulse was pounding as I hurried for a closer look in the failing light.

There was no question about it. I knew immediately that he was the biggest of the many whitetails I have shot in my half a century of hunting them. Even in the dusk I had made one mistake, though. The deer had nine points, not 10. One tine had been broken off, probably in a fight with another buck. Still, I knew the rack would score at least 150 by the Boone and Crockett system. The odds are that I will never shoot a better buck.

Buck D has a high-horned, nontypical rack. There are 21 points over one inch in length. He would undoubtedly score more than 150 by the Boone and Crockett system. This rack is most difficult to judge.

Buck E would likely score the highest of the lot. This remarkable buck has 17 points, heavy main beams, and a two-foot spread. The rack would probably score between 180 and 190 in the typical class.

Buck F is another unusually fine whitetail with 14 points and heavy beams. Notice how the rack extends well beyond the ears. I believe this deer would score 170, and he is my choice for No. 2 in this group.

The All-Time No. 1 Whitetail

Ron Schara

J im Jordan stared at the fresh deer tracks in the snow. He figured that three, maybe four deer had recently shuffled by. But one set of hoof marks caught his eye. The snow-molded hoofs were huge; the toes splayed outward like the legs of an overloaded chair.

Jordan cradled a .25/20-caliber Winchester in his arms and took a deep breath of cold morning air. If the tracks were any indication, he had crossed paths with a huge whitetail buck. Jordan peered at the tracks again. He had never seen such massive hoofs. He knew he had to follow the inviting track. That decision launched him on a bizarre deer hunt that really lasted for 64 years.

The tracks Jim Jordan followed on a November morning in 1914 were made by the world-record whitetail buck. But for more than six decades, a series of strange twists of fate kept Jordan from being recognized as the man who shot the great buck.

Past editions of *Records of North American Big Game*, the record book, stated that the name of the hunter who took the world-record typical whitetail was unknown. Those editions also indicated that the location was Sandstone, Minnesota, which has turned out to be a mistake.

For more than 60 years, about the only thing known about the No. 1 set of antlers was that they were discovered at a rummage sale in Sandstone. When Jordan heard of that discovery, he knew that the record really belonged in his name. He had written down the story of the hunt the day the record buck was killed, and he remembered vividly. But events made him give up hope of being listed in the records.

When the locomotive whistled, the deer raised their heads from their beds in the snowy grass. Jordan put his sights on the great buck's neck and fired. But the buck ran, and Jordan fired again and again.

Several years ago, I wrote a column for the *Minneapolis Tribune* pointing out the mystery of the world-record antlers. Later, I got a call from a reader who said that the hunter might be an elderly man who lived near the St. Croix River, which flows between Minnesota and Wisconsin. I looked the man up; his name was Jim Jordan. I wrote about the story he told me in the *Tribune* in 1977, and that attracted the attention of officials of the North American Big Game Awards Program, administered by the Boone and Crockett Club. They investigated, and in December of 1978, the Boone and Crockett Big Game Committee recognized Jordan as the man who shot the record buck.

The story begins on November 20, 1914, in north-western Wisconsin. Jordan, who lived on a small farm near the little town of Danbury, woke up particularly early. He looked out and liked what he saw: his farmyard freshly covered with snow. It was the opening day of Wisconsin's deer season, an event that Jordan never missed. He was 22 years old, a woodsman, logger, and trapper, and he loved deer hunting most of all.

Jordan hopped out of bed, dressed quickly, and hustled out to the barn to harness his horse to a buggy. He wanted to be ready when Egus Davis rode up. Davis arrived on schedule, unsaddled his horse, and threw his gear into Jordan's buggy. Together, the two quickly headed into Danbury, bought their 50¢ deer licenses, and turned the horse and buggy southward toward the Yellow River. When they arrived where they wanted to hunt, Jordan tied his buggy horse, and the two hunters headed into the aspen timber on foot. They had hunted in the familiar woodlands during previous deer seasons. Today, they planned to hunt together rather than split up; Davis discovered that in the rush to open the deer season, he'd forgotten his hunting knife.

As Jordan expected, the hunting conditions were ideal, thanks to the new snow. Quietly, softly, the two trudged toward the Yellow River. They hadn't walked far when Jordan spotted a doe, raised his rifle, and fired. The big doe fell. Davis was elated by the quick success. He suggested that they drag the doe back over the short distance to the horse and

buggy. But Jordan was impatient. He handed his hunting knife to his friend.

"Here's my knife. You can have the doe, but you also can take the deer back by yourself. I want to keep going," he told his hunting partner. Davis nodded his approval, and Jordan, minus his hunting knife, headed off by himself. He hadn't gone far when, up ahead in the virgin snow, he spied a string of pockmarks meandering through the aspen thicket. From a distance, he knew the tracks had been made by deer, and—because of the overnight snowfall—he knew they were fresh.

His attention was drawn immediately to the set of supersize hoofprints. He couldn't resist the temptation to follow. He checked his Winchester lever-action rifle one more time; it was loaded, but the magazine wasn't full. The buck that made those imprints in the snow might not be far away. He quickened his pace. The fresh deer tracks wandered southward for a few hundred yards and then turned back north toward Danbury and closer to the Soo Line railroad tracks that roughly paralleled the course of the Yellow River. Jordan continued until the deer trail led toward an opening, the railroad right-of-way. The wandering deer—there were three or four sets of tracks, including the giant buck—had probably crossed the railroad and continued, he thought to himself.

Suddenly, Jordan heard the familiar whistle of an oncoming Soo Line freight train. He paused near the open swath in the aspen. A quick glance at the trail told him the deer had not crossed the tracks. The fresh sign ambled along the grassy strip between the tracks and the timber's edge. He had a good, clear view, north and south, on his side of the railroad bed. Still, he couldn't spot the deer that had made the tracks he'd been dogging. The train whistled again, still a long way down the track.

Suddenly, just ahead, Jordan saw movement—heads raised out of the heavy, tall grass along the railroad tracks. The bedded deer were alerted by the oncoming train. There were three deer or four, Jordan wasn't sure. His eyes were already glued to the third one that appeared above the snow-laden clumps of grass less than 100 yards away. It was a huge buck.

Jordan didn't hesitate. He quickly shouldered his .25-caliber Winchester and steadied the iron sights on the big buck's neck. The deer remained motionless, listening for the train, and unaware of Jordan. The buck was poised, head high, his enormous head ornament shining in the sunlight of the cloud-free morning. Jordan squeezed the trigger.

The rifle bucked, but Jordan's eyes never left the huge deer. The does bounded for the jungle of aspen. The buck went in the opposite direction. Jordan fired again, then again. Once more, and that was the last cartridge in the rifle. The speeding buck disappeared.

Jordan was quite sure he'd hit the buck once if not twice. What's more, tracking conditions were still ideal. He figured he'd catch up with that buck

THE 64-YEAR DEER HUNT IN BRIEF

1914—Jim Jordan shoots an enormous whitetail buck on November 20. George Van Castle offers to mount the head for $5. Jordan agrees, and Van Castle takes the unskinned head to his home in Webster, Wisconsin.

Later, Van Castle moves to Hinckley, Minnesota, but does not inform Jordan.

Years later, Jordan visits Hinckley to see Van Castle, but the taxidermist has moved to Florida.

1964—Robert Ludwig, a distant relative of Jordan, buys the Van Castle mount for $3 at a rummage sale in Sandstone, Minnesota. The cape has deteriorated. Ludwig shows the trophy to Jordan, who is sure that it came from the buck he shot in 1914.

Ludwig measures the rack and sends the Boone and Crockett form to Bernie Fashingbauer, an official B & C

measurer, who measures the antlers again at a score of 206 5/8—a world record. The rack, later measured by a B & C committee, is officially recognized as the No. 1 typical whitetail, hunter "unknown."

1968—Ludwig sells the rack to Charles T. Arnold of Nashua, New Hampshire, a collector of antlers. Arnold still owns the trophy, which he refurbishes with a new cape.

1977—as a result of a story by Ron Schara in the *Minneapolis Tribune*, the Boone and Crockett Club begins investigating Jim Jordan's claim.

1978—The club officially recognizes Jordan as the man who shot the world-record typical whitetail, with a recalculated score of 206 1/8. Jordan died two months before the recognition.

Jim Jordan with his wife, Lena, when he was 21. He shot the buck the next year.

Charles T. Arnold, who owns the trophy. He later refurbished it with a fresh cape.

again, sooner or later. Sooner, probably, if the animal was seriously wounded.

He quickly picked up the buck's trail. Anxiously, he followed the buck's bounding footprints, looking for blood. Then he remembered his empty rifle. He paused and dug frantically in his coat pockets for more ammunition. He had, he discovered, only one more cartridge. His last shot would have to be fired at close range.

Jordan continued to follow the buck's trail. He found blood, not much, but some. He trudged on. The buck seemed to be heading toward the Yellow River. Jordan didn't mind at all, for the river flowed not far from his farmstead. Suddenly, about 150 yards away, he caught a glimpse of the giant whitetail. He raised his rifle, then lowered it. With only one shot left, he decided to wait for a closer shot.

The whitetail headed for the river, where it turned west. Jordan was not far behind. Now he saw the buck most of the time as it stumbled toward the river. At the river's edge, the buck stopped, his massive head and neck arched low above the ground. Jordan continued to close the distance between them. Suddenly, the buck plunged into the shallow river, struggled awhile against the current, and

then stepped out on the far bank. By that time, Jordan had reached the river's near edge. The mighty whitetail, again alerted, raised his head and looked back.

"He looked right at me," Jordan told me years later. "I aimed at the backbone this time because he was such a big deer; I didn't think my rifle could bring him down if I didn't hit him there." Indeed, Jordan's Model 1892 Winchester, firing the pipsqueak .25/20 cartridge, was really inadequate for deer hunting.

Jordan fired his last shot, and the huge whitetail collapsed.

Jordan rushed across the shallow river, oblivious to the icy water that poured into his hunting boots. The buck hadn't moved. For the first time, Jordan could take a close look at the marvelous whitetail. Never had he seen such a set of antlers. Never had he seen such a heavy deer. He reached for his hunting knife, and then he remembered. He had loaned it to Egus Davis.

No problem, Jordan thought. If his calculations were correct, he wasn't much more than a quarter-mile from his farm. He'd walk back to find Davis and get his knife.

Davis had already returned to the farm with the horse and buggy and the doe. Jordan told of his hunting luck. Then he and Davis hurried back toward the river where the big buck had fallen. But when they arrived, there was no buck in sight.

"The buck must have flopped one more time and slid into the river," Jordan explained. "I went down to the bend of the river, and there he was—hung up on a big rock. I waded out in water waist deep to get to him. Later, it took a whole bunch of us to pull him home. I can't remember if he weighed just a little over 400 or just under 400 pounds."

The news of Jordan's mammoth whitetail spread quickly. Neighbors and town folk rode out to take a look. One of them was George Van Castle, who lived in Webster, about 10 miles south of Danbury. He worked on the Soo Line Railroad, but he also did taxidermy work in his spare time. He greatly admired Jordan's trophy and offered to mount the head for $5. Jordan accepted. He'd seen plenty of big bucks, but none as big as his. Van Castle picked up the unskinned head and caught the Soo Line south to his home in Webster. Jordan didn't know it then, but he would not see his prized trophy again for more than 50 years.

Shortly after Van Castle agreed to mount the head, his wife became sick and died. Troubled by the loss of his wife, Van Castle decided to move to Hinckley, Minnesota. But he never told Jordan, who waited for months and heard no word about his mounted trophy. Finally, he made a trip to Webster, where he learned that Van Castle had gone to Hinckley, and so had his mounted whitetail.

Jordan considered making the trip from Danbury to Hinckley to reclaim his deer, but such a trek was not easy. Although the towns were only 25 miles apart, they were separated by a long bridgeless stretch of the St. Croix River. Time passed. Eventually, a new bridge across the St. Croix connected Danbury and Hinckley. But by then, Van Castle had married again and moved to Florida.

"I never heard from Van Castle again," Jordan recalled. He gave up all hope of seeing his whitetail trophy again. He and his wife, Lena, moved to a small acreage near Hinckley, along the Minnesota side of the St. Croix. He was not a young man any more, and life had not been easy. Still, he hadn't lost his interest in deer hunting. He shot his share of good bucks. Their many racks hung from the rafters of the Jordans' home, and he could easily tell when, where, and how each had been taken. He started collecting deer antlers as a hobby. That hobby led to still another twist of fate.

One day in 1964, a Minnesotan by the name of Robert Ludwig was strolling down Main Street in Sandstone, a small town about eight miles from Hinckley. Ludwig was a shirt-tail relative of Jordan's and also collected antlers. He came to a rummage sale on a vacant corner lot. The goods—dishes, antiques, furniture—were the usual assortment. One item, however, caught his eye. It was an old, dusty,

decrepit, mounted deer head. Ludwig looked it over. The mothy head had been stuffed with yellowed newspapers and homemade plaster, and it had been sewed up with twine. But the antlers were magnificent. Ludwig couldn't believe their size. The rack, massive and perfectly shaped with five equal points on a side, was larger than any he had collected.

Ludwig paid $3 for the head and took it home. His wife was less than overjoyed at his bargain. The mount was beyond repair.

Ludwig, a forester for Minnesota's Department of Natural Resources, became curious about his $3 antlers. He got a form for measuring typical whitetail racks and measured the huge rack himself. He wasn't sure what the total score meant, but he sent his results to a St. Paul naturalist, Bernie Fashingbauer, an official measurer for the Boone and Crockett awards program.

Fashingbauer thought Ludwig's measurements must be wrong. If they were right, the rack qualified as a new world-record typical whitetail buck. He contacted Ludwig and arranged to see the big rack and to take his own set of measurements: an unbelievable score of 206⅝, a world record.

The score was submitted to Boone and Crockett officials, who asked for measuring by a panel of experts. The experts came up with the same score. Ludwig had indeed found the new world-record typical whitetail rack. He couldn't wait to tell his friends and relatives—particularly Jim Jordan, since Jordan was also interested in big antlers.

Jordan looked at the record rack when Ludwig showed it to him. He was stunned. It was the same rack he had lost 50 years ago to Van Castle, the taxidermist.

Ecstatic about the discovery, Jordan had a picture taken of himself with the record antlers. He showed it to old friends who had seen the head five decades earlier. They agreed it looked like the same buck. Ludwig, however, disagreed. Four years later, in 1968, he sold the record head for $1,500 to Charles T. Arnold, a deer-antler collecter from Nashua, New Hampshire. Arnold still owns the record rack, which has since been remounted and refurbished with a new cape.

So Jordan was separated from his trophy, although he continued to insist it was the same buck he killed in 1914. He also insisted he wasn't interested in any of the money Ludwig received for selling the world-record head.

"I just want to set the record straight," Jordan told me in the fall of 1977. Of course, the record eventually was set straight when the Boone and Crockett Club credited Jordan with killing the world-record whitetail buck. The score was recalculated at 206⅛. But the long hunting adventure took one more bizarre twist when the announcement was made in December 1978.

Jordan never heard it. Less than two months before his record claim was officially accepted, Jordan had died at the age of 86.

Freak Antlers

Jim Zumbo

One of the oddest and most fascinating big-game animals is a deer with freak antlers. Called nontypicals for record-keeping purposes, these zany racks grow in absolutely unpredictable formations. A few are magnificent and awesome trophies. Some are nothing but a curious conversation piece. And some are downright ugly—repulsive examples of how nature sometimes makes mistakes.

Why do some deer grow deformed or nonsymmetrical racks, while others develop normal, typical antlers? Are freak bucks rare? Can deer be induced artifically to produce nontypical racks? The answers may come as a surprise to you.

To fully understand this strange phenomenon, let's start with a brief look at what's involved in normal antler development.

All normal North American male deer, including giant bull moose, grow antlers, which are shed annually. The whole process is controlled by two hormones. One is produced by the pituitary gland, which is situated in the brain. The other, called testosterone, is manufactured by the testicles.

Scientists have shown that the amount of daylight regulates production of the hormones. As the length of daylight increases in spring, the antlers begin to develop, and they grow rapidly through late spring and summer. During this time, they are covered with a blood-rich skin called velvet. In late summer, the buck's testicles enlarge greatly and release testosterone, which causes the velvet to crack and shed.

Deer with undeveloped or removed testicles often grow abnormal racks and rarely shed their velvet normally. I once shot a mule deer in late November that had velvet-covered, badly deformed antlers. It had a total of seven points, growing at grotesque angles from the main beams. When I rolled him over to field-dress him, I learned the reason for his strange antlers: His testicles had failed to develop completely. Otherwise, though, the buck appeared normal. He was in excellent condition and weighed about 200 pounds after he had been dressed.

Many more deer grow typical antlers than nontypical ones. But enough odd ones exist that the North American Big Game Awards Program, which keeps records of big-game trophies, recognizes special categories for nontypical mule deer, whitetails, and Coues deer. There are no categories for nontypical moose, elk, caribou, or blacktail deer, apparently because too few good nontypical trophies are taken.

A typical whitetail rack is symmetrical. It consists of two main beams and one or more points spaced along each beam. All points usually are counted on a whitetail.

Studies of thousands of whitetails show that most have even-numbered racks. Six, eight, or 10-point bucks are more common, for example, than five, seven, or nine-point bucks. Only about one buck in 50 has 11 or more points. One in 1,200 has 15 or more points, and only one in 5,000 has 17 or more points.

Interestingly enough, some areas produce a greater proportion of odd racks than others. In parts of Texas, for instance, a buck with "double drophorns" is considered a highly prized trophy. A drophorn is defined as an antler with a tine that an-

Why do some deer have zany racks like this one, with points jutting crazily in every direction? Read about the fresh insights and new theories on this curiosity.

haven't been able to prove their hunch, but they suspect that certain plants growing on granitic soils cause hypogonadism.

Biologists have observed that normal bucks are much more aggressive than velvet-horned bucks. Normal males won't allow an abnormal one within 10 feet, and they sometimes charge more than 60 feet to drive away velvet-horns. A Texas hunter once killed a velvet-horned buck that was being chased by six normally antlered bucks, which had "already hooked its rump bloody."

Velvet-horned bucks never respond aggressively to challenges by normal bucks and always keep their distance. They approach feeding grounds cautiously and allow normal bucks to have their fill first.

Injured deer commonly develop abnormal antlers. Often, the relation between the injury and the deformed antler is contralateral. In other words, an injury to the animal's left side resulted in an odd right antler, and vice versa. This isn't always true. One buck observed for three years had lost the lower part of a front leg. Each year the injured animal grew a spike on the side of the injury and a typical, branching antler on the other side.

An injury to the antler itself can cause a deformed rack. Deer kept in wire-fenced pens, for instance, often grow odd-shaped antlers because they scrape their growing racks against the fence.

Nontypical racks also result from genetic factors. In other words, a buck with freak antlers is more likely than a normal buck to sire nontypical bucks.

Mule deer have a different antler structure from whitetails. A mature male typically grows a doubly forked antler on each side. Only the points on one side are counted. Most Westerners don't include the brow tine or eye guard, although this practice varies in some areas. Thus a four-point generally has four tines and one brow tine on each side. A whitetail hunter would call this a 10-pointer. Most muleys have the same number of points on each side, but three or five points on one side and four on the other are common.

In some areas, mule deer grow a single tine sticking straight to the side. Often three to six inches long, this tine is often called a cheater because it raises scores in Western big-buck contests, in which the greatest outside spread is scored. Several sporting-goods stores in Utah sponsor such contests each year, awarding four-wheel-drive motor vehicles as top prizes. Invariably, a rack with a cheater wins. To be in the running, a hunter usually needs to take a deer with a 40-inch or wider outside spread. Few of these racks, however, score high enough to be listed in "the book," *Records of North American Big Game,*

gles straight down. The tine is often situated midway on the beam. If each antler is a drophorn, the deer is called a double drophorn. Such animals are extremely attractive, especially if the rack is heavy.

The Central Mineral Region in Texas has an unusually high ratio of deer with hypogonadism, which is the scientific word for undeveloped testicles. Bucks with this condition have velvet antlers, and they behave distinctly differently from normal bucks.

Curious about what might be causing the high ratio, biological researchers examined each deer taken by hunters in this region for seven years. Each kill site was located on soil maps. The results? Of 1,605 hypogonadal deer, 1,474 or 91.8 percent were taken on soils composed of granite. Half the remaining abnormal deer were killed within 1½ miles of granitic soils. This finding indicated that their home territories probably included granitic soils.

What in the world does granitic soil have to do with abnormal antlers and testicles? The scientists

Some freak racks are striking trophies. This is No. 1 nontypical whitetail. It was taken in Texas in 1892.

One mystery of nontypical deer is that their antlers usually take on the same shape each season. It stands to reason that freak racks are just that—freaks—and you might figure they should grow in different designs each year. But this sort of thing doesn't happen. A pen-raised nontypical deer grows surprisingly similar antlers each year.

In 1962, Del Austin, a Nebraska bowhunter, killed what was then the third-largest nontypical whitetail ever taken. It earned first place in the Pope and Young Club's records, which are restricted to bow-killed game. The two sets of antlers shed by the buck before he was killed were amazingly similar. When this deer was taken, he had 19 points on one antler and 18 on the other. The rack had the amazing score of 277 $\frac{3}{8}$.

Some antlers are so grossly deformed that they endanger the life of the deer. A drophorn buck, for instance, often must cope with obstructed vision, a weakness that makes him more vulnerable to predators, including man.

Occasionally, a buck actually is injured by his wildly growing tines. One whitetail shot in Pennsylvania was unable to open his mouth more than half an inch because his antlers curved tightly under his jaws. It almost certainly would have died of starvation in the winter had it not been killed.

More than one buck has been blinded in one eye when a tine grew into it. More common is infection brought about when points pierce the skin.

It is probable that an antler tine can grow in such a way that it pierces the brain, killing the animal. Naturalists have noted bighorn sheep that have been

because they don't have the necessary mass and main-beam length.

In the past, Western cowboys occasionally lassoed male fawns and castrated them. Some of these bucks grew no antlers at all. Others sprouted fantastically branched racks. Sometimes they never shed their antlers.

The cowboys did not necessarily castrate deer as merely a cruel prank. Altered male animals generally grow more quickly than normal ones, and their flesh is said to be of higher quality. To this day, millions of cattle and sheep are neutered each year for this reason.

An altered buck often grows what is known as a "cactus rack," a confused mass of branches and nubs covered with velvet. Most cactus racks have no distinctive beams and appear to be spongy. Few hunters consider one a trophy.

While riding horseback in Utah once, I jumped several deer in a small cluster of piñon pines. One deer seemed to have entwined a sagebrush plant in his antlers. From closer range, I looked over the buck through my binoculars and discovered that he was a cactus buck. He had no discernible antlers, only a grotesque, burly mass of velvet. I saw this buck two more times that fall, both times during breeding season. But he had no does with him and never had a rut-swollen neck. I suppose he was incapable of mating.

This queerly antlered buck was in danger of losing the sight in his left eye and of having a tine pierce his throat.

killed by ingrowing horns and muskrats that have died when their teeth curved into their skulls.

An especially odd antler formation is palmation—the development of a flat "web" between tines. A moose's antlers, of course, are typically palmated. Both mule deer and whitetails sometimes grow antlers so palmated that they look much like those of a moose.

Some deer grow a nontypical antler on one side and a typical one on the other. A few bucks develop no antler at all on one side and a tremendous, many-pointed one on the other side.

Then there are bucks that never grow antlers. This failure is usually caused by hormonal abnormalities, but apparently the tendency can be inherited. Anterless bucks turn up frequently in certain areas. Sometimes only a tiny nubbin appears where each antler should be.

On the other hand, some does carry massive racks. Biologists believe most antlered does do not produce enough female hormones, which are thought to suppress antler growth. A rare cause of antler development on female deer is a tumor that releases male hormones.

Another type of freak deer is a hermaphrodite—an animal with both male and female sex organs. Hermaphrodites seem to be increasing in numbers in some areas, particularly in the Northeast. If a hunter ever shoots a hermaphrodite or antlered doe, he should immediately call a conservation officer. By studying the glands and reproductive organs of bisexual deer, scientists hope to learn enough about hermaphroditism to prevent the condition's occurrence in humans.

An extremely rare type of freak deer is one with three antlers. This occurs among both whitetails and mule deer. The classic *Lives of Game Animals*, written by noted naturalist Ernest Thompson Seton, contains line drawings of two "three-horned" deer. One, a whitetail, was shot in December 1897 near Brainerd, Minnesota. This animal's left and right antlers are massive, typical but slightly deformed. Below the left one protrudes another antler, which forks once.

The other buck is a mule deer, taken near Meeker, Colorado, in 1892. His odd antler juts straight up from the skull, exactly between the two "normal" antlers. This third antler has at least seven points. In addition, this buck is a double drophorn—a long tine angles downward from each main beam.

Not all extra antlers grow out of the cap of a deer's skull. Duwayne Statzer, hunting just outside Craig, Colorado, some years ago, knocked down a four-point mule deer that had a third antler growing under its left eye. The tine measured 6¾ inches long, and velvet still covered the last two or three inches.

A well-known buck that lived until 1928 in Yosemite National Park was perhaps the strangest of all. Known as "Old Horny," this mule deer was first noticed when he sprouted a third antler halfway between his nose and forehead. This extra horn came out first as a single spike, covered with velvet. That winter, he shed this antler and developed in its place a pair of horns, still velvet-covered. Next year, these antlers were discarded and gave way to a third two-pronged set. For at least four years, this buck roamed the park, attracting a great deal of attention until he became sick and died.

The next year, another three-antlered buck was seen in Yosemite Valley. A weirdly jutting prong

NONTYPICAL RECORD-BOOK DEER

Whitetails				Mule Deer	
Saskatchewan	38	Pennsylvania	5	Colorado	68
Wisconsin	34	British Columbia	4	Idaho	36
Minnesota	26	Idaho	4	Arizona	29
Montana	17	Maine	4	Utah	22
Nebraska	17	New Brunswick	4	Montana	15
Ohio	15	New York	4	Wyoming	15
Washington	14	Arkansas	3	New Mexico	13
Texas	14	Georgia	3	Saskatchewan	10
South Dakota	11	Nova Scotia	3	Oregon	9
Alberta	14	Oklahoma	3	Washington	9
Iowa	9	Louisiana	5	Nevada	7
Wyoming	9	Virginia	2	Alberta	5
Illinois	9	Kentucky	1	British Columbia	5
Kansas	7	Maryland	1	California	3
Manitoba	6	South Carolina	1	Nebraska	2
North Dakota	8	Tennessee	1	South Dakota	2
Michigan	6	West Virginia	1	Kansas	1
Missouri	6	Mississippi	1	Unknown	3
		Unknown	2		
		Total	240	Total	240

grew from the middle of his forehead. So striking was his resemblance to Old Horny that he was called "Unicorn Junior." His existence seems to be evidence that such characteristics as three antlers can be inherited.

A freak whitetail shot near Bracketville, Texas, in 1906 actually had two complete sets of antlers. One set grew beneath the other set. Both are somewhat typical. This buck is a 20-pointer.

Some hunters still believe the old myth that the age of a buck can be determined from the number of points on his antlers. Nothing disproves this tenacious fib more firmly than the existence of freak heads. Some cactus bucks have as many as 1,000 points! Though very few deer live more than 10 years, racks with 20, 30, or even 50 points turn up once in a while.

Many hunters falsely believe that the record system does not penalize differences between antlers of a nontypical trophy. The rack is first measured as if it were a typical one. But then the score on abnormal points is *added* not subtracted as in the typical category.

In both categories, though, differences between the two antlers at specified locations are subtracted. Thus, a nontypical buck with a huge, many-pointed, nonsymmetrical rack may not make the record book.

The world-record nontypical whitetail was killed in 1892 by Jeff Benson at Brady, Texas. It had 23 points on the right antler and 26 on the left and scored 286 points. Strangely enough, nontypical

An interesting deformity is palmation—the growth of a "web" between tines. This whitetail's antlers resemble those of a moose.

record whitetails don't seem to be getting scarce. Of the top 15 bucks, seven were killed in the 1970's.

The world-record nontypical mule deer was killed by Ed Broder in 1926 near Chip Lake, Alberta. It scored 355 2/8 and had 22 points on the right antler and 21 on the left.

Unlike whitetails, truly large nontypical mule deer haven't been making the record book in recent years. Of the top 15 heads, only two were taken after 1970.

Outstanding nontypical specimens seem to come from the same areas that produce record-class typical deer.

The top five states or provinces, in terms of producing record-book typical whitetails, are Saskatchewan, Texas, Minnesota, Wisconsin, and Nebraska, in that order. Saskatchewan also leads the nontypical listings. It is followed by Wisconsin, Minnesota, Montana, and Nebraska. But Texas is still high on the nontypical list—No. 8.

The mule-deer situation is similar. One state—Colorado—leads both lists. The next six states are the same in both categories. Only their sequence is different.

It's tough to judge a record-book nontypical deer as it races through the underbrush, or even as it stands on an open hillside. But the sight of one will make any hunter's adrenaline flow. Despite the odd rack, a big buck with funny horns never lacks for admiration and amazement from wide-eyed observers.

This is a so-called cactus buck, easily identified by the grotesque mass of points. Hormonal abnormalities cause this condition.

PART 7

FINDING THOSE HIDDEN BUCKS

Where the Bucks Go

John Weiss

Where the bucks go after opening day, and how they manage to evade throngs of hunters still prowling the woodlands, remains a mystery to many people. But sometimes small fragments of the puzzle fall into place, enabling savvy hunters to take very nice bucks—even on the last day of the season.

My friend Clyde Beltner had one of these eye-opening experiences a few years back. On his small Morgan County, Ohio, farm, well before opening day, he had pegged the routine of a handsome six-point buck using a trail through a narrow hollow all choked with honeysuckle. Yet after Beltner patiently waited on stand the entire season, the deer never showed, and Beltner's license went unfilled that year. Because guns had been hammering all around and a local newspaper reported that 24,000 hunters had infiltrated tiny Morgan County that year, Clyde was certain "his" deer had been taken by another hunter on a neighboring farm.

Two days after the season closed, Beltner grabbed a handsaw and hiked to the very center of an old meadow to cut down a Christmas tree. A small, raised patch of ground—no larger than a front porch—stood there, almost entirely shale and not capable of growing anything except a few pine trees that Clyde had planted years before as seedlings. Only one of those evergreens took root and survived. The lone pine, its branches drooping low to the ground, stood like a lone sentinel watching over acres and acres of open meadowland.

Beltner's mind was on unfinished holiday shopping when suddenly the same six-point buck he'd been hoping to collect days earlier jumped up from beneath the low pine boughs and bounded away. For a long moment, Clyde just stood there shaking his head in disbelief: That buck had probably been holed up right there for the entire season.

This hunter took his buck because he knew how deer react when something upsets their routine.

Clyde left that pine undisturbed and later *bought* his Christmas tree in town. He also saw his buck many more times as the months passed. The following autumn, the deer was sporting a still larger rack—and still used the same trail through the same nearby hollow.

At the onset of the hunting season, Clyde went to his favorite stand; gunshots again rang out in all directions. After two days of not even catching a glimpse of his buck, however, Clyde knew exactly where to go. This time he was armed for the task at hand. After hiking halfway across the expansive meadow, he stopped and took a brief peek through his binoculars.

Sure enough, the buck was bedded beneath the branches of the lone pine tree, his chin flat against the ground. Beltner quickly assumed a steady kneeling position, and with a single shot from 85 yards, collected his winter supply of venison.

Clyde now realizes, along with many other veteran hunters, that preseason scouting in the usual manner is increasingly becoming a waste of time. The only exceptions are when planning for a wilderness hunt or a bowhunt. Strategies planned for these hunts are seldom interfered with.

Unfortunately, the opposite is true when hunting whitetails on those tracts of land just beyond the city limits, especially on property open to public hunting such as state and national forests, timber-company holdings, mining leases, and utility company lands. These lands remain relatively fixed in number, yet each year they must somehow accommodate more hunters than the season before. The end result is akin to cramming six pounds of apples into a five-pound bag. Something, obviously, has to give, and in a vast majority of states, that "something" is a hunter-success rate that steadily diminishes.

An enterprising whitetail hunter will leave plenty of boot tracks when scouting such congested areas to determine if huntable numbers of animals are indeed present. Then he'll want to locate bedding areas, feeding sites, breeding scrapes, and major trails the deer use.

One common shortcoming of most hunters, however, is failure to consider still another crucial element in the scouting equation: the sudden presence of countless other hunters in the immediate vicinity.

In whitetail habitat that has been quiet and undisturbed for the previous 11 months, suddenly convoys of vehicles are traveling seldom-used trails and back roads. Hunters themselves are tramping around, saturating the woodlands with man scent, climbing trees, cutting brush for ground level blinds, cutting firewood for camp, hollering while making drives, sending out fusillades of shots, and chasing the animals through the woods.

Obviously, a day or two of such blatant intrusion will completely spook the deer, disrupt their normal behavior patterns, and force them into hiding. Survival now becomes their foremost concern. Feeding and other activities become secondary.

One locale that hard-hunted whitetails frequently retreat into is any kind of marshy lowland, swale, or swamp containing at least several inches of standing water. Biologists believe whitetails under pressure intuitively head for water, perhaps obeying some primitive genetic instinct to use water as a means of covering their scent trails and evading predators.

Not many deer hunters dress appropriately for gunning in swamps. Fewer still have the desire to go sloshing through sometimes knee-deep water, muck, and mire. It's cold and wet, it stinks, and it is difficult to negotiate on foot. As a result, most hunters elect to bypass such hellish places altogether, or at least widely skirt their perimeters to stay on high and dry ground. Yet the bold, willing hunter will discover that shortly after the opening-day rifles begin cracking, junglelike marshland may act as a magnet to deer inhabiting the immediate region.

I discovered not long ago in South Carolina's Francis Marion National Forest just how many deer seek refuge in swamplands. Because of prior commitments, Benny Wilson and I were unable to join forces until the fourth day of the deer season. We didn't bother to scout or install portable tree stands in the forest's wooded regions; instead we donned chest waders and began slowly sneak-hunting through flooded black-oak timber and cypress bogs.

During the early morning and late afternoon, we saw dozens of browsing deer, standing hock-deep in the tannin-stained water. We discovered that during the midday hours, these deer like to find small, dry, slightly elevated hummocks and ridges where they can bed down.

A stealthy swamp hunter, because there are no brittle twigs or dry leaves underfoot to betray his location, can often approach feeding or bedded deer quite easily. A hunter who wades slowly, hunts into the wind, and uses intervening cover to conceal his approach can move along as silently and inconspicuously as a wisp of woodsmoke.

If swamps are the premier locations for finding hard-hunted whitetails, second place must go to pine forests and plantations, which speckle the whitetail's habitat from coast to coast.

Whitetails have a distinct preference for long-needle species such as white pine and red pine, but the real key is to find the immature, closely planted trees no taller than eight or 10 feet. These young trees generally have dense whorls of branches close to the ground, which create a thick understory that whitetails find ideal to hide under. Conversely, stands of older, towering pines block sunlight penetration to the ground, causing the lower branches to die and fall, leaving no understory cover at all.

One pine plantation near Eau Claire, Wisconsin, contains such a density of young trees that a walking hunter could not see six feet in any direction. After several days of unsuccessfully hunting nearby birch ridges where tracks pockmarked almost every square yard of ground, our party quickly realized that the pressured deer just had to be hiding in the pines. To overcome the difficulty of not being able to see any appreciable distance from ground level, we hung portable stands high in trees surrounding the perimeter of the plantation and posted ourselves during the hours of dawn and dusk. From elevated vantage points, we could easily see long distances down and through the aisles of pines. By the end of the next day, four additional bucks were hanging from our camp meat pole.

Because there were six hunters in our group, maybe staged drives would have also produced well. But the point driven home was that when hunters become evident, it doesn't take wary whitetails anywhere very long to realize they're in serious trouble. Because most whitetails have relatively small home ranges, they will remain in some type of security cover until the heat is off.

As Clyde Beltner discovered, however, security cover doesn't necessarily mean large tracts of impregnable terrain. It only needs to have enough cover to conceal a deer, be situated so it won't arouse the interest of most hunters, and all the while give a crafty buck the assurance that he is safe from whizzing bullets. A classic illustration of this whitetail trait occurred once in Iowa.

Throughout most of the year, the deer cling to the very few woodlots and thickets that separate wide tracts of croplands. Yet when hunters begin swarming through these places on opening day, the deer seem to vanish. The woodlots and thickets become barren of whitetail activity. All the terrain that surrounds them is flat and open—but that's exactly where the deer are!

One fall, our group found deer in unbelievable places. They would belly down in small depressions and ditches, lie in the shade of a rock pile, or hunker down near a stack of old fence posts. Much hiking was needed to check each isolated feature, and we had to be prepared for quick action when a deer finally bolted from its hideout and began streaking away across the flats.

We also found numerous deer secluded between rows of unharvested crops such as corn and soybeans, particularly where puddles of rainwater had collected. Nearby food and water, plus surrounding cover for total concealment, make crop fields ideal hiding places.

Hunting bean fields for these deer is relatively easy because a stand hunter can station himself somewhere around the perimeter during the early and late hours of the day. Or groups of hunters can walk between the rows of beans (be sure to get permission), hoping to either jumpshoot animals bounding away or drive them to partners stationed along the far edge.

To hunt in standing corn, on the other hand, is very difficult. Even attempting to drive the animals may be a futile endeavor because cornfield deer are inclined to eternally circle and dodge hunters without ever actually leaving the cropland. Standhunting is probably the best bet, especially if the hunter can find a place where the corn butts up directly against a woodlot or brushy lowland. By selecting a stand right where the field edge meets native cover, the hunter can watch over a considerable distance to both his right and left—maybe as much as 700 yards of total coverage. Any deer that happens to just momentarily peek out along that edge should present a clear shot.

In numerous other regions, growing numbers of deer-hunting parties are pursuing their quarry in yet another way, and they're enjoying tremendous success. The first day of the season, everyone in the group waits on stand. The deer have yet to be extensively pressured, so watching well-used trails, breeding scrapes, and feeding sites yields many handsome racks.

But beginning with the second day, these hunters cloak themselves in fluorescent orange, spread out in a drive line, and begin marching cross-country. No standers are placed as in a conventional drive, though, because hard-hunted whitetails simply will not allow themselves to be pushed any significant distance. Instead, they merely run short distances away from the drivers. The drive line must maintain quite close ranks. Otherwise, the deer won't run at all but will hunker down and not budge an inch unless they're almost stepped upon.

I participated in one of these "rabbit hunts" for whitetails in Kentucky and was amazed at the results. Five of us spread out about 15 yards from each other and began tramping the length of a stream bottom, where thick clumps of willows and tall weeds offered perfect midseason hiding conditions for deer.

First a doe bounded out in front of us. She ran no more than 30 yards, quickly came to a stop, and then ducked back down. Several minutes later, a forkhorn buck popped up, which I brought down with an easy, close-in shot. As we approached the buck, the same doe we'd previously flushed got up again, ran another 30 yards—and spooked a six-pointer farther ahead. That buck scurried along belly-tight to the ground for only a short distance before hitting the deck. Later, Bob Wilson tagged that buck by simply walking him up and kicking him out of hiding.

Any hunter should be able to enact approximately the same strategy even when hunting alone. It's not necessary to be quiet, walk slowly, or worry about to which direction the wind may be carrying your scent. Just find brier patches, stands of alders, swatches of tall buffalo grass, or similar cover. Then you bull your way right on through, relying upon the hard-hunted whitetails' reluctance to move from their chosen hiding spots until a hunter is so close he almost trips over them.

Hard-hunted whitetails are indeed a challenge to the big-game hunter. Yet even on the last day of the season, success is still possible for hunters who believe that a buck you can't see isn't necessarily a buck that isn't there.

The Secret Life of the Cottontail Deer

John Madson

If there's anything dull about a whitetail deer, I don't know it. I like everything about him. His biology is fascinating. So is his management, his history, and the old legends and grandpa yarns.

I like to talk about whitetails with hunters, and with such seasoned deer men as Jack Calhoun of Illinois and Bill Severinghaus of New York. I admire a deer rifle that shoots true and handles easy. I've got a hunch that good tracking snow and prime roast venison may just help a man live forever. And as the years go by, I become more and more absorbed with the essence of the whitetail—the cunning inside that makes him what he is.

The whitetail is the only big-game animal that has succeeded in our woodlots and field edges, and he's made it because he's sharp. His senses of smell and hearing are acute beyond belief, and his vision is probably as sharp as ours even though it's believed by a lot of people to be in black and white.

His success, however, depends on not just the sensory information that he soaks up but also on the ways that he plugs it in. Those keen senses detect the slightest changes in the deer's home range. And how he knows that home range! He knows every little break in terrain, the open ground and its edges, and each windfall, thicket, rootwad, spring seep, berry tangle, cutbank, and mire. No human hunter can possibly know the deer range as well.

Knowing that range, and sensing an alien presence there, the whitetail reacts in many ways. He may lie doggo, watchful and waiting, or sneak cat-like around an intruder. He may explode into action, white banner astern, making spectacular leaps over obstacles and racing headlong through heavy timber—only to stop somewhere just beyond and fade into a thicket off to one side to resume lurking and spying. He has a particular genius for melting into cover that couldn't possibly conceal a deer.

A few years back, my old friend Keith Kirkpatrick was on a whitetail hunt with several friends. They were driving some farm timber known to have deer, but they hadn't seen any. One of the group, a young man who had never hunted deer, asked the farmer where the deer were. The farmer didn't know, but he figured that somebody ought to hunt a brushy draw that ran from the timber out into the fields.

The new hunter worked through this cover, coming out into an open field where there was a little pond. It didn't look like much. But as he stood there wondering what to do, he heard quail chirping in the fringe of foxtail and sloughgrass. He shucked the deer slugs from his shotgun, slipped in some bird loads, and stepped into the grass. The covey roared up. And at the same instant, a big buck broke cover a few yards away. He tore across the fields and vanished, leaving our hero with a gun full of bird loads and egg on his face.

It was a standard whitetail trick. We should be accustomed to it by now, especially out in the Midwest where good deer populations thrive in woodlots, thin fringes of creek brush, and all manner of little cover scraps. Still, it's always a surprise to find deer there. Even more surprising are the people who share their land with these superb animals and never know it.

There was a certain place in central Iowa where I usually could count on a pheasant or two late in the

150

The whitetail's survival depends on how well he uses the information that his extraordinary senses feed him. Those senses pick up the slightest changes in the deer's home range. (Erwin A. Bauer photo)

season. It was a little dimple in the rolling farmland that couldn't be seen by road hunters. It was in the exact center of the mile-square land section, half a mile from any road, the remnant of an old farm dump that was set about with sumac and undergrown with giant foxtail.

I hunted up to it one day in late December, working into the wind on an inch of snow. By the time I was within gun range of the little covert, I could sense that empty, birdless quality that a long-time pheasant hunter learns. But I played out the hand anyway. I stood in the fence corner for a couple of minutes, looking things over, knowing that this might do as much to flush a hiding rooster as any cover-kicking. Nothing. I jacked open the Model 12 and swung up to sit on the fence.

He came to his feet in one fluid, powerful move-ment and was instantly on his way with that buoyant grace that even very large whitetails have. He had been lying beside a roll of rusty fencewire, his antlers melting into the sumac around him. He couldn't have been 50 feet from me. If he'd been a pheasant's head, I might have seen him. I was hunting pheasants. I hadn't expected anything like him.

I knew him for what he was. I was a professional wildlifer by that time. In fact, I had just finished working at the Lansing check station for five days, and we had weighed and aged many deer, including a dozen bucks that would take any hunter's breath away. But nothing like this one.

His broad back looked as if it might hold water in a heavy rain, the gray neck seeming as thick as a Holstein bull's. And though he wore a typical rack, I haven't the slightest idea how many points there were. It was the sheer weight of antler that stays in my mind. Between burr and brow tine, each main beam was as thick as my wrist, arching out and forward in great curves, with broad webbing where the tines arose. Ten days before, we had weighed a buck that would have gone 250 pounds, and this one was bigger.

He rose weightless out of his bed and ran off down the fence line, making no sound that I can remember. It was easily the largest whitetail I had ever seen. He left me there on the fence, heart pounding, breath coming short, and legs trembling.

I casually asked two farmers living on that square mile if they'd seen any deer around, especially anything big. Yeah, they'd seen a few deer earlier, but the hunters must have killed them all. I told the local game warden, a good friend. He was keenly interested, but he hadn't seen such a buck nor heard of anyone who had. Same with several good local hunters.

That deer was probably never taken by a hunter. There'd have been no keeping it out of the record books. Nor was he killed on a road during the antlerless season. We'd have known that, too, for no car could have survived it. The point is this: an incredible stag was living in an intensely farmed and hunted region and had not been detected. For all I knew, I was the only person who ever saw him up close.

The secret of the whitetail's success is simply his success at keeping secret. Given an option, he'll always play it sly.

I once started a whitetail buck near the head of a timbered valley. Flag up, he ran out of sight around a bend of the creek. I tracked him in the new snow. As soon as he was out of sight, he began walking slowly uphill, stopping now and then to look down his backtrail. At the top of the hill was a three-wire fence that the deer had crawled under. The bottom wire was just 17 inches from the ground. I measured it. To appreciate this feat, try crawling under a low fence with a small rocking chair strapped to your head. That's about what this buck did. He could have jumped that fence from a standing start. It would have been far easier, but it just wasn't the sly way to handle a fence with me coming up behind.

In manner of escape and evasion, the whitetail deer can be remarkably like the cottontail rabbit. (It's not unusual for deer to hide in big brushpiles in heavily hunted farm country.)

The cottontail starts with a burst of speed that quickly outdistances men and dogs. Then he slows or even stops and ambles around in a circle to his starting point, even though a couple of Beagles may be singing down his trail. It's much the same with the cottontail deer—the flashy start and the sly circling back to home base.

Hunters who are long experienced in chasing deer with hounds report that such deer may not even run. At least not flat-out. Archibald Rutledge once said that in all his years of hunting, he had seen only two or three deer in full flight before dogs, and in each case the deer was wounded and about to be caught. In front of hounds, Rutledge said, deer usually loaf along, dodge, make a few showy feints and spectacular jumps, but generally play it cool. He once watched a big buck at the head of a drive suddenly "appear like an apparition and then, with extraordinary skill, efface himself from the landscape." It was later found that the deer had turned and sneaked to safety between the hounds and the hunters.

I once played tag for four hours with a buck on a Mississippi River island. It was only about eight acres, but heavily covered. I was alone, hunting steadily and carefully, and I had one quick glimpse of the deer at the beginning and another just before I quit. So I knew that he hadn't left the island during the hunt. We were perfectly synchronized; if we hadn't been, I might have killed him. But when I stopped, the deer stopped; when I sneaked, he sneaked. We must have cut each other's tracks a dozen times. By the end of the day, I was kicking willows and saying things not for the young to hear.

I came back the next day with Joe Martelle, my old river friend. You guessed it. The buck had left.

The whitetail's ability to adjust to man's doings is uncanny. A deer can even adjust to gunfire—if it's not being directed at him.

My son Chris and I were bowhunting one late October morning in the Glades, a wild tangle of Illinois River backwaters and bottomland not far from the Mississippi. We were on tree stands in big silver maples looking out over a cornfield that had been sharecropped.

There were local mallards and woodies back in the swamp, and duck blinds only a couple of hundred yards behind us. We hadn't counted on that. In the frosty dawn, the big shotguns were thunderous. And yet, stealing down a cornrow toward us came a fat whitetail buck. At each salvo of the 12-bores back in the Glades, the buck lowered his head a notch and kept walking directly toward the guns. He was alert but not particularly nervous. He must have had a good reason. Probably trailing a doe. Anyway, it was clear that he knew the shooting wasn't at him. When we last saw him, he was still heading back into the swamp in the direction of the gunfire.

The whitetail is one of a kind, a big-game species that thrives in small-game habitats. No other large mammal could have done it; only the whitetail has that unique set of qualities and responds so well to management. In most states today, this deer is the biggest and most prized of wildlife. It has special meaning to the ordinary hunter, not just as big game, but also as available big game. It is the common man's chance for high personal adventure—and often his only chance.

There's all that, and something more.

Whitetails aren't often hunted in real wilderness. They are often hunted in the tamest of farmlands.

In most states today, the whitetail is the hunter's only big-game opportunity. The whitetail lends a special wildness to whatever land he lives in.
(Irene Vandermolen photo)

But even in a horseweed patch at the edge of a cornfield, a deer lends special wildness to the land. Wherever the deer is found is a truly wild place. Deer carry wilderness entangled in their antlers; their hoofprints put the stamp of wildness on tame country.

When I was growing up in the mid-1930's, our part of central Iowa held a lot for an outdoor boy. But deer weren't part of it. About the only deer we had was a little fenced herd in the Ledges State Park on the Des Moines River. They were interesting, but they didn't offer much to small boys who loved to prowl the woods. They were park deer, kept deer. They were not real deer, if you see my meaning.

I was about 14 the time Dad and I were fishing the Des Moines River, and I took a shortcut across the inside of a big sandbar. There was a dead buck lying at the edge of the willows. There was no sign of injury. The buck was just dead, maybe four or five days dead, fly-blown and swollen. It was the first wild deer I had ever seen, dead or alive, and it instantly changed my world.

He was imposing. His rack, still with some tatters of dried velvet on them, seemed huge. I had never been so close to a deer. There was no fence around this one. He had been ranging free, leaving his great heartshaped prints at muddy creek edges, and finally leaving his corporeal being here for a boy to find. Buzzards and possums would soon remove that, but something of the deer's presence would stay to renew the spirit that had faded from the valley 60 years before.

An almost tangible change had come over the sandbar—that thing that comes when a boy is touched by genuine wildness for the first time. It's something like falling in love. Windows had opened in my horizons, revealing wonders out back of beyond. Up until then I had played at imagining this valley to be a wild place, though I knew it wasn't. But to find a wild deer there!

That has been well over 40 years ago, and I still vividly remember the quality of light on the sand and the striped willow-shade that lay across the dead deer's flanks. There suddenly seemed to be a dusty quality to the light, and a hush and suspension of all moving things. It was the old spell of wildness that other boys have felt in all other times, and it must always be the same.

I dropped my fishing rod and tore off to fetch Dad. He was as impressed as I. We must have hung around there for an hour or more, marveling and speculating and not knowing what to do about it. Dad told me all he knew about deer, which wasn't much, but it was impressive at the time. So was the sudden revelation that inside my stern, graying father was a boy my own age. I suspected then, and know now, that men and boys are about the same when confronted with genuine wildness. It makes boys older somehow, and men younger, and they may come together at a common point on common ground.

I prize the whitetail as huntable game. There is none better. I prize his fine meat and soft leather, and I waste neither. But even more, I cherish the whitetail deer for breathing wildness into our bland, tame countrysides—reminding us of old times and old doings and the meaning of being young and free.

Finding Those Spooked Muleys

Hartt Wixom

Many hunters believe that after first week of deer season, chances of finding buck with respectable antlers are next to nil. They're wrong. (Erwin A. Bauer photo)

The puzzle was familiar. Every deer hunter will experience it sooner or later. With the quest for mule deer well into its second week, bucks were no longer running surprised and bewildered. Human scents and sounds had transformed the bucks' activities from sheer flight to sophisticated hideaway. So sophisticated, in fact, that after a day of hunting and searching, the same question remained: Where do deer go when spooked?

I was probing proven mule-deer country in western Wyoming, an area less pressured than many deer areas I've hunted. And I could visualize the big racks I might have looked at here on opening weekend. But even with the late start, I had ample company: hunters who thought they had been on the wrong mountain, some who found game but hadn't connected, and others who sought better racks. Now, though, even the veterans among them began to complain by end of the first week that "the area was all shot out."

I knew better. I remembered another day in this same general region when I saw two hunting parties—one on a ridgetop trail, the other some 400 yards below on the canyon bottom. My vantage point was midway up an opposite slope. I was only scouting that day, but in some ways I learned more than if I'd been hunting.

As I glassed the ridge between the advancing hunters, I noticed several dozen deer. There were bucks, including a four-pointer. At the first noise, every pair of muley ears perked up. Then ears and heads went down, especially on the bucks, as they slinked into a brushless indentation scarcely deep enough to be a gully. There they could apparently see no danger, and more importantly, vice versa. After the hunters passed by, the deer returned to their browse. That night those hunters told me they had seen no bucks, only a forkhorn miles from where I'd last seen them.

That incident crossed my mind now as I rode with other hunters toward some timber where we were to make a drive. I was tempted to hurry along with the main group. However, something on the ground attracted my attention. It was not merely the presence of deer tracks, but the fact that they didn't seem to head for any distant location. I dismounted, tied my horse, and took a closer look.

Then I made my way carefully down the snow-covered and treacherously slippery slope. I had to use a skier's tactic to "hold" the hill—that of weighting heavily the upslope edge of each foot. I hadn't gone far, however, when I was aware of a dark object less than 60 yards away. Bedded in a fold of the hill that could not be seen from the trail, yet devoid of any cover, was a wide-antlered buck. The buck put so much confidence in his previously successful ploy that he did not seem to realize the vulnerability of his position. The buck finally spooked and ran downhill against white sage, the only cover on that ridge. I wondered how many hunters this muley, and others like him, had eluded by literally disappearing into the earth. It reinforced an old conviction: once you're in actual deer country, never hurry. Take time to study everything, especially places other hunters might miss.

My home is near the Wyoming-Utah-Idaho border, and I've had the opportunity almost daily to observe mule-deer movements. Right up to the very eve of the mid-October hunting seasons in those three states, I watched bucks raiding alfalfa fields and haystacks at dawn, at dusk, and sometimes in broad daylight. But when the hunting started, those deer disappeared.

Because the surrounding terrain where I saw the deer most frequently was undulating sage, many hunters didn't think it would be too difficult to find bucks. At first I included myself in that number. We were all wrong.

A frustrating factor was that the only "typical" cover around, aspen and oak on high ground, held no deer. And it had been empty for some time. Shortly after the seasons closed, heavy snow and cold weather hit the entire region and the bucks returned to their old familiar farm-edge haunts. In many ways, these muleys behaved like antelope. Yet there was one exception: The pronghorns were visible almost all year long, but the deer came and went. I was determined to find out where the muleys hid after winter's end and where they ran to when alarmed.

About the time I could once more hear Canada geese from the river bottoms and smell April sage, roadside deer were a rarity. Finally, I turned my attention to fishing—and that's when I found the mule deer, with the geese and trout. Far more bucks than we realize live much of their lives in riverside brush, willows, tamarisk, and irregular-shaped banks. This holds true along the Colorado River, the Green River, the upper Missouri, even smaller streams like South Dakota's Belle Fourche or Utah's Dolores. If you can't float to these deer, the best method is to glass from bluffs or cliffs within shooting range. Without streams or cover, some bucks will seek refuge in gullied sage slopes. Some little-noticed draws and arroyos offer more deep, shadowed sanctuary than hunters realize.

After years of scouting and hunting, I've concluded that muley bucks take full advantage of anything nature (or man) offers. Muley habitat may include rock outcroppings, canal or ditch banks, tall grass, cactus, knolls and shelves, timbered edges, even cliffs. Often all of these places are near "standard" muley habitat such as higher elevations that have cover.

Near the end of one mule-deer season, I could find no bucks, even though I was obviously in good cover. Lowland aspens appeared as a vague gold tapestry, while at my elbow, leafless quaking aspen fingered up tapering canyons into converging saddles. I was about to leave for better pastures when I stopped to think about how many hunters had trodden here. Where would I go to escape them? Then I realized I had avoided a cliff that towered above me and might harbor more than boulders.

Ten minutes after climbing into them, I detected the sound of gently rolling pebbles. I looked up just in time to glimpse a giant rack. Then I saw another. I wish I could say I bushwhacked one of those bucks, but they both disappeared over the ridgetop. In any event, I had found where some muleys go under pressure. Of course, if I was to score on such animals, I would have to climb high and then hunt on the way down. Deer least expect danger from that direction, and you can see a great deal more.

Of course, it is not always true that bucks hide uphill or down. Sometimes the first shots simply steer them farther from roads, or into more rugged terrain. When alarmed, bucks often move to different areas from does. On one hunt, I was disappointed that bucks were not where I'd scouted them 2½ weeks before, although does were about where they had been. The problem was that warm weather and dry roads allowed easy access, with more than the usual number of noisy campers. The bucks were not at 7,500 feet. We began locating them at 9,500, where they most likely had moved the night before opening day. Once there, my partner and I found bucks where conifers met rockslides.

One reason the bucks are often below the slides is that they don't like to get in them. In addition, they may not take refuge in logjams that restrict flight, but they will often use them as a barrier to bed beside. They know that anything crashing through would provide ample warning. Likewise, they often bed with a cliff or high ledge at their backs. One rock wall on a Great Basin mountain yielded many bucks on the second weekend of the season when they could be found in few other places on the sparsely vegetated range. When you're scouting, these are places to check.

It is known that wise bucks will grow old by bedding just beneath ridgetops. No matter which way you approach, a single bound puts a buck out of sight. But I saw another variation of this tactic when a big buck took one leap from a timber patch. When we emerged from a drive, he bolted into the trees. It is one thing to get a shot within the lace of limbs, but we faced an impenetrable wall. There are no surefire prescriptions for tagging such a buck.

Steven Kearl, Utah conservation officer in a region with both mountains and sage flats, says that after several days of pressure, larger bucks opt for the little-trammeled flatlands. After patrolling for part of the hunt, he often scores later on bucks that hide in low-lying brush. "They have a confident style that makes you think those critters get away with it more times than not," Kearl emphasizes.

I've also observed high-antlered bucks eluding hunters by flattening themselves out in treeless terrain or crawling in a single oak bush. One Arizona four-pointer I studied from the Colorado River dug into soft sand to bed down half-hidden. Another buck I watched remained statue-still while novice shooters fired on every side. The animal trotted away unscathed only when the hunters began shouting and waving at close range.

These deer don't resemble the doltish muley of hunting folklore. First, even if any deer behaved that way on the opener, he isn't the one you are looking for now. You are seeking survivors, animals that have outlasted predators, winter weather, dogs, vehicles, encroaching civilization that diminishes or destroys habitat, hunters, and poachers.

In developing that art, a mule deer can rarely depend on its legs, however swift, for they may take the deer into more danger. Not always does a muley seek to elude hunters by distance. Frequently the deer uses a particular type of vegetation. It can be conifer forests if under constant harassment, but there is little, if any, feed there. One sanctuary used more and more by pressured bucks is mountain mahogany. This tree offers head-high cover for deer, giving them a feeling of security, with browse brush underneath. An advantage to the hunter is that deer legs, or parts of them, are visible.

Mahogany was where I found bucks on one short hunt near a large metropolitan area. Sitting down with binoculars, I began searching for thin brown legs among the larger mahogany trunks. I figured the law of averages was with me, and kept looking. Then I found them. The entire patch was alive with deer! They were so comfortable in their beloved mahogany that I could move around to several vantage points—so long as I stepped no closer. Most of the deer never moved, seemingly convinced that they remained invisible that way. I focused my Weaver 2×-to-7× variable scope on a buck at less than 150 yards, and the rest was easy.

If mule deer are not easy to find, don't make the mistake of assuming they aren't there. One hunting season, I helped nonresidents locate bucks. But traditional hotspots weren't accessible, because of rain-slickened roads. It seemed that the hunt was over, and some hunters hurriedly packed, heading home empty-handed. But one group would not give up so easily. They decided to hike from camp into what appeared to be a hostile maze of rock and strewn timber. On closer examination, they found hidden terraces with bitterbrush and other deer browse. They also found six of the heaviest-tined bucks I'd seen in a long time.

The next season, I abandoned the usual hunting grounds on the third day of the hunt to try my luck in there. I bagged a buck with a 30¼-inch spread.

When bucks are spooked, a muley quest can turn into an equipment hunt. Those hunters with four-wheel drives and pickups with chains can get into the least-searched pockets. But big bucks are often closer than we think. On one hunt, my guide told me he had observed a four-pointer near a certain arroyo all year long. But when we searched, the buck wasn't there. Finally, on the evening of the last day, my guide suggested we look again—but this time from a greater distance to avoid letting him know we were around. Sure enough, there he was. Good thing I'd been practicing at longer ranges that

autumn. I took the buck at a measured 334 paces.

There is also what I call a "Wednesday factor." After weekend pressure subsides, bucks often are likely to return once again to open, south-slope feed. But the hunter must allow time. It is wise to plan on doing more than walking the weekend woods. Wait out storms. Deer do not like rain, soggy snow, or wind any more than humans do. Bucks that have lain low during those times may grow bolder with hunger pangs, moving into openings and clearings.

While much attention is paid to watching known muley trails, it does not always pan out after several days of stiff hunting. Mule deer do not confine themselves to as narrow a chunk of real estate as whitetails do. Yet even if they're not using a given trail repeatedly, the muleys could still be nearby. Studies done by the Utah Division of Wildlife Resources, including one on Oak Mountain, found that muleys rarely move more than a few miles. Our party once hunted miles from camp, then returned after dark to find a four-pointer browsing within sight of our tent!

Phantom muley bucks can die of old age in slightly hilly terrain or low-lying mountain ranges where few hunters suspect they might exist. One day during off-season, I was hiking not far from rolling ranch country when I noticed two giant bucks about 500 yards below me. Then I was distracted by several deer bolting from a thicket at my right. A quick search located no fleeing bucks, so I turned my attention back to what I thought would be two bucks with no place to go.

They weren't there! Yet I had a commanding view of the entire hillside. I could see no way they might go anywhere without my noticing. Walking where I had last observed the pair, I discovered a slight depression with slightly higher-than-usual wheat grass. The bucks had apparently used it to work their way right up behind where I had been.

Another time, southeast of Smoot, Wyoming, I saw a great muley rise like an apparition from what seemed a level meadow to join three does. As he scurried off into a line of brush, I studied the geography more closely. The buck had been hiding in a ditch, another example of the magic a muley employs to blend with the landscape. Most hunters never bother to hunt or scout for deer in that kind of area.

Frightened deer will sometimes slip into north-slope thickets. It is difficult to hunt for them there. I have found it possible to sneak in after them only following a rain, or newly melted soft snow. But if a hunter is patient and has enough time, the best approach is to wait the deer out. Sooner or later, even spooked muleys will move again to timber-edge browse. So pay special attention where the solid wall thins out into scattered fringes.

One thing is for sure. The deer must be somewhere. Chances are they have gone where the other hunters haven't.

Stalking Bedded Muley Bucks

Erwin A. Bauer

It is near the end of a bleak day late in a bleak November. I have reached the crest of a granite ridge in the Wind River Mountains, and I pause to give battered, complaining leg muscles a break. This range is well named, I muse, because a biting wind snarls through a gunsight-shaped notch. Thanksgiving is only a couple of days away, and here I am, teeth chattering, on top of Wyoming. I'm looking for a big buck deer somewhere out there in that lonely wilderness.

What I'm *really* searching for is a buck in his bed, a huge male muley unaware he has been spotted, maybe dozing or asleep. I want a buck with a bigger head than the one hanging on the kitchen wall at home. During a week of steady hunting, I've seen several good candidates. One was sneaking up a narrow canyon, and two others were racing in highest gear toward Colorado.

It is already dusk in the Cottonwood Creek bottom far below the ridge, and darkness is slowly creeping up the mountainside toward me. That is when I see a strange glint on another finger ridge to my right. After I study it for a moment, my pulse begins to pound because that glint is a white antler tip. Beneath the tip is the kind of impossible buck that artists paint for calendars. The only trouble is that the deer is too far away—450 or 500 yards—for a shot.

The next 20 minutes are a frantic scramble against time. Backing down from my original position, I make a wide circle around the deer, keeping out of sight and trying not to kick loose rocks into the dark abyss below. One advantage is that I am not cold and shivering anymore. The adrenaline is pumping. When I finally reach a point about 200 yards from my target and peer over an edge, the bed is empty.

My great buck has vanished. It is a bitter moment, and I have no choice but to retreat again to a cold camp. With hands nearly numb, I coax a fire from dry, dead branches of a Douglas fir.

If that whole incident some years ago seems like madness, it probably was. "Venison chops," someone wrote, "are as good from a creek-bottom buck as from a ridge runner." Maybe so. But why do a few anglers try to catch big brown trout on No. 20 dry flies when a hairy streamer fly usually does the job better? Why do some men hunt only with a bow and arrow? And why do some fanatics fish for 100-pound tarpon and sailfish with a fly rod and streamers instead of a boat rod and bait or lures? For the same reasons, I submit, that a growing number of mule-deer hunters have refined their own goals to make deer hunting more of a challenge.

An unofficial cult has quietly formed among serious mule-deer hunters. It is something like the catch-and-release cult of trout fishermen. The objective of the hunters is to hunt a buck in his bed and nowhere else. The game isn't likely to deplete our mule-deer populations.

Mule deer are no longer as abundant as they were 10 or 15 years ago when the limit was two or even more deer per season in several Western states. Then it was no big deal to take a good buck. Those golden days, I'm sad to say, may be gone forever. One reason is that much blue-ribbon mule-deer country from New Mexico northward to Montana is being heavily mined. This activity and the exploitation of coal, oil, and natural gas have destroyed a lot of prime range.

There are fewer deer to hunt nowadays. In many parts of the Rockies, a hunter must now apply for a permit awarded by lottery instead of simply buying

This big buck stayed in his bed as I moved closer and closer to take photos. I had plenty of time to study rack. It would have been easy shot.

his license. Other restrictions have been tightened. As is usually true when a wildlife resource is in short supply, some conscientious sportsmen voluntarily make the hunting a little tougher. In doing so, they reduce the harvest and also improve the quality of the sport.

The mule deer of western North America is a superb game animal that lives in lofty, scenic real estate. Much of the mystique of muley hunting lies in roaming the Rocky Mountains as autumn blends into early winter, when aspen leaves and snow begin to fly. Hunting mule deer in the backcountry anywhere can be a rich and rewarding experience, even if you do not score. That is doubly true when trophy hunting.

A lot has been written about taking the biggest trophy deer at low elevations. Yes, it does happen. But year in and year out, nine in 10 of all better-than-average male mule deer are going to be taken at high elevations.

The best single bit of advice to any trophy hunter anywhere is to hunt high. Some of the finest bucks I have ever seen were roaming bighorn-sheep range. My friend Mont Harmon, who has been guiding in Wyoming's Thorofare for his entire adult life, recalls that the largest mule deer ever packed out from that region was shot well above treeline under a bare, wind-scoured ridge. The same is true almost everywhere else.

The biggest of all mule deer stay on top of the landscape until the annual rut or deep snows drive them down. By that time during normal years, the hunting seasons are closed. So the ultimate in mule-deer hunting is to stalk a big buck where he spends most of his life during daylight hours—in his bed.

There are several ways to do it. Perhaps the surest and easiest way, particularly for a nonresident hunter, is to engage a good outfitter who specializes in trophy deer.

Another way is to arrange to be packed into remote deer country on horseback, set up your own base camp, and hunt on foot. On a prearranged date, the packer comes to pack you out. Still another choice is to backpack. If you can manage it, that is

the most challenging and rewarding way to hunt.

Backpack trophy hunting has suddenly become quite popular, especially among young hunters. The success rate is probably the lowest of all. During a recent October, I saw a pair of very big bucks collected this way. One of the hunters, Tom Haas of Oakland, California, spotted his deer bedded beneath a ledge three days before he finally managed to get close enough to try a shot. Only after he shot did he see two other equally large deer that had been bedded nearby. Both jumped up and ran when Haas approached his own deer to field-dress and drag it downhill. It is common for old mule-deer males to live in small bachelor groups. Some of these deer may be past breeding age.

Searching for a buck in his bed can be very difficult. It means making plenty of footprints vertically, often on thin game trails, if there are any trails at all, just to get to high country and lookout points. It also means starting out well before daybreak in penetrating cold so that you can reach a good area by sunup. After that, it is a matter of sitting motionless for long hours, glassing an alpine landscape that is often devoid of deer. You focus field glasses or spotting scope on every niche that might hold a motionless buck.

Starting a vigil at first light has a lot of advantages. Although a buck may be already bedded down for the day and may therefore remain motionless for a long time, he can be betrayed by the first slanting rays of the morning sun reflecting on ivory antler tips. More than one fine trophy started a trip to the taxidermist this way. Early morning also is good because the shadows are long, and living creatures are more clearly outlined against their backgrounds. Later in the day, the bucks blend into their settings, and glare often makes spotting them very difficult.

Outfitter Larry Moore of Jackson Hole, Wyoming, with whom I trophy-hunted several years ago, revealed another reason why he likes to be on a lofty ridge in the Gros Ventre Mountains at first light on the coldest, clearest mornings.

"A buck can stay motionless," he noted, "but he

cannot stop breathing. I first found two of my biggest deer by spotting the vapor breath on the still morning air. One was about 600 yards away and invisible, except for its white breath."

George Smith, for many years the boss at Canyon Creek Ranch near Melrose, Montana, is another guide who for many years produced an awesome number of trophy mule deer by hunting bedded bucks. His technique differs from Larry Moore's. After an autumn snowfall, Smith rode the slopes of steep mountainsides, following a contour. His eyes were on the ground, searching for large tracks heading uphill. When he located such sign, he rode to a vantage point, tethered his horse, and then studied the mountain above him to see if he could spot the bedded buck. He was successful so often that he devoted much of his time to scouting this way before the hunting season opened and clients arrived in camp.

"It is very important to sit down in a comfortable spot and study any likely bedding area very carefully," Smith told me. "At long range, it is often possible to look right at a deer and not see it. I have glassed the exact same spot several times before finally discovering the deer lying there so still he seemed to be carved from the mountain."

The big bucks bed high up, but never right on a crest so that the animal is silhouetted or skylighted. Nearly always, the deer will be lying beside, just beneath, or behind brush. He will be in total shade, or irregular shadows will fall across face and body to provide a baffling camouflage. Almost always, the bed will be in a position from which the occupant can watch the landscape for a great distance below him.

Once, when I was hunting sheep in southern Alberta, I reached a high ridge from which I spotted a deer just below me. The deer was facing away from me. At first, he seemed to be asleep, and maybe he was. Even so, with 10× binoculars, I saw his big ears moving and twisting ever so slightly to pick up sounds from all directions. Otherwise, the buck was motionless.

Suddenly, some vagrant breeze or sound brought a message. Up on four feet, the buck turned directly

toward me for an instant before racing away around a rimrock. I heard rocks clattering long after he was out of sight.

If the new group of deer hunters has a high priest among outfitters, he is Ken Clark of Afton, Wyoming, who has had uncanny success with bedded deer. He hunts wilderness where few others are willing to go, and much higher up. That means getting started earlier in the morning, riding farther on poorer trails, and covering more steep terrain on foot. The rewards have often included the largest mule deer taken in Wyoming during several different seasons, plus several entries in the state records.

Clark concentrates on searching for bucks in their beds and enjoys an advantage while doing it. He has learned that when they are not hunted too much and driven from their home ranges, trophy mule deer tend to bed in the same preferred areas year after year. For example, if a client collects a bragging-size deer on a certain ridge in October, another buster buck will usually be bedding there the following October. It's also true that a good bedding area may harbor more than one trophy buck. Clark does not have to waste valuable time exploring unproductive locales. His long experience is invaluable to a client.

It's true, of course, that some big deer do not inhabit steep mountain ranges. Some also thrive in dry foothills, canyon country, river brakes, and eroded badlands on the edges of deserts and ranchlands. You are likely to find at least a few almost anywhere in the still undeveloped, unpaved West, but one fact does not change. The biggest of the bucks anywhere will almost always be in the highest, most remote parts of any given territory. If you are hunting in a lowland area, focus most of your attention on the highest ground.

Even though hunting the big bucks in their beds is very challenging, there are certain advantages. If you do spot a deer in his bed, and the animal is undisturbed, you have time to study his antlers before deciding whether or not to take the shot or make a stalk. If you're trophy hunting, you can evaluate the rack carefully. That's next to impossible if you jump a deer. Many a trophy hunter has taken a quick shot at a moving buck under the impression that the antlers would make the record book, only to find later that the dream buck had mediocre headgear.

Another advantage is that it's easier to hit a bedded buck than it is to score on a moving animal. You can take your time and perhaps roll up a jacket for a rifle rest and assume a solid shooting position. Because you can fire a carefully aimed shot, it's possible to score at longer range than you would attempt when firing at a moving deer.

These few advantages aren't really important. The new breed of hunters try for bucks in their beds because of the challenge and because they're more likely to take a big deer. If you do take a wall-hanger buck while he's bedded, you have proven that you have mastered one of the most difficult forms of hunting. 🦌

A recent wet snowfall makes it easy to track a deer to its daytime bed. But deer may see, hear, or scent you.

PART 8

SECRETS OF TOP BOW- HUNTERS

Bowhunting Open-Country Muleys

Dwight Schuh

The morning was dark as Mike Cupell and I crunched along a graveled hillside 50 yards from camp and then plopped into the sagebrush. It was late August, the third morning of the bowhunting season. We shivered in the cool air of the 9,000-foot Great Basin desert mountains in Nevada and whispered to each other softly as we waited for light. The pungency of sage and sweet fragrance of mountain mahogany saturated the humid morning air.

Within half an hour, the rising sun cast shafts of yellow light onto the highest peaks, and the foothills slowly took form in the dawn. Miles of sage, broken only by scattered clumps of mahogany and scarce juniper, stretched before us. The country was wide open, seemingly barren. It was ideal for bowhunting.

With the coming of light, it didn't take long for us to spot seven bucks and two does feeding on sage a quarter-mile away. To the south, six bucks foraged in a draw. More and more deer became visible as the dawn broke. By 9 a.m., Mike and I had seen enough. We slipped back to camp for a late breakfast. Mike was smiling.

"Dear Diary," he said, dictating mock notes. "Opening day wasn't so great. We saw only 25 bucks from camp. Today we saw 33." He laughed. "I like this open-country hunting."

That experience wasn't unusual. Many times I've seen 30 or more bucks during one day. It always has been in vast, open areas, in lands that I call big-sky country. The horizon is far away, and scarcely a rock or tree is to be seen. I rarely see other bowhunters,

Best place to do your glassing is high in rocks that break up your outline. Biggest advantage a bowhunter can have is to spot a deer before it sees him.

probably because most hunters think this is country for riflemen and that you need dense vegetation to provide cover if you want to bowhunt deer.

While planning one desert hunt, I talked to a dozen biologists and hunters. Without exception, they said the best bowhunting was done in areas with dense cover—such as mountain mahogany, junipers, oak brush, and aspen. They figure, I suppose, that a bowhunter must get close to deer for good shots, and that the denser the timber, the better his chances for getting close.

I don't think that reasoning is quite on target. The biggest advantage a bowhunter can have over a deer is to see it before it sees him. That way, he can stalk within close range and take time to make a deliberate, well-placed shot. Unless you're hunting from a tree stand, dense cover favors a hiding deer more than it does a moving hunter. In wide-open spaces, however, you easily can spot a deer before it sees you. Not one of the 33 bucks that Mike and I saw had seen us. We had the upper hand.

Open country is ideal for trophy hunting, too, because you have time to size up the deer's body and antler condition. Perhaps best of all, you don't have to waste time scouting before the season, looking for tracks, droppings, and other sign as you do in forests, where you would stillhunt or take a stand. You hunt by sight alone, so you combine scouting and hunting simply by looking for deer. Mike and I arrived in the dark the night before the season opened in a region we'd never seen before, yet we had action the first morning.

This kind of hunting offers nearly unlimited po-

tential. Perhaps the greatest opportunity lies in the limitless expanses of desert mountains and hills covering parts of Oregon, Idaho, Nevada, Utah, Arizona, and California, but the same hunting principles apply to the prairies east of the Rockies and to the wide-open alpine country found in all major Western mountain ranges. Couple the breadth of this prime mule-deer country with generous bow seasons—as long as 30 to 40 days in many states—and you have the greatest hunting opportunity since the days of the pioneers.

Efficient hunting starts with equipment. Binoculars in the 7×-to-10× range are essential for seeing deer that are a mile away. Nearly as useful is a 20× spotting scope for glassing longer distances and for sizing up trophies.

But if there's one reason to scout open country, it's to locate good spotting points, such as hilltops or rimrocks that overlook several square miles of deer country. Wind direction may seem irrelevant if you're looking at a deer a mile away, but I'm convinced that deer can pick up your scent at that distance, so don't glass from points that are upwind of the area you plan to hunt. Just as important, keep the sun to your side or back. You won't be able to see anything if you're looking east early in the morning—the sun will blind you. And make sure you're in a place where you can make a clandestine getaway to start a stalk. It does little good to spot 100 deer if they all can see you and then run off when you make your first move.

One point should go without saying—if you're in position by dawn, you'll see far more deer than at any other time of day. Early morning is when deer are in open areas and moving. You may see nearly as many deer at sundown, but then you rarely have time for a stalk before dark, so hunting is not as easy.

On the other hand, don't give up just because you haven't seen Mr. Big by 10 a.m. One advantage of open-range hunting is that you can spot deer all day. Throughout the day, bucks will get up to stretch, nibble a few twigs, and move from sunlight to shade. If you are patient, you'll see deer.

You also will be able to spot bedded bucks. Most Western bow seasons run during hot weather, so first look on north slopes or in shady spots under rimrocks or trees. That technique worked for my friend Larry Jones in Oregon's Wallowa Mountains, where a certain alpine area is so barren I've dubbed it "the moon." One ridge is coated with granite gravel and has only a dozen stunted whitebark pines for cover. While hunting one day, Larry climbed that ridge to look for deer. He started at the top and worked down into the wind, glassing the shade under each of the scattered pines. Eventually, he spotted the antlers of a bedded two-point buck. After an hour-long stalk, he shot the buck at 35 yards.

Deer, however, don't always lie down in the shade. Bucks may bed in the wide-open sage under a blistering sun. Using a 20× scope, I've found many bedded bucks by studying sage flats and looking for the tips of antlers rising from the brush.

Efficient glassing takes time, especially when you are looking for bedded deer. You may detect only the white of a leg or a silhouetted antler tine. Even in early morning, you can overlook animals if you're not thorough. Give the deer time to move around and you eventually will see deer that you couldn't see only minutes before. I usually glass for at least an hour from a position before moving on.

Let's assume you've spotted the buck you want. Maybe he's feeding in a patch of bitterbrush, lying under a rim, or wandering up a timberline ridge back. To me, this moment of spying on an unknowing buck is the moment that distinguishes open-country hunting from other forms of hunting. You can watch the buck nibbling twigs, scratching his back, sparring with another buck, and twitching his hide. Through a 20× scope you feel as if you're right beside him. You feel a little smug.

But guard against haste. That buck looks so real, so accessible, so unaware, you may feel you can't go wrong. If you were a rifleman, you'd just roll into a prone position and drop him. But for a bowhunter, he still is hours away. You need to take your time.

There's another precaution you must take. You undoubtedly can see more than one buck. You may see 32 others as Mike and I did. All those deer may tempt you to "flock shoot," much as a novice shotgunner does on mallards. With so many deer around, how can you fail if you just sneak among them, or if you and your buddies get them moving

every which way? The results of that approach are about as sure as those a beginner gets when shooting at a flock of mallards.

When you concentrate on one buck rather than a herd, your chances of success are far greater. This type of hunting works best one-on-one. Go for the one shot you can make at the one buck you want.

If you've spotted a buck early in the day, you must decide whether to go after him now, as he's feeding, or to wait until he beds for the day. In general, stalking a bedded buck is easier than stalking one that's feeding because he's most likely blindsided by a tree or cliff, and from his low point of view, he can see less than if he were standing. A bedded deer also will stay put for several hours, which gives you time for a careful stalk. I often sit tight and watch a buck until 10 or 11 a.m. After he beds down, I stalk him. On the other hand, if he's wandering out of my sight, or if he's feeding among rimrocks or cliffs where he'll be no harder to stalk while feeding than if bedded, I'll stalk him immediately. It's a matter of judgment.

Once you've decided when to stalk, you need to plan it. Any hunter knows that wind direction gets first priority, and you must stalk from downwind. During the day, when thermal currents rise, that usually means starting from above and stalking down.

Open country offers more cover than is first apparent. Use your binoculars to pick out draws, outcroppings, knolls, and rims—any feature that will hide you. Carefully mark the buck's position and note landmarks. Once you've moved, the land around the buck will look different, and relocating him can be hard. Don't trust your memory. When hunting by myself, I carry a notebook and pencil and sketch a map of my stalking route. If you are hunting with a partner, you can work out hand signals and take turns guiding each other. My wife has directed me to several deer.

When you plan, try to spot all the other deer near your buck. Unseen animals can be a real thorn in the side. One time above timberline in Oregon's Blue Mountains, I spotted two fine bucks feeding in a ravine. By staying below the lip of the ravine, I could walk right to them. It was so simple I didn't hesitate, and it would have worked except for one thing—a third buck. As I neared the two bucks, the unseen deer ran out from brush not 10 yards away. The deer I was stalking spooked, and I was left talking to myself. If I'd taken a few minutes to look, I'd have seen the third deer and could have either stalked it or sneaked around it to the two others.

When you're ready to stalk a buck, you often can move quickly at first. Mule deer have fair eyesight, but if you're more than half a mile away, you can walk in plain view and they probably will pay little attention to you. In most areas, topography is varied enough so that from the back of a hill or a draw you can walk within 100 yards of a deer with little trouble.   Just beware of other deer and go out of your way as necessary to keep from stirring them up.

Once you get close to your buck, relocating him is a challenge. You've probably circled a mile or more, and from up close the perspective is unfamiliar. That's when your map or your hand-signaling partner is invaluable.

Even when you're sure where the buck is, you may not be able to see him. Now's the time to start stalking at a tortoise's pace. Take one small step at a time, and use your binoculars constantly. Try to identify every detail. Look for antlers above the brush or any small speck of brown or gray hair, and sensitize yourself to see movement. During early bow seasons, flies are bad. Deer constantly flick their ears and tails.

If you don't see the buck right away, don't give up. You may be tempted to concede that he has picked up your scent and spooked or that he has wandered away. More than once I've given in to those doubts and made a quick move, only to have the buck dash off very nearby. If you haven't seen or heard him run off, keep looking. Eventually you'll see him, and he probably will be no more than 50 to 100 yards away, as contented as an Angus bull, chewing his cud and drowsing in the midday heat. That's when your heart starts to thump.

Now the real stalk begins. Of course, you already have got the wind in your favor, but you still need to get past the deer's eyes and ears. To do that, picture yourself as a stalking cat. Cats slink unseen and unheard within quick striking range. That's the approach you need to take. Keep yourself low and move as slowly as a cat. Use every bit of cover to your advantage. To improve your odds, camouflage your clothing, hands, face, bow, and arrows. Getting close to a rimrock may be a simple matter of quietly walking to the edge of a cliff, but on a sage flat or open, shale-covered slope, you have to crawl. Take your time, move ahead by inches and not by yards. It may take two hours to travel 100 feet. But if you go slowly enough, you can get within good bow range of any buck.

To be consistently successful, follow the cat's example one step further. One reason a cat moves so quietly is padded feet. Give yourself the same advantage. Shed your boots, slip on a pair of heavy wool socks, and stalk in stocking feet. Stocking feet absorb noise and allow you to feel the ground so you can avoid loose rocks and twigs.

No matter how good you get at stalking, however, sooner or later you'll make a wrong move and get caught off guard. Remember that mule deer are more curious than spooky. Unless they catch you in the wide open at close range, they won't bolt. When a buck sees or hears you crawling through the brush, the best thing you can do is freeze. Most bucks will stare at you for several minutes and then return to what they were doing before they were interrupted. The stalk still is on. It's useless to try a quick shot at a suspicious buck. He'll bound off before you can get your bow half drawn.

When you get within good range of a buck—25 to 50 yards—it makes little sense to throw away the hours you've invested by taking a poor shot. If the wind is steady, make yourself comfortable, and wait for the buck to get up to feed or stretch to provide you with a good shot. If the wind is unstable, waiting too long is risky. To get a buck out of his bed, I hide and bleat on a predator call. The deer gets up. But when he can't see the source of the sound, he usually wanders off to feed and presents a good shot. When you're looking just over the brush tops, as you frequently are in open country, judging the range can be difficult. You may find a bowhunter's rangefinder helpful. If you've practiced shooting your bow all summer, you ought to have no trouble collecting your deer.

Hunting deer this way may seem too difficult and troublesome to be feasible, but it's not. More than anything else, it requires patience, but it demands no more patience than sitting in a tree stand and waiting for a whitetail to walk by. I collected a buck on that hunt with Mike Cupell just this way.

At 7:30 on the fourth morning, I spotted a small four-point buck feeding near the bottom of a canyon, a quarter-mile away. Circumstances looked just right for an immediate stalk. I sneaked back over the hill out of sight and hiked to the bottom of the canyon. Now the buck was hidden behind a low knoll and couldn't see me. I quickly walked toward him and at 7:45 came to the knoll just opposite him. He was within 150 yards.

I slipped off my day pack and boots, pulled on wool stalking socks, and crept up the hill. The dirt was soft at first, but loose shale covered the top of the knoll, so I began to move each padded foot with great care. After each step, I looked through my binoculars to study the area ahead. The palms of my hands grew clammy and cold, and my muscles drew tight. That buck had to be within 50 yards, but he was nowhere in sight.

In the next half an hour, I sneaked a mere 20 yards. I knew that to get my shot I'd have to see the deer before he saw me and that he'd hear even the tiniest sound. Finally, at 30 yards, I spotted the tips of his velvet-covered antlers bobbing up and down just beyond the crest of the hill. I nocked an arrow.

Slowly the buck fed uphill into full view. A couple of times he looked at me but paid no attention to my still, camouflaged figure. When he was broadside and looking away, I drew the bow, held for 35 yards, and let the arrow fly. It hit him square. The deer sprinted 100 yards and crashed headlong into the sage. The time was 8:30.

I've had many similar experiences since my first big-sky hunt more than a decade ago. You can, too, if you'll break with tradition and stay away from those timbered regions considered "best for bowhunting." Instead, head for the open spaces where the sky goes on forever and trees are scarce. And you'll learn that big-sky country is really the place for a bowhunter.

Big Bucks Or Nothing

Larry Mueller

Yeater poses with the fifth deer he has taken with the same arrow. He shot it at a range of 25 yards, although he prefers shots no longer than 100 yards.

A long, low, bleating *ur-r-r-rp* sounded from just behind a veil of trees. Kenneth Yeater's grip tightened on his bow. He had heard this same noise two evenings earlier. And immediately afterward, three does had crossed a pair of fences in single file, followed shortly by the biggest buck Yeater had ever seen. The distance had been too far to risk a shot.

This time, all three does passed under Ken's tree stand as they jumped the fences. A moment later, Yeater began drawing his bow as the buck emerged from the trees. And then he relaxed. It was a respectable buck all right, but not the huge deer he was expecting.

The four animals disappeared and left Ken with nagging regrets.

"Should have shot," his alter ego kept saying.

"You're hunting the big one," he kept reminding himself until he had his nerves under control.

Four minutes passed. Ken began to relax. And then once more a bleating *ur-r-r-rp* raised the short hairs on the back of his neck. An enormous buck ghosted out of the trees, jumped the first fence, and stood broadside.

Ken drew his bow, but a small sapling covered part of the deer's chest. It could deflect the arrow.

The buck jumped the second fence and stood again. Ken shot, heard a thump, and saw his arrow fall. This time his alter ego was name-calling.

"Idiot! After all of that, you get your chance and *miss!*"

Ken grabbed a second arrow. The buck turned to see what had made the thump. Ken glanced at the bow sight as he nocked the arrow. Bent! Must have hit it against something. This time he shot instinctively and heard the sound of a good hit.

After 84 yards of trailing, Yeater found his buck—a trophy big enough to be listed in the Pope and Young records.

"That typifies the way I hunt," Yeater said. "Find the buck I want and let the does and inferior bucks go by. I'm not deer hunting; I'm hunting one *specific* deer."

That tactic has brought Yeater remarkable success. Nine times he has killed the specific buck he was hunting. Five of those years he took the biggest buck reported from his county. His 1971 buck was recognized by the state of Illinois as the largest nontypical whitetail taken by a bowhunter.

Yeater, who works for the Army at the Rock Island Arsenal, has also scored well on the archery range. He has won six state indoor archery championships in Illinois and Iowa, and one year he was the outdoor archery champion in Illinois. But when fall approaches, he has one thing on his mind: finding another big buck.

Yeater divides hunting season into three parts: the first three weeks of October, the rest of October through the first two weeks of November, and mid-November through December 31.

Although the third period covers half of the bow season in his home state of Illinois, Yeater rarely hunts then. Shotgun season in mid-November breaks up the herd's daily habits. The bucks go out of rut, making them even more unpredictable than they normally are. Yeater puts all of his time and effort into the more productive first two periods.

During the first period, leaves are still on the trees. Corn is in the fields. It's warm. And in Yeater's experience, when temperatures are above 55°F., most deer move late in the evening or at night. But Ken is in the woods almost daily, anyhow. He isn't seriously hunting. He's looking over the herd by comparing tracks. He's deciding which animal he wants. He's learning where that deer hangs out.

The next thing Ken adds to his formula is getting onto the buck's merry-go-round at the right time of day. Whitetails travel in circuits. Usually not circles. Probably long ellipses. Yeater observed one that made a long, narrow figure eight. Some deer travel their routes every day, others every second day.

"What you have to find out," says Yeater, "is where the buck stays at a time you can be there, too."

To analyze deer movements, Ken uses a daily log. Recording all the details of each hunt—where, when, weather, various animals seen, and so on—provides a broad view that can be studied for patterns.

One such pattern didn't suggest itself to Ken until after he'd spent four years recording weather data. His records suggested that clear, pretty skies make for poor hunting.

Ken found that although days were overcast and rainy only 24 percent of the time during hunting season, he saw deer on 45 percent of those days. Deer were seen only 27 percent of the days that were clear or somewhat cloudy, and these weather conditions were prevailing 76 percent of the time.

Another note in the log illustrates Yeater's persistence. He spent 6.88 hours in the tree stand for every deer seen during a recent season. But he hunted 82.5 hours before he got a chance at the buck he wanted.

Yeater begins his annual analysis by hunting in the worst possible places to kill a buck: the feeding areas such as corn, bean, and alfalfa fields. Deer are often going in and out of these fields. It's almost impossible for a hunter to get into a tree along the edge of a field without disturbing the deer. But mostly, Ken checks tracks, getting a line on an animal he wants. When he finds those tracks, he learns where the buck goes in and out of the woods. He follows the trail for a short distance to get an idea of where the deer rests. But he doesn't follow far enough to spook the buck off its bed. That mistake could make the deer change its habits.

Ken is now watching for the direction of his buck's fresh tracks. If they're pointed both ways on a trail, he assumes the deer is moving in and out of a feeding area. If the tracks go one way, and toward the feeding area, they lead away from the resting area. One-way tracks away from the feeding area point toward the bedding grounds.

Following the one-way tracks along a well-worn trail generally leads to a small secondary trail. This leads to or from the bedding area. Ken puts a tree stand 10 yards or more from this junction. He chooses two or three more stands that can be used when winds are from different directions.

"It isn't always possible to tell what time the bucks are using these trails," the meticulous Yeater says, "so I carry a spool of dark thread and tie a length across every trail that interests me. I check these threads twice a day. This way, I know whether the threads were broken at night or during the day. Some are morning places for the deer, and others are evening places. When I'm pretty sure about a spot, I hunt it for three days to give the buck more than enough time to travel his circuit. If nothing happens, I look for a new stand."

All of this activity is recorded daily. He assigns numbers to his tree-stand locations because he uses too many to remember by name. Some trees are used year after year in bedding and mating areas. Others are added and subtracted because trails to feeding areas change annually when farmers rotate crops.

Old reliable stands are usually reconditioned in late summer. Ken uses homemade portable seats, but the climbing boards and foot rests are checked.

The seat is about 15 feet above ground on each tree. If a seat is lower, the deer easily sees hunter movements. If higher, the shooting angle is too steep.

Yeater, once among the top 24 archers in the country and winner of state tournaments, indoors and out, won't put a stand more than 30 yards from a trail. He prefers 10 yards. A shot longer than 30 yards gives the deer enough reaction time to escape the arrow. During one recent season, he passed up three 40-yard shots at the buck he wanted.

To further guarantee his shot when the chance comes, Ken clears limbs and saplings.

"Too often, we hear about a neck or gut shot because the arrow deflected off a limb," Yeater told me. "There's no excuse for that. But don't clear too much, or the deer will notice it. And if there's an awkward place around the stand where a deer will be difficult to shoot, put those limbs on the ground as barriers to guide the deer where you want him."

Yeater was never one to trust hunch, instinct, or feel. Back before the days of compound bows and sights, when he was only a high-school boy in his first serious competition, he beat the state champion in instinctive shooting because the other fellow just pointed his arrows and shot. Ken noticed sunlight on the floor of the archery range on the first day and used it as a point of aim. He still leaves nothing to judgment.

Using a 50-foot tape measure, Ken places strips of white plastic at 10, 20, and 30 yards along each shooting lane. Red or orange plastic is used as five-, 15-, and 25-yard markers. Yeater then knows the exact range of his deer and how to hold his bow sight.

All range measurements are made on the ground. The actual path of the arrow will be a little longer, but gravity will speed the downhill flight, equalizing the point of impact.

Yeater's only noticeable impatience is with other hunters who aren't using good sense. They get recorded in his log as "coughing his way through the woods" or "waiting on the ground for a deer, straight-jacketed in a sleeping bag for warmth."

Inept hunters can be used to advantage, however. Invariably, they hunt the feeding grounds and spook the deer on the way in. Ken is already in his tree stand on his buck's escape route. And Yeater doesn't go to his stands by the shortest routes. He walks a wide circle around, avoiding the feeding areas, and comes in from a direction rarely traveled by deer.

Occasionally, however, Ken may deliberately spook deer off of their feeding grounds so they'll change daily habits that make them inaccessible to him. Or he may hunt the feeding grounds for an evening or two to learn what time his target buck

first comes out of his bed. But when he does this, his tree stand is 10 yards from the edge with shooting lanes to the field, not right on the edge where deer can easily see him.

By the end of the third week in October, usually after two hard frosts, S marks—indicating buck scrapes—begin appearing on the neatly drawn maps in Yeater's log. He ignores rubs because he thinks bucks don't return to them. But the locations of scrapes are important. The bucks are coming into rut. Instead of moving only early and late, bucks may be active any time of day.

The first scrapes along edges of fields or the little ones in trails are made by bucks advertising their presence. Some are made by young bucks. But when the scrapes become nearly three feet in diameter with a hoof print in each, and they're made near regular trails with paths going to and from them, this is serious business. The mature bucks are now advertising for does. Ken looks for mating scrapes in flat, wooded areas of 30 yards square or more that are open and free of underbrush.

"I've watched bucks make these scrapes," Ken told me. "They go one, two, three with the right front hoof, the same with the left, and suddenly there's a bare circle of dirt. Some bucks urinate in the scrape and step in it with one foot to leave a print. It happens so fast it appears to be done almost on the run. One young buck made scrape after scrape and was back within an hour expecting results."

Yeater puts his tree stands near those scrapes. And after years of keeping records, he has decided that as long as the woods and other natural barriers remain the same, the breeding areas don't change much either, especially if deer are undisturbed.

Ken's senses are incredibly sharp. He sees a

At left, Yeater uses a tape measure to determine the exact placement of range flag. Above he drenches with deer scent a cloth he has tied to his shoelace.

Yeater likes to have stand at least 15 feet above ground so deer are less likely to spot him. One choice spot: near a scape.

mashed or turned-over leaf. Under it is a track. A wet leaf among dry or just moist ones may be sniffed for the somewhat cowlike odor of urine left by a doe in heat. By the slight irregularity in the pushed-aside leaves, he recognizes a scrape without having to go to see the bare dirt.

Ken never scents a scrape to "enhance" it. Nor does he throw leaves on it to encourage the buck to "police" it and prove he's coming back. These tactics only alert the buck. Yeater keeps his distance from trails as well as scrapes. And when he is in the area, pieces of shoestring tied to his boots will be drenched with doe-in-heat scent.

Of scents in general, Yeater says he believes they work until the deer have had time to associate the smell with the hunter and his movements. For this reason, he uses scents only during the rut.

Ken airs his hunting clothes outside every night and puts them in a plastic bag when he leaves for work. He washes them every two or three days in plain water. He says that soaps smell too much.

Yeater checks the wind direction before he chooses his tree stand, of course. But when he's in the tree, he also ties a length of light-colored thread to a limb so he can monitor changes. Ken hopes for a light, steady wind that carries his scent in one direction, but isn't strong enough to prevent him from hearing deer move. Ken hardly ever sees deer on a calm day, he says.

His tree seat is homemade. It has rubber strips between the joints to prevent squeaks. For silence, pieces of carpet are tied to the foot rest, to the tree behind Ken, and also to where his elbow might

scratch against the bark when he draws his bow. Ken uses a compound bow because it gets the arrow on target faster than a stick bow. Ken's bow has a stabilizer because early tournament archers found that stabilizers cut bull's-eye misses in half. Masking tape painted in several colors of flat latex wall paint camouflage the bow.

Yeater has sewn little socks to cover white fletching on his arrows. The broadheads are sharpened with a file to produce a burred edge. The razor insert is sharpened on a stone.

Ken has sewn extra material on arms and legs of his coveralls to protect wrists and ankles against mosquitos and to help him avoid shivering when it's cold. A net covers his face, and tree branches break up his outline. Nothing is too extreme for Yeater's Germanic thoroughness if it will keep him motionless, silent, and unseen.

When he sees a buck, he never stands or draws a bow unless the deer is moving. "When a deer walks," he says, "it appears to him, just as it does to us, that the trees are moving. It's hard for him to tell if the movement is you or the trees.

"You know if you're doing everything right," he says, "if the doe gets past you. She has the buck to protect. She's sniffing, looking, and really alert. If she gets through, the whitetail buck assumes it's safe and follows. And don't shoot the squirrels. They're your buddies during deer season. Several times a squirrel's barking has alerted me that a deer was coming."

But what should you do if you follow Yeater's pattern to the letter and still can't connect with the animal you want?

Well, try what Ken did when the woods were dry a few seasons back. He saw the big tracks on October 2. For the next month, he saw nothing but two chance glimpses of his target buck. Deer left no tracks where they walked through the woods. It was impossible to learn the buck's circuit.

But Yeater did finally locate a big doe with two large fawns in a valley that was listed in his log as a favorite breeding area. Ken decided that the doe, when in heat, might lure the buck to him. He saw the trio repeatedly after that, but nothing else.

Finally, on November 12, the last morning of his vacation, the doe and her fawns passed the tree stand quietly, walked up a hill, and vanished. Fifteen minutes later, all three came racing down the hill 30 yards from the blind. Yeater noticed the tails weren't up. Yeater got ready.

Suddenly the buck appeared and ran to the bottom of the hill, tongue hanging out and panting. He was at 20 yards, but behind a small tree, looking for the doe. He moved to 10 yards. Ken drew back as the buck walked. It turned for a quartering shot, and Yeater let go.

Once again, this time with the help of a Judas doe, Kenneth Yeater had succeeded, upholding his 70 percent kill record (despite letting unwanted deer pass) in a state where even firearms hunters achieve only 25 percent success.

Bowhunter
with a Heap
of Record Trophies

Dewey Haeder

Here I was in Stanley, Idaho, among 550 other archers competing in the Idaho State Bowhunters' annual jamboree. Amid a forest of trailers, campers, and tents was one big trailer that was drawing a crowd of gawkers. It looked like an oversize horse trailer. I walked over to see what was so interesting.

Inside the trailer, the walls were covered with antlers, horns, and skulls. All of them were impressively big. There were two goats, eight antelope, 27 mule deer, and 12 elk. Under one tremendous 8×9-point elk rack was a plaque that said it scored 359⁷/₈ according to the Pope and Young Club system, even after losing a count of almost 30 to penalties! While it scored seventh in the world at the time it was taken, the rack would have been a world record but for the heavy penalty deduction.

But most amazing were the mule-deer racks. An entire side of the trailer was covered with them, a blizzard of four, five, six, and up to 10-point racks. Under each set of antlers, inscribed on a brass plaque, was the score, date killed, and the trophy's ranking in the Idaho record book. Every one of them, I noted with awakening awe, was big enough to make the Idaho book. All but seven were big enough to qualify for the Pope and Young Club's book of record-class bow-killed game.

On the other side, hanging in almost commanding isolation among the other species' heads and racks, were the really big muley racks. The *really big* racks. In the middle were two phenomenal heads. One was a beautiful 5×5 with wide, symmetrical antlers, and the other was a huge nontypical 8×9. I mistook their Idaho rankings on the plaques for errant scratches, but when I looked closer, I could see that both numbers were deliberately stamped. And they were both No. 1s!

I walked around the far side of the trailer and looked at the heads there, then went back to the front where a man in Western clothes was talking with two young, camo-clad archers.

I was still 10 feet away when one of them asked, "And you killed all of these in Idaho?"

The man nodded and said, "Yup, every one of 'em."

Wait a minute! How could one man . . . ? How could this guy . . . ? But the truth was there. This amazing collection of bowhunting trophies belonged to this one bespectacled gentleman!

Such was my introduction to Cal Coziah of Soda Springs, Idaho, one of the most successful trophy bowhunters in the world. His accomplishments read like "Who's Who in Trophy Bowhunting." Cal Coziah's story is almost unbelievable.

Cal started hunting with a bow in 1937, when he was 12. He hunted for three years before killing his first deer, a little 2×3 muley. He took it with a homemade bow, a wooden dowel fletched with Rhode Island Red chicken feathers, and a picked-up obsidian arrowhead that had been tied to the shaft with rockchuck hide.

In the next 25 years, Coziah shot many deer. He became strictly a trophy hunter and passed up hundreds of does and small bucks in his quest for record-book racks. "I could've had a lot more big deer if I'd known how to shoot in those days," he told me.

In 1965, he met a California dentist, Dr. Everett Watkins. Doc, as he'd come to be known, told Cal, "You could very well be the world's best hunter, but there is no doubt that you are also the world's worst shot."

Cal accepted the criticism and worked hard until he became an excellent field archer. Now he has a

Cal Coziah has taken more than 20 mule-deer trophies that most bowhunters would give a right arm to take. But he has never entered them in Pope and Young competition.

great deal of confidence in his shooting ability and no longer suffers from buck fever as less experienced archers often do.

His bowhunting equipment is a tribute to his ingenuity. Every piece, from his bow to his eyeglasses, bears evidence of his I-can-make-it-better credo. Take for instance, his old Allen compound bow.

It was new and shiny once—the technological Cadillac of the archery world. But now it shows

many signs of wear. It has been used to beat snow off brush, lift hot lids from dutch ovens, and rap hardheaded horses for bad behavior. It has been a stave and walking stick. It creaks, groans, and protests like an arthritic cricket when it's drawn. It looks old, a relic among the split-limb, totally adjustable bows that are now standard equipment for many a bowhunter.

The limbs are cracked. It's been bolted, screwed, taped, and hose clamped, but it still unleashes a 568-grain broadhead at a chronograph-proved 190 feet per second. The bow has probably killed more record-class animals than any other bow anywhere in the country.

Cal shoots 32-inch-long Bingham Binglass H-55 shafts, his only factory-produced piece of equipment that hasn't been altered. His Bear Razorheads, however, which he uses almost exclusively, undergo major changes.

Dissatisfied with their factory design and thinking that a wider blade would be more effective, Cal and Doc use Doc's 15-amp orthodontist's welder to spot-weld a Shick injector blade onto each blade of the Razorhead. The weld is then coated with Pliobond cement and baked for 45 minutes at 250° until the cement sets. The treatment has proved so tough that the 1½-inch-wide head remains intact through heavy bone.

Cal touches up the edges with an eight-inch file. He completes the job with eight to 10 strokes of an Eze-Lap Diamond "M" steel, bringing the entire cutting edge to hair-shaving sharpness. He demonstrated the technique to me, even sharpening badly dulled razor inserts from my Satellite broadheads. It left me a believer.

Cal's quiver looks like a piece of moth-eaten foam pad glued onto a cut-out section of aluminum irrigation pipe. Surprise! That's exactly what it is. The carrying harness is made of GI canvas webbing.

But how has Cal managed to shoot a record-class animal practically every year when 99 percent of hunters never even see such a trophy?

To find out, I talked with Cal for many hours and with many of his friends and hunting partners. I also read his book, *Bucks, Bows and Campfires—Forty-Four Years of Hunting Trophy Bucks.* I pinpointed five reasons for his uncanny success. They are:

1. a good hunting area and a thorough familiarity with it;

2. an outstanding hunting ability;

3. an intimate knowledge of his quarry;

4. patience; and

5. a refusal to shoot any but the largest deer.

Knowing where to find trophy bucks is the first step. Big racks are the result of soils rich in calcium, usually limestone, and it's exactly this antler-building mineral that makes up much of the southern-Idaho mountains.

But area is only a small part of the story, for there are many hunters who tramp these same hills every year. Of these, only a minute fraction get a shot. Almost nobody ever kills one.

COZIAH'S TROPHIES AT A GLANCE

Mule Deer, Typical

(Pope and Young minimum score: 145)

Year Taken	Score	Antler Points	Rank in Idaho Records
1980	192$7/8$	5 × 5	1
1979	171$3/8$	5 × 5	14
1976	178$0/8$	5 × 6	8
1975	161$7/8$	5 × 5	33
1974	156$4/8$	5 × 5	41
1971	172$6/8$	5 × 5	11
1970	167$0/8$	5 × 5	18
1969	150$2/8$	5 × 6	52
1968	168$7/8$	4 × 5	16
1966	162$3/8$	5 × 5	30
1964	151$4/8$	5 × 5	50
1961	163$1/8$	4 × 4	29
1961	157$6/8$	5 × 5	40
1958	160$6/8$	6 × 7	36
1955	145$7/8$	4 × 7	58
1949	166$6/8$	5 × 5	19

Mule Deer, Nontypical

(Minimum score: 160)

Year Taken	Score	Antler Points	Rank in Idaho Records
1981	207$0/8$	8 × 8	3
1973	181$6/8$	7 × 10	9
1969	213$5/8$	8 × 9	1
1954	169$2/8$	7 × 8	10

But Coziah does. Almost every year.

Part of the reason lies in his hunting ability, the product of a half-century's experience in the woods. As a child, he was taken by his father on long hunting trips and told, "You'll learn a lot more out here than in that schoolhouse." Cal never objected. Instead, he learned from his teacher the ways of the woods and animals.

He began trapping at age 6 and, later, after graduation from Utah State University, worked as a fisheries biologist and hatchery superintendent for 23 years with the Idaho Fish and Game Department. This added volumes to his already bulging storehouse of knowledge. And over his many years of exclusively trophy hunting, the know-how became almost legendary.

Cal is convinced that motion, especially fast movement, is the culprit that ruins many a stalk.

"Show me a hunter who can get from here to there without apparent movement, and I'll show you a successful archer," he says.

Coziah has elevated slow movement to the level of an art. While he covers nonproductive areas at a fast walk, he slows considerably when he gets into gamey country. Frequently, he sits and waits, so inconspicuous that he almost becomes a part of his surroundings.

On one hunt, in the final successful stalk of what he calls his S-horn buck, Cal stalked to within 10 yards of the giant buck where it lay bedded in a lodgepole pine jungle. Unable to shoot even at that range because of the tangle of branches, he inched forward in half-inch steps for an hour until he was within *five yards!*

Cal's ability to move so inconspicuously is matched by his uncommon patience. He can sit in a blind or stalk an animal noiselessly for hours, waiting for that critical moment. He bides his time, moving extremely slowly and watching the wind.

Cal wears little or no camouflage, saying that clothing makes no difference in the outcome of the hunt. He has had many experiences that illustrate his point.

"One time, a big four-point mule deer ran up to within 20 feet of me," he said. "There was new snow, and I had no cover. I was wearing my red-and-black-plaid hat and mackinaw, as I always do in cold weather. I was within extremely close range of a very nervous animal. He never saw me, even after the arrow hit."

Cal also eschews scents, saying they're unnecessary if an archer hunts properly with the wind in his face. "And if the wind comes from behind, the scents will probably be of little benefit anyhow." Many archers will vehemently disagree with this opinion and Cal's thoughts on camouflage. Coziah doesn't discount camouflage, however, nor does he talk disparagingly about any equipment or technique that helps.

"If it works and it gives you confidence, use it," he says emphatically.

Another reason for Cal's success is his intimate knowledge of deer behavior. He knows where the big bucks are and what they're going to do, usually long before they do. He enthusiastically passes on all of this know-how to anybody who asks.

An illustration of this ability to anticipate deer movements occurred in 1969, when he killed the biggest nontypical buck ever taken by a bowhunter in Idaho. He'd seen the 8×9-pointer several times during the hot, early-September season, and he knew the movements of the buck and his two four-point consorts revolved around their need for water. Their daily pattern was to drink early in the morning and then retreat to the safety of an alpine fir jungle to bed for the day.

After establishing the deer's travel route and schedule, Cal went back the next morning and hid in a trailside blind. An hour passed before the two four-pointers fed into view. He could have arrowed either one, but he was determined to kill the big buck. The huge animal followed half an hour later, and Coziah missed it.

A few days later, he missed again. Then he had to wait until the late season in December. The buck was still in the same area of cliffs and shale rock when Cal returned, and it was now in full rut. Cal knew the deer was interested in one thing and would ignore almost everything else.

Cal watched the buck chase a doe in heat. The

deer repeatedly moved through a notch in a rocky cliff. Cal moved near the notch. Forty-five minutes dragged by before he heard the *Thump! Thump! Thump!* of an approaching deer. A second later, the doe came through the notch. Cal drew his bow and waited. Long moments passed, and then the buck came swaggering through the notch, his neck swollen to twice normal size and his nose to the ground.

Cal released, and the arrow cracked through one rib and sliced through both lungs. The deer whirled around and looked up the hill, apparently unaware that it had been hit. Then it turned and continued walking after the doe. Ten yards later it collapsed and tumbled end over end. The massive beams spread 39½ inches. The rack scored a whopping 213⅝. At the time, it would have been a world record, but Cal never entered it in the Pope and Young Club's record book. None of his other trophies, except two elk, have been entered in the books. "Why?" I asked him.

"Well, at the time I just wasn't interested, and now it'd cost over a thousand dollars to enter them all," he replied.

Cal says only big bucks make scrapes and only early in the rut. It's common knowledge that whitetail deer make scrapes, but few hunters know that mule deer do. Cal says big muleys make many more rubs than small bucks, and the trees are rubbed cleaner and higher. He says big bucks chew off branches and twigs above the rubs.

Wary old mossyhorns are becoming more like whitetails in other ways, too, Coziah says. Where big mule deer once lay exposed all day on open hillsides, they now bed in heavy timber. Often they never leave this cover except during darkness.

"Timber jungles are terribly hard to hunt," he says, "but that's where the deer are during the time of day I normally hunt."

Coziah rarely gets up early, preferring instead to sleep later and work harder during the day. The deer are usually already bedded in the jungles when he arrives.

Cal also rarely makes late-afternoon or evening hunts. The possibility of losing the blood trail because of failing light is too great, he feels, except in exceptional circumstances.

He says deer also are wising up to the quiet danger of archers. Twenty years ago, they would continue to stand after an arrow went past. But now, he says, it's rare to get more than one shot before they run.

Like many archers, Cal carries a pocketful of small rocks to divert or distract a deer. Throwing a rock beyond an otherwise unapproachable deer has often brought it running toward him. He also has killed deer by using the rocks to divert a deer's attention long enough to allow him to draw and shoot.

Bucks that aren't badly spooked rarely go far in Cal's country. A mildly spooked buck often thumps away out of sight and earshot, then sneaks back in downwind half an hour later to locate the hunter.

Cal has played that habit to a successful conclusion more than once.

The most significant aspect of big-buck behavior that Cal has discovered is that big muleys are attracted to rutting elk. This habit has allowed him to take both a buck and a bull in the same area on at least five occasions. Once he killed both at the same time without moving more than a few feet.

It happened as he was trailing a herd of elk, and a four-point mule-deer buck was evidently interested in the cows. Cal killed the deer and was prepared to gut it out when he heard an animal above him on the same trail on which he'd just shot the deer. Looking up, he saw a six-point bull elk walking back to check the disturbance.

Cal grabbed his bow and nocked an arrow as the bull went behind a tree. When it emerged, he drove the Razorhead through both lungs. The bull stood for several seconds, then walked off uphill. Fifty yards away, it fell and started sliding downhill toward him. It slid to within 50 feet of where he stood over the buck.

Cal has observed that bucks usually bed within 200 yards of an elk herd, and usually uphill. He tries to get into an ambush position between the two, and takes the deer as they make their frequent investigations of the elk herd. The bucks' interest, he feels, is triggered by the great amount of elk estrus scent in the area and by the bulls' rutting behavior. He says this combination usually sends the muley bucks into a "prerut condition," and their necks swell and their testes enlarge.

The deer become careless, as they do when they rut with their own species later in November, and become easier to approach. "They're like college freshmen," Coziah says. "They're very undependable about when they'll come home, dragging their feet, their eyes rheumy and nose running, and they have a tendency to bed down whenever and wherever the chance occurs."

The last characteristic of this trophy hunter, the refusal to shoot any but the largest bucks, has been the cause of more than one dry season. But it's also the reason for the huge nontypical buck he killed recently.

Cal had passed up many mediocre bucks, including some that would have made the book. On the final weekend of the season he'd resigned himself to not killing a deer at all, but then he saw the big buck feeding toward him.

The deer approached slowly. At 50 yards, Cal knew the animal would come no closer. It was a difficult shot, but 44 years of shooting trophy-size muleys had prepared him for the moment and he was calm and confident. The arrow shot noiselessly out of the old Allen and penetrated completely. A few panicky, pogo-stick bounds, and the 35¾-inch buck went down.

The bespectacled bowhunter, who'd left camp at 8 that morning, dressed in red-and-black plaid, had taken another record-class buck.

PART 9

MEAT FOR THE TABLE

How to Have Tasty Venison

J. Wayne Fears

The age of the deer, its sex, and the time of year it is shot will influence the quality of deer meat. But these factors usually are beyond the control of the hunter. The legal hunting season restricts the time, hunting often is restricted to bucks only, and it's almost impossible to tell the exact age of a deer without examining its teeth.

Several factors, however, that are under the control of the hunter will markedly affect the palatability of venison. These are the quickness of the kill (stress), field-dressing, skinning, and cold-storage aging. Sometimes the hunter can also elect to shoot a doe rather than a buck.

A recent study conducted by graduate student Joyce Hosch in the food-technology department at Texas A & M University provides information that is of great value to deer hunters who want high-quality venison.

Under the supervision of the Texas Parks and Wildlife Department, 36 whitetail deer were shot under controlled conditions and grouped as follows:

Group I: Five young male animals that were not stressed. These were field-dressed right after the kill and skinned immediately, but the carcasses were not aged.

Group II: Six females, not stressed, field-dressed and skinned immediately, not aged.

Group III: Six females, not stressed, rapidly field-dressed, delayed skinning, not aged.

Group IV: Seven females, stressed, rapidly field-dressed, skinned immediately, and not aged.

Venison can be delicious for a holiday feast or any meal. (Stan Trzoniec photo)

Group V: Six females, not stressed, delayed field-dressed, skinned immediately, and not aged.

Group VI: Six females, not stressed, rapidly field-dressed, skinned immediately, and aged.

Here are the definitions of the factors that were tested in this study.

- Not stressed—shot through the neck or shoulder to assure a quick, clean kill. These animals usually died immediately.
- Stressed—shot through the gut so that death was delayed. Animals in this group often ran 50 to 75 yards before death.
- Skinned immediately—skinned within two to four hours of death.
- Delayed-skinning—skinned 12 to 16 hours after death.
- Field-dressed immediately—all internal organs were removed within two hours of death.
- Delayed field-dressing—the internal organs were not removed until the animal had been dead four to 11 hours.
- Aged—the gutted carcass was placed in a cooler at 40° and left for one week before being butchered, packaged, and frozen.
- Not aged—soon after the animal was field-dressed, the carcass was butchered. The hams, backstraps, and shoulder trimmings were wrapped in PVC plastic and then in freezer paper. The meat was then placed in a freezer.

Two cuts of meat were used in the taste testing—backstraps and ham steaks. A taste panel was selected, and its members were trained as taste-testers. All testers ate samples from the same cuts of meat during each panel session. After testing each sample, the testers rated the sample on the intensity and desirability of flavor, juiciness, tenderness, and overall satisfaction.

Flavor intensity can be described as the degree of "gamey" flavor the meat possesses. Sex is an important factor in determining the intensity of flavor in venison. The male animal has a more gamey flavor. As for **flavor desirability,** aging produced a flavor that was more desirable than the flavor of venison that wasn't aged.

The testers agreed that venison is characteristically dry. **Juiciness** scores were low in all the groups studied. The dryness of venison is explained by the small amount of intermuscular fat. Perhaps the most important factor influencing the juiciness of cooked meat is the cooking procedure. By lowering the internal temperature of cooked meat to 158° before serving, the juiciness of the meat was greatly improved.

Tenderness has been cited by several researchers as the most important palatability factor in the acceptance of any type of meat. Stressing the animal was detrimental to the tenderness of the meat.

Stress at the time of death causes muscles to enter rigor mortis in a more contracted state. Contracted muscle is tougher than muscle that is relaxed. Stressed animals also enter rigor mortis at a faster rate, and this causes a decrease in tenderness. The animals that were gut-shot and died slowly were stressed. There were significant differences in tenderness between the meat of stressed animals and meat of animals that died quickly.

Keeping the meat in cold storage significantly increased the tenderness of venison. The aging process retards rigor mortis and extends it over a longer period. It also tends to increase the water-holding capacity of the meat and causes the breakage of muscle fibers.

Boning of the hams seemed to decrease the tenderness of the meat. The bone serves as a muscle attachment. When the bone is removed, the muscles contract more, and this contraction reduces the meat's tenderness.

Overall satisfaction is the combination of all the palatability attributes. Group IV scored lower more often than all other groups, while Group VI always rated in the top two.

Of the five variables evaluated in this study, aging in cold storage and stressing of animals caused the greatest effect. Aging enhanced the flavor and increased the tenderness of the meat. Stress decreased the quality.

The data gathered in this study demonstrated that one combination of factors ensures very palatable venison: Shoot a doe in a way that assures immediate death, field-dress as soon as possible, age the carcass at about 40°F. for a week after skinning out and butchering, cook the meat carefully to preserve the flavor.

Of course, doing all this is not always possible, but anything you can do along these lines helps to put good meat on the table. For instance, a young buck shot through the neck and properly field-dressed, skinned, butchered, aged, and cooked is going to taste a lot better than a tough old mossy-horn shot in the paunch at the height of the rut, no matter how you handle the old-timer.

TASTY RECIPES

Roast venison

5- to 7-lb. venison leg
¼ lb. fat salt pork
salad oil
For marinade
1 qt. water
1½ cups vinegar
2 onions, chopped
1 pared carrot, diced
1 clove garlic
1 tsp. dried thyme
4 sprigs parsley
12 whole black peppers (peppercorns)
1 tbsp. salt

First make marinade by bringing to boil in saucepan the water, vinegar, onions, carrot, garlic, thyme, parsley, peppers, and salt. Simmer covered one hour, then cool.

Cover venison leg with cooled marinade and refrigerate leg in the marinade 24 hours or longer before roasting.

To roast, preheat shallow, open pan in 450° oven. Meantime, take venison from marinade and remove skin and any visible tough sinews. Sprinkle meat with salt and cover with slices of fat salt pork. Place meat in preheated pan, adding salad oil to cover bottom of pan. Roast uncovered, basting meat with salad oil.

Allow about nine minutes per pound for very rare, 15 minutes per pound for medium rare, 25 to 30 minutes per pound for well done.

Braised venison

Use steaks cut ¾- to one-inch thick. Pound flour into both sides with head of camp ax and put in skillet or Dutch oven containing a small quantity of hot fat. When bottom has browned, season top with salt and pepper, and turn steak. Brown the other side, season again, add half a cup water or tomato juice, cover tightly, and let simmer slowly until meat almost falls apart when pierced with fork. This will require two to 2½ hours, and more liquid may be needed occasionally to prevent burning. Prepare one-half to three-quarters of a pound per person.

Venison steak

Cut steaks ¾-inch thick, trim off tendons and tallow. Pound flour into both sides, using edge of saucer or plate if a regular steak pounder is not handy. Melt enough butter in skillet to give a depth of one-quarter inch, and fry meat in it from 10 to 20 minutes, depending on how well done you like it. Season both sides with salt and pepper at the last turning, remove and place on heated platter. Dot with butter. Serve three-quarters of a pound per person.

Breaded venison steak

Venison steaks
1 egg, beaten
Bread crumbs
Salt
Pepper

Pound steaks until about ¼-inch thick. Dip each steak into egg and coat with bread crumbs, working crumbs into meat with fingers. Season steaks and fry quickly in hot fat, turning once. Serve immediately.—*Dan Klepper.*

Deep-fried venison backstrap

1 strip venison tenderloin
3 cups flour
Salt
Pepper
2 cups milk
2 eggs, beaten

Slice tenderloin cross-grain into very thin pieces. Soak in milk-and-egg mixture for 30 minutes. Dip individual pieces into seasoned flour and fry in hot vegetable oil. For garlic flavor, add garlic salt to flour. Serve piping hot.— *Peggy F. Brady.*

Venison creole

1 pound ground venison
4 tbsp. shortening
1 large onion, chopped
2 tbsp. chili powder

1 tbsp. black pepper
1 (16 ounce) can red kidney beans
1 (16 ounce) can tomatoes
¼ tsp. garlic salt
Dash salt
3 cups cooked rice (preferably brown rice)

Brown meat and onion in shortening over medium heat. Add remaining ingredients, except rice. Cook on high heat until steaming. Reduce heat to low and cook about 30 minutes. Serve over rice.—*John E. Phillips.*

Venison hot tamales

2 pounds lean venison
½ pound beef suet or 3 tbsp. margarine
4 tbsp. chili powder
4 tbsp. paprika
1 tsp. oregano
2 tsp. ground comino (cumin) seed
1 tsp. ground cayenne pepper
2 tsp. black pepper
1 tsp. salt
4 garlic cloves, minced
1 cup bouillon

Brown meat in suet or margarine. Add seasoning and simmer for 30 minutes. Set aside.

Paste mixture
1 pound tamalina or white cornmeal
½ pound shortening
4 tbsp. salt
2½ cups bouillon, warm after boiling

Mix ingredients to form a thick paste.

Shucks
Soak 50 to 60 corn shucks, green or dried, for several hours in hot water. With scissors cut to 2 × 6 inches. Brown paper bags can be used if shucks are unavailable.

Layer paste over top four inches of shuck to a depth of ⅛ inch. Spoon a heaping tablespoon of meat sauce to the center of paste and roll loosely like a cigarette. Fold or tie empty end of shuck with string. Steam over boiling water for one hour.—*Peggy F. Brady.*

Venison stew

2 lb. cubed venison
1 small onion, sliced
1 clove garlic, minced
1 tsp. salt
¼ tsp. pepper
Pinch of thyme
¼ tsp. parsley flakes
1 cup diced celery
4 medium potatoes
4 carrots, diced
4 small onions
1 tbsp. flour

Dredge venison in flour and brown in hot fat in Dutch oven. Remove, and in remaining fat sauté sliced onion and garlic for three minutes. Return venison to oven and add boiling water, salt, pepper, thyme, parsley, and celery. Simmer 1¾ hours. Add medium potatoes cut into small pieces, carrots, and the small onions (these may be omitted). Cook 30 minutes longer. Thicken pan juices with flour and a little cold water. This makes 4 servings.

Field-Dressing Your Buck

Here's an easy way to dress out your deer in jig time, using only your knife and a piece of twine. With a little patience and care, you'll wind up with fine venison without spoiling a scrap of meat.

BE SURE HE'S DEAD!

NO NEED TO BLEED DEER

FOR QUICK DISPATCH, SHOOT HERE.

A SMALL, VERY SHARP BLADE IS BEST.

TAG DEER IMMEDIATELY (WHERE LAW REQUIRES)

DO NOT CUT OUT THE LEG GLANDS SIMPLY AVOID TOUCHING THEM

ROLL DEER ONTO BACK, RUMP LOWEST, IF POSSIBLE.

UNLOAD GUN AND SET IT ASIDE!

1

Remove penis and scrotum with shallow cuts. Do not pierce body cavity.

2

With tip of knife, cut completely around the rectum to free it from rest of skin.

3

Pull rectum outside body and tie off to prevent feces from reaching meat.

Illustrations: Ken Laager *Information:* Dick Fagan, Pennsylvania game department

176

Carefully cut abdomen open from rear to sternum (where last ribs join). Hold intestines down with fingers and back of hand so that you do not cut or pierce the intestinal tract or the paunch as you proceed.

Cut the bladder out very carefully. Try not to spill urine.

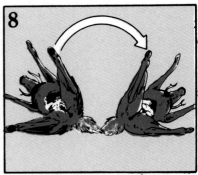

Pull rectum inside cavity, and cut tissue holding it in place.

With deer lying on one side, cut all tissues that hold the intestines in place all the way down to the animal's spine.

Now roll the deer over so that you can free the intestines the same way from the other side.

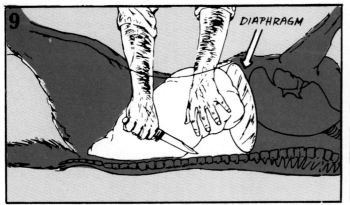

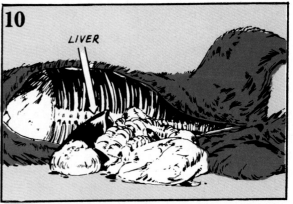

Repeat Step 7. Little cutting is needed. Then sever gullet in front of stomach. Do not spill contents. If you do, immediately wipe clean.

Contents of abdomen come out in one big mass. Retrieve liver, and cool it quickly in open air or water.

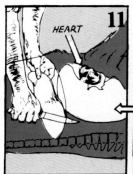

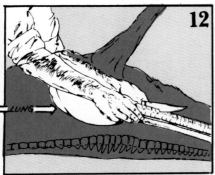

Cut out diaphragm (wall between abdomen and chest).

Reach up inside chest and sever gullet and windpipe. Pull them out with lungs, heart.

Wipe dry. If day is hot, it's better to split breast, open neck, and cut out rest of windpipe and gullet to avoid spoilage. If, however, head is to be mounted, "cape out" (skin) neck first.

Skinning Your Deer

A few important additional points should be borne in mind. After skinning, it's important to cut out and discard all bloodshot meat around bullet holes. Such meat is inedible and spoils quickly and may contaminate the rest of the meat. Pick off all deer hair on the skinned carcass. It lends a truly horrible taste when meat is cooked. The skinning method shown here results in a raw deer hide suitable for tanning and use in a vest or jacket. If you want to have a head-and-shoulders mount of your buck, you must "cape out." The cuts used for that purpose are shown in circular inset in panel 13.

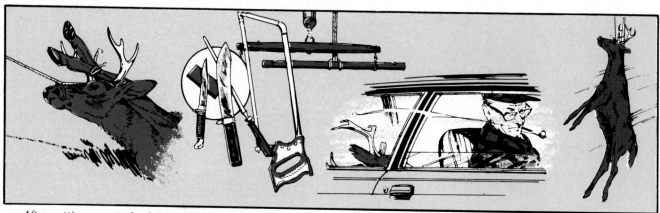

After gutting out, tie forefeet together over neck to streamline carcass. Drag out with rope around antlers and half-hitch around upper jaw. In vehicle, never subject carcass to heat. Don't use heater; keep windows open. Most hunters hang deer in cool place (41° to 45°) for a week with the hide still on to tenderize meat and enhance flavor before they skin out and butcher.

1 *With point of knife, cut hide from abdominal cut to just below both joints. Don't touch leg glands.*

2 *Skin out both thighs. Try not to cut meat or inner side of skin.*

3 *With deer still lying on the floor, skin out thighs to top of legs.*

4 *Saw off lower legs just below the joints. Use a meat-cutting saw or crosscut wood saw.*

Illustrations: Ken Laager   *Information: Dick Fagan, Pennsylvania game department*

5 Hang deer with gambrel or stick in each leg between bone and tendon.

6 If it wasn't done during field-dressing, cut H-bone of pelvis with your saw.

7 Continue skinning. Leave tail on hide by tunneling under it between hide and back.

8 Hide in this area usually comes off quite easily. Pull on hide and then cut.

9 Sever tail near body inside hide. This avoids cutting the hair, which you'd have to pick off meat.

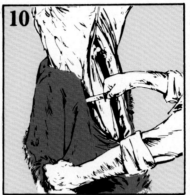

10 Use knife to separate hide from thin muscles near the abdominal lengthwise incision.

11 Hoist deer higher. Pull with one hand and "fist" hide.

12 Saw off lower forelegs. Split breast and neck, and cut out the gullet.

13 Slit skin of forelegs to the breast cut. If you want deer mounted, inset shows the cuts.

14 Skin out the legs and the neck. Neck is hardest area to skin.

15 Pull hide down, and then use knife. Continue to base of skull.

16 Saw off head. Again, doing it this way avoids cutting the hair.

17 Clean carcass (see accompanying instructions) before butchering.

18 Hide still has head and tail attached. Cut head off. Wipe inside of hide dry with cloth.

19 Sprinkle borax or salt on inside of hide. Roll up hide, hair side out. Send package to the tanner immediately, or store in refrigerator or freezer till you can do so.

Butchering Your Deer

The assumption in this chapter is that you're starting out with a skinned carcass that has been carefully cleaned of all dirt and hair and that all bloodshot meat around bullet holes has been cut off and discarded. Deer can be butchered in many different ways. This method is employed by many experienced hunters. It's very easy. After you have cut your deer into table portions, wrap them in aluminum foil or special freezer paper, seal the packages with freezing tape, and (very important) label each package so that you'll be able to find what you want to eat. If you don't have a freezer, there are other ways to keep venison on hand—smoking, pickling, making sausage or jerky, and even canning.

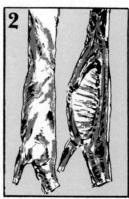

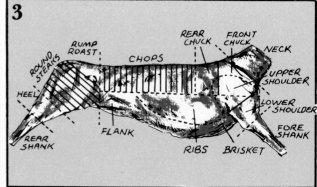

With meat-cutting saw or fine carpenter's saw, cut carcass in two. Start where tail was severed.

Cut spine in half lengthwise. Cut can be corrected if it wanders.

Dotted lines show major cuts. Solid lines indicate secondary cuts that divide roasts into two or separate steaks and chops. This is right side. After cutting the whole side, repeat cuts on left side.

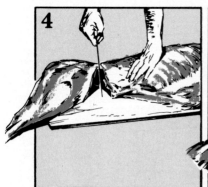

Divide haunch from loin. With all cuts, use knife first. If you hit bone, use saw to complete cut. A cleaver is handy but not essential.

Cut rump roast off haunch. Make a neat straight cut. It determines angle of cuts for round steaks.

Cut thin or thick round steaks as you prefer, but keep cuts parallel.

Down toward joint, meat is tough, and it doesn't pay to cut more steaks. Instead, take off a chunk called the heel, usually used for stew.

Illustrations: Ken Laager   *Information:* Dick Fagan, Pennsylvania game department

8 Now for the front part. Cut entire shoulder and foreleg off the side where the shoulder joins the body. Knife blade is horizontal.

9 There is no ball-and-socket joint, so this cut is easy.

10 Separate shoulder from shank at joint or close to it. You need the saw for this cut. The shank is used as chop meat.

11 The shoulder is usually divided into two separate pieces for pot roasts or stew meat.

12 Cut off the neck. Neck is tough like shank or shoulder and is best as chop meat or stew.

13 Saw ribs off. This long, angled cut is made where thin meat between ribs thickens toward spine.

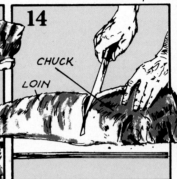

14 Separate chuck (under the meat cutter's left hand) from the loin. The loin is cut into chops; chuck is usually cut into two roasts.

15 Cut the loin into chops, as thick as you like. They resemble lamb chops. These cuts are started with the knife and completed with saw.

16 Trim thick fat off chops. Heavy fat should be trimmed off all cuts. It has an unpleasant flavor.

17 Cut the chuck into two equal portions. It's too big to cook whole (usually as pot roast) unless you have a big family.

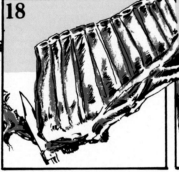

18 This long cut starts parallel to first rib and outside it and then circles around the tips of ribs.

19 The cut completed. It separates brisket and flank from ribs. Brisket and flank go into chop meat.

20 Separate ribs. Knife slides along bone to one side so all the meat between two ribs stays attached to single rib.

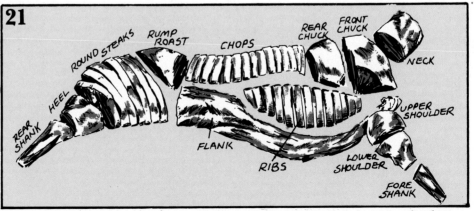

21 Here are all the cuts from right side, properly trimmed. If you do mangle a piece, remember that you can always bone it out and grind it up for chop meat or mincemeat or chop it up into chunks for stew.

Index